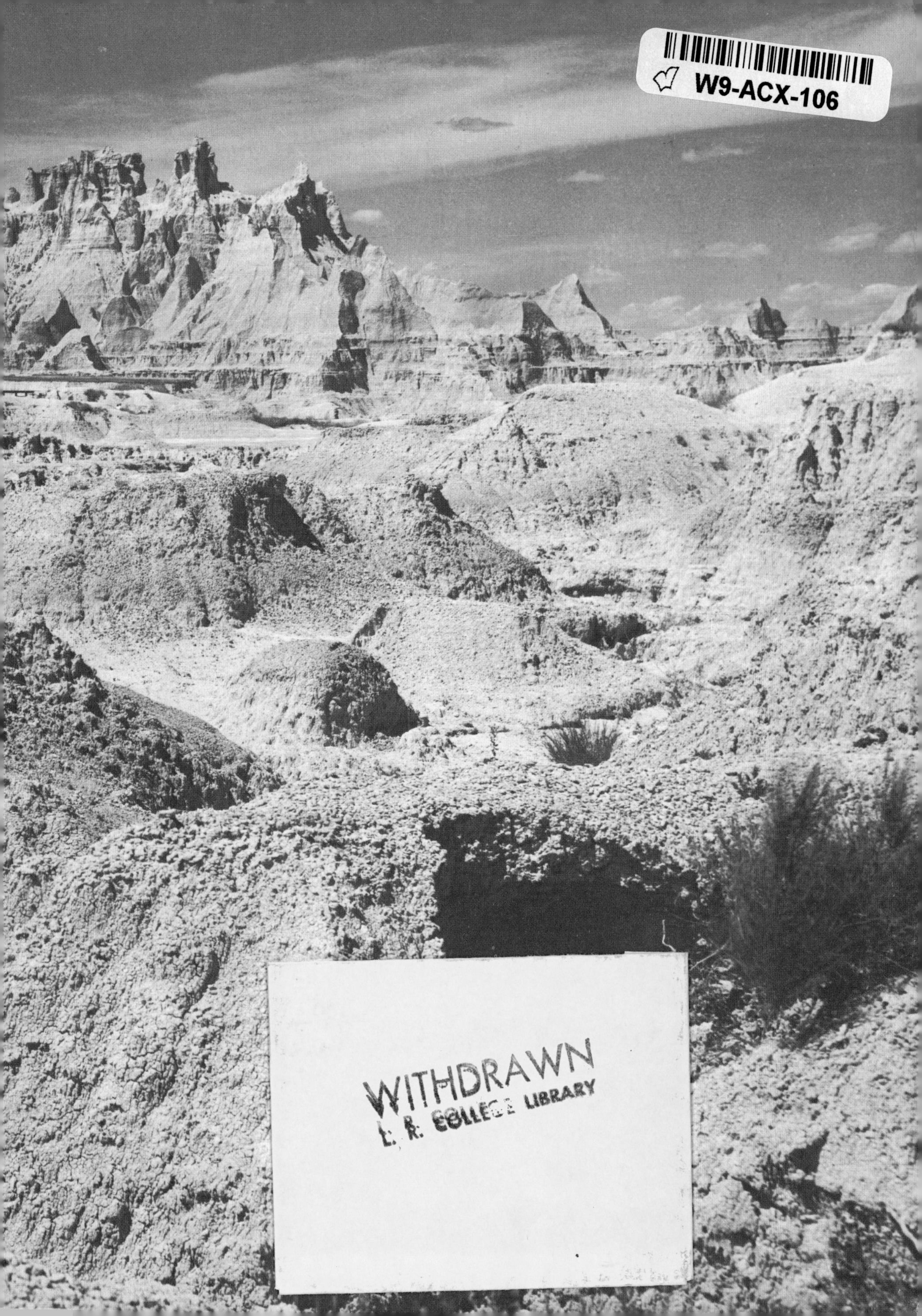

Facing:
Giant panda; the symbol of the
World Wildlife Fund; a rare and
protected animal of China, where
it has bred in captivity.

Overleaf:
The planet Earth from space,
photographed from Apollo 11.
If man had reached the Moon
a century ago with optical
instruments of the quality available
then he could have followed
not only the seasonal vegetation
changes through the years, but
gross vegetational changes due
entirely to the lumbering, forestry,
agriculture and industry of man.

Wildlife Crisis

H.R.H. The Prince Philip, Duke of Edinburgh,
and James Fisher

Forewords by H.R.H. The Prince of the Netherlands and Peter Scott
Epilogue by Stewart L. Udall

Published with the cooperation of the World Wildlife Fund

Cowles Book Company, Inc.
NEW YORK

SBN 402–12511–8

Library of Congress catalog card number 76–116129

This book was designed and produced in Great Britain by
Rainbird Reference Books Limited,
Marble Arch House, 44 Edgware Road, London, W.2

Published in 1970 by Cowles Book Company, Inc.,
A subsidiary of Cowles Communications, Inc.,
488 Madison Avenue, New York, N.Y. 10022

Published in Canada by
General Publishing Company Limited,
30 Lesmill Road, Don Mills, Toronto, Ontario

Printed in Great Britain by
Jarrold and Sons Limited, Norwich

First Edition

Contents

Maps

The maps were drawn by Crispin Fisher.

Colour Plates

Foreword

by H.R.H. The Prince of the Netherlands

As President of the World Wildlife Fund International I am
delighted to be associated with this book, which I believe will do
much to spread the basic concepts of conservation throughout the
world. The idea that the survival of the human species is inescap-
ably linked with the survival of all other forms of life is relatively
new; yet the more we study it the more this basic truth becomes
evident. What, then, should be man's relationship with nature, of
which he is no more than a part? Do his intellectual capacities
impose a responsibility to conserve the rest of the natural world?
On formal occasions such as the Council of Europe's inaugural
conference for European Conservation Year at Strasbourg in
February 1970, I found myself trying to answer these and other
questions, and I should like to bring some of the answers into this
foreword.

At the outset it may be worth defining the word "conservation,"
which already seems to have acquired many connotations in
various parts of the world. As I understand it, conservation deals
with the preservation, and the management, and the wise and
rational use of the natural resources of the earth, and in particular
the living, renewable natural resources – the animals and plants
which share this planet with us, and which are self-perpetuating,
provided that we humans, with our greed and our carelessness,
and our sweeping technological power, do not prevent their
self-perpetuation.

We, who are concerned about conservation, are usually called
"conservationists." For those eager to exploit our earth without
much regard for the long-term future, we are the enemy. But just
as the exploiters are the product of evolution in the human species,
so, too, are the conservationists.

One among many of the subjects that are of particular concern
to conservationists is the extinction of species. There are those
who suggest that it is not a subject about which we should
exercise ourselves too greatly. After all, the dinosaurs became
extinct without human intervention – why should we worry too
much about the threatened species of today? Is this not merely the
process of evolution at work – the survival of the fittest? If the
human species makes the environment no longer fit for these
"delicate" species to survive in, that is their look out – not ours.

I do not subscribe to this view.

Survival has a meaning for all living things, and there are many
among us who feel that we, as the first species to develop conscious
reasoning, have already acquired some degree of responsibility.
Be that as it may, the variation through which evolution by
natural selection operates has thrown up among human beings a
kind of animal called a conservationist – who believes, among
other things, that species – the end-product of 2,000 million years
of evolution – should not be exterminated in a few decades by the

thoughtlessness and ignorance of the human race itself. Those people believe that unless we give a great deal more attention to the conservation of our environment and of the natural world, the future may be pretty bleak for our own species.

I think we should establish that, whatever our personal motivations, nature is something which exists in its own right and which demands our respect and attention. Our attitude to it – as Dr Frank Fraser Darling has pointed out in his remarkable Reith Lectures for the BBC – is a measure of our consciousness of the whole situation, of which our survival is only a part, not the "be all and end all."

This is a point of view that is beginning to be recognized, and UNESCO's Conference on the Biosphere in 1968 brought the matter to the attention of scientists and governments very effectively. The follow-up conference in 1972 will bring together the political leaders of most of the nations of the world under the banner "Man and the Biosphere." Then perhaps we shall see concerted action in defence of the biosphere – this thin layer over our earth which supports life. It requires a stout defence against wanton or careless destruction, against pollution and against the disaster of unrestricted human population increase. The biosphere is limited in extent and it cannot be significantly increased in size.

For many years there have been voices crying from the wilderness – not the wild wilderness of nature (of which all too little is left to cry from!), but the wilderness of ignorance and apathy.

Now suddenly people seem to have begun to listen. What has brought about this change? I believe the major eye-opener has been pollution – pollution for all to see – pollution of the atmosphere, visible as smog; pollution of the fresh waters, visible as detergent foam or as rainbow films of oil; pollution of the oceans, visible as slicks or as black sludge on the beaches; and pollution of the soil with persistent poisons, visible occasionally as a "die-off" of wildlife. Of course, there are varying kinds of pollution which are not visible, and which are much more insidious because they creep up on us unseen, or at least unnoticed by any but specialist scientists. We ignore their warnings at our peril, but here, naturally, there is frequent controversy. All too often there are powerful interests whose business is directly affected and whose energies will therefore be devoted to casting doubt on the findings of the scientists. They will find other scientists who will put forward a different view. They will tell you they do this in order to protect the interests of their shareholders. Lord Ritchie Calder has described pollution as "a crime compounded of ignorance and avarice." When things begin to threaten the survival of the human species, it is time all the people are alerted to the dangers facing them and their children. The pollution of the biosphere is such a danger – only one of the threats to human survival, but at present probably the greatest and most immediate. The effects of carbon dioxide buildup are only now beginning to be recognized and assessed, and we shall have to take a long hard look at the whole question of the burning of fossil fuels.

In my view we should be paying much more attention than we do to the collection and storage of solar energy, so that, in terms of power, we could live on income rather than on capital.

Clearly, conservationists must be concerned with root causes of the threats to the biosphere, such as the effects of a too rapid escalation in technological power, and the exponential curve of human population increase. If these problems are not solved in the long term, then all short-term conservation achievement will be set at naught.

However, we all have to make some assumptions – we have to have some faith that solutions will be found. If one were to suppose that these great problems were insoluble, we might as well give up altogether. But if we believe that they can and will be solved, then, my friends, we have work to do – work in two directions: first, to stimulate and expedite the solutions to those main causal problems, and second to perform a "holding operation," to save as much as we can of what is irreplaceable, while the solutions are being found and brought into effect. In the first area, it seems to me that conservationists must establish strong lines of communication with the organizations working on these basic solutions. For example, we should have close liaison with the various demographic bodies and in particular with the International Planned Parenthood Federation.

The "holding operation" part of conservation involves a whole host of quite small efforts – the saving of individual areas, of individual species, of animal and plant communities, of unspoiled countryside, of a wetland here and a woodland there – a river cleared of pollution, a smoke-abatement measure, a new method of cleaning out oil-tankers' tanks – things which by themselves do not always seem to be very great achievements, but which in the aggregate amount to solid conservation progress.

In each case conservation must be precise and specific. It must have well-defined, attainable objects, and because so much needs to be done and there are so few dedicated people and so little money to do it, conservation must have its priorities very carefully worked out and firmly based on scientific research.

In this connection I would like to pay tribute to the work of the International Union for Conservation of Nature and Natural Resources, which has been operating, more or less on a shoestring, since soon after the end of the Second World War. I believe that the new awareness of the problems of conservation on the part of governments and of the general public can be attributed largely to IUCN.

The organization of which I have the honour to be President – the World Wildlife Fund – has the function of trying to raise voluntary money for all aspects of conservation. I am happy to say that between WWF and IUCN there is the closest possible collaboration. IUCN is the scientific and technical arm of world conservation, while WWF is the fund-raising and campaigning arm. We like to think of the two as running in double harness.

Many people feel that a subject so vast can be financed adequately only by governments, and certainly there are many aspects of the defence of the biosphere which fall directly on the shoulders of governments, and which call for substantial support from them. But I believe there is an important part to be played by volunteers, by dedicated people whose philosophy gives high priority to man's treatment of his environment and of the natural world. These are still in many cases the pioneers, the pathfinders, and the moulders of public opinion – and the efforts of these volunteers and their collective organizations are going to continue to need support.

I am very pleased to know that the royalties from this book will go to the World Wildlife Fund and thence out into the field to deal with the mounting list of urgencies and emergencies – the factors in human behaviour, in intentional and unintentional human activity, which threaten the survival of all life on earth. These are problems of vital interest to humanity – literally vital.

Foreword

by Peter Scott, First Vice-President and
Chairman of The World Wildlife Fund

"Do you think," said Stanley Flink of Cowles Book Company,
"that Prince Philip would write a wildlife book in European
Conservation Year for our firm, if the royalties went to WORLD
WILDLIFE?"

"Pretty unlikely," said I. "He'd never have the time, and he'll
have no truck with ghost writers. But I suppose we could always
ask. . . ."

And so we asked, and the Duke of Edinburgh agreed to write
two chapters (later expanded to three) and the captions for those
of his photographs that would be used. When I say write I mean
literally that, because he wrote them in longhand. And this
foreword gives me a chance to express the gratitude of the World
Wildlife Fund for this latest help which His Royal Highness has
given to our organization.

Back in the summer of 1961 Prince Philip injured his leg in a
polo accident and had to cancel his engagements for a couple of
weeks. At that time the World Wildlife Fund was in the process of
formation, and I thought his accident might give him time to
advise us on the establishment of the new body we were creating.
I took the various papers to Buckingham Palace and H.R.H. said
he would give me his conclusions a week later on July 19 when,
because of his injured leg, the monthly meeting of the Zoological
Society of London, over which he was to preside, would be held at
the Palace.

Before the meeting, Prince Philip handed me a sheaf of notes on
our proposals and agreed to become President of the British
National Appeal of the Fund. Later the same day he telephoned to
say that if I went quickly to Claridge's Hotel, H.R.H. The Prince of
the Netherlands would receive me and might be prepared to
become President of World Wildlife International. An hour later,
Prince Bernhard had accepted the invitation.

It is scarcely possible to overestimate the contribution of these
two men to the subsequent success achieved by the World Wildlife
Fund. Since then Prince Philip has also become an International
Trustee.

WWF was conceived as a campaigning and fund-raising arm of
the international conservation movement, to give financial help to
(and to be advised by) the relevant international scientific
organizations, especially the International Union for the Conservation of Nature and Natural Resources and the International
Council for Bird Preservation. We described ourselves as a
foundation for saving the world's wildlife and wild places and as a
new Noah's Ark. In the context of the name, "wildlife" means
anything that is alive and wild – thus encompassing plants as well
as animals. Our symbol is a giant panda (drawn by me from a
suggestion by Gerald Watterson, then Secretary-General of IUCN)
and to many people wildlife suggests big-game or fluffy animals,

but the scope of WWF has always been much wider. It covers, in effect, the whole spectrum of nature and natural environment. At first, our main activity was to raise the money so badly needed for conservation on a global scale, through National Appeals in those countries where voluntary money could be found for such purposes. But soon it became clear that the distinguished people who had become associated with the organization were in a position to represent the conservation point of view to heads of state, government ministers, international organizations, and leaders of thought in many walks of life. Often this brought about the achievement of conservation measures which no money could have bought.

WWF has continued to support IUCN, ICBP and many other organizations, international and national. It has bought extensive areas of wild country for nature reserves and national parks, normally passing them on to other organizations for management. It has provided equipment for conservation – aircraft, boats, vehicles. It has commissioned scientific studies to make sure that the right conservation measures are adopted and that money is not wasted on wrong measures. It has supported educational programmes for children and for adults – and more particularly for the training of wildlife management personnel. It has supported the promotion of international conventions aimed at arranging for conservation measures and for the survival of endangered species.

The last subject is the particular concern of one of IUCN's six commissions – the Survival Service Commission of which I have the honour to be Chairman. Its object is to prevent the extinction of animal and plant species. "Survival" is a word with a meaning for all of us. Too often these days the word needs a question-mark after it. New potential threats are constantly arising to the very survival of all life on earth.

Many scientists believe that the point of no return may already have been passed – that we may already have irreversibly damaged our biosphere, the bubble-thin layer round our earth that supports life. The results of the thalidomide error were detectable in a few months, X-ray burns took longer to be discovered. How much irrevocable harm may have been done which will not take effect until years hence? Perhaps none, but no one will deny that big chances have been taken in the name of human avarice, and the mad scramble for what we choose to call economic progress.

In the past, man has frequently done many irreversible things without knowing it. Almost all of the 358 kinds of mammals and birds which have become extinct since 1600 (and many before that back into Stone Age times) were exterminated by people who neither knew nor cared what they were doing. Nowadays, people mostly feel that the ethical, aesthetic, scientific and even economic arguments for trying to avert species extinction are compelling. One of the most striking features of the conservation scene in recent years has been the support given to the Survival Service Commission by some 150 scientists from forty countries. Their time is given free – and they give much – to examining the prospects for survival of the 817 mammals and birds, and the still uncounted reptiles, amphibia, fishes, invertebrates and plants that are currently threatened with extinction.

14

A prominent and active member of the Commission is James Fisher. We have known each other since schooldays (his father was my headmaster), and we have often been together on field trips – including a notable summer in Iceland. I am especially pleased that for a significant part of this book we have been able to draw on James's immense scholarship. In a most authoritative way he has set the activities of man in the perspective of geological time. His application of the science of palaeontology to the present survival situation gives a fascinating new dimension to the whole question. Incidentally, he, too, wrote his part of the book in longhand.

Although most people these days are broadly in favour of conservation and recognize the general need for more of it, when we get down to detail the controversies begin to arise. Just what steps should be taken, just whose interests must be sacrificed, just how is it all to be paid for and by whom? And it is going to cost a lot to defend the biosphere, to defend our spaceship Earth – probably as much as it costs us to defend our frontiers and our national sovereignties.

In the end, of course, the money will have to come from governments and international aid programmes – for what we are talking about is, in the long run, nothing less than the survival of our species. Our survival is bound up with the survival of the other animals and of the plants which, with us, make up the spaceship's crew. Until this issue of survival is fully understood and the necessary steps to ensure it are generally accepted by the people and their governments, it falls to the world's conservationists, and the voluntary bodies they have created, to sound the alarm, to find the way, and to provide the money to carry on until the governments are ready to shoulder their own responsibilities.

You have already helped by buying this book, and you will also help by reading it – because the more people are well informed the more will be achieved. The problem must be widely discussed, and the dangers must be understood so that they can be averted. A greater value, it seems to me, must be placed on the quality of human life and on the higher aspirations of mankind. There must also be more action – more precise and specific conservation measures in the field. In our planning the long-term future of the environment must take precedence over short-term exploitation.

I believe all these things will happen in the end, but then I have always been an optimist. I am pleased to have been allowed to contribute this foreword to a book which will assuredly help to change man's attitude towards spaceship Earth.

Peter Scott.

Slimbridge 1970

Preface

by H.R.H. The Prince Philip, Duke of Edinburgh

taken from an address made to a conference in Strasbourg, February 9 1970, for European Conservation Year

Europeans have never restricted their interest in conservation to their home countries. Colonial administrations had an excellent record in the protection of forests from exploitation and in the establishment of nature reserves to protect populations of wild animals. This policy has been successfully continued in most of the newly independent countries and in many cases it forms the basis of a prosperous tourist trade and a key factor in their economies.

It is worth remembering that most of the world's flora and fauna were catalogued and classified by Europeans. I suspect that the rest of the world still looks upon dedicated bird watching, or the collection of everything from Acephalan molluscs to Zabrus beetles as a form of madness.

Today interest in our natural environment is as great as ever and in Europe the Council for Europe's initiative in calling this conference reflects the concern felt by the present generation. The problem facing us today is that there are some entirely new factors that are changing Europe's already artificial balance of nature.

People realize that the last hundred years have witnessed a scientific and technological explosion. Most people are now aware that there has also been an increase in human population to almost plague proportions.

What is less obvious, perhaps, is the penalty we have to pay for the enormous improvement in human material standards. The fallout from the technological explosion has littered Europe with immense industrial complexes belching pollution into the air and into the water, while the increase in human population has created cities bigger than the world has ever known and produced intense overcrowding in almost all parts of the Continent.

By a strange irony it is the growing urban populations, and not country people who will be the first to feel any deterioration of the environment.

Between them technology and mankind have created a vast network of road, rail and air transport systems, along with a problem in refuse and waste disposal which has completely defeated our efforts to control it. Meanwhile, increasing leisure has released millions of people into the mountains and on to the beaches.

For years we failed to notice the effect all this was having on the environment. Now we are facing a crisis situation. We have suddenly become aware that European land-locked seas and lakes are in greater danger of becoming deserts than the land. It is said of Lake Erie in the United States that it is so polluted that if anyone falls into it they don't drown, they just decay. This could happen here.

For generations agriculture has been a partnership with nature. Today, the pressure to increase output is so intense that farmers have to grasp at every chemical and mechanical means of increasing production, and they have to bring every available acre into use. Intensive research helps to destroy pests and weeds, but their destruction inevitably interferes with some long-established, delicate food chain. Many people, described until recently as cranks and crackpots, have been trying to give warning of the dangers for quite a long time, but it was probably Rachel Carson who managed to ring the loudest alarm-bells with her now famous book *Silent Spring*.

In 1961 a group of far-sighted people led by Prince Bernhard and Peter Scott established the World Wildlife Fund to help the work of the International Union for the Conservation of Nature and Natural Resources which was becoming increasingly concerned about the future of wild populations, both plant and animal.

In Britain many organizations were conscious of the dangers to their own particular interest but it needed a National Wildlife Exhibition sponsored by a Sunday newspaper in 1962 to begin the process of cooperative study and action. The exhibition was part of a National Nature Week intended to interest people in natural history. It succeeded far beyond its expectations. People came to see in the usual way but left deeply disturbed by the picture of man's intense and destructive pressure on the countryside and on wild populations. They also noticed the almost complete absence of any co-ordinated attempt to cope with these serious problems. Out of this exhibition grew the idea of holding a conference of all the parties, societies and interests concerned with the use of land and water: industry, urban communities, agriculture, forestry and leisure.

In 1963 the first "Countryside in 1970" Conference was organized in London and for the first time the full extent and seriousness of the situation became apparent. This was the beginning, in Britain, of a comprehensive and organized concern for the whole environment.

Since that time voluntary organizations, industrial and agricultural interests and government departments have been working together to repair some of the worst mistakes and to prevent any further avoidable damage. This is an immensely difficult process because conservation is to do with people. Every restriction, every control, and every development inevitably makes a direct impact on the life of particular individuals or groups of people.

We are only at the beginning, and all over Europe there are some formidable problems still to be faced and overcome. In the first place we need to assess the legitimate demands for land for industrial and city development and for water storage. We need to strike a balance between the control of pests and the destruction of wildlife, bearing in mind that animals don't know much about frontiers between nations.

We must find a way to control the exploitation of wild fish stocks in the open oceans. We must decide whether our inland seas are to continue to sustain life or slowly become polluted rubbish dumps. We need to decide whether we want to use our rivers and lakes as a supply of domestic water, or for sport and recreation, or as carriers of recycled industrial water, or whether

The Spanish lynx may now be the sole surviving race of its species, the pardel lynx, and confined to the delta of the Guadalquivir in southern Spain where *c.* 150–200 in the Coto Donaña Reserve form the main population.

18

we should let them rot as sewers. They cannot be used for all these purposes. We have got to learn how to handle our own waste products and effluents.

In any case, the natural supply of water will soon be unequal to the demand and we shall have to develop other sources of supply. We must decide how much pollution of the air, the land and the water we are prepared to tolerate. We must make a fair allocation of land and water for agricultural purposes and for different types of leisure occupations and recreations.

In order to make these decisions we need to create an administrative system which is capable of formulating a sensible and comprehensive conservation policy, which can take – hopefully – the right decisions and which can eventually carry the policy and decisions into effect. It must distinguish between those aspects of conservation which can be dealt with by advice and encouragement and those which require legislative action. I need hardly add that the system must make it possible to agree upon and enforce international controls where these are found to be necessary. Above all we have got to face the unpalatable fact that the conservation of our environment is going to cost a very great deal of money, and the denser the human population becomes the more expensive it will be.

It is no longer a question of stimulating interest and concern, or of discussing present mistakes and future dangers. People are already showing signs of boredom with all this talk about conservation. Even without any further research we know enough to be able to put many things right. If we establish the right administrative structure, it should be possible to see that plans for future development are not unnecessarily destructive. We also know quite enough to be able to say in which direction research programmes should be aimed.

More research is certainly needed but we must, at all costs, guard against the temptation to allow research programmes to become excuses for doing nothing else. Research and action must go on at the same time.

The fact is we cannot postpone decisions any longer. The process of destruction of living things cannot be reversed. The burden of responsibility for the future of Europe rests squarely on us and our generation.

It is just as well to recognize that any measures taken to protect our environment are bound to be unpopular in some quarters and they will inevitably cut across national boundaries. They will certainly be condemned as unwarranted interference or for preventing necessary development. Some will be called politically inconvenient, others will be dismissed as administratively awkward. It will be extremely difficult, but we must find ways to compromise between conservation and development.

The "starving millions" are always used as justification for the use of any agricultural toxic chemical. The public interest in the short term can always justify yet another encroachment, yet another water-storage scheme, yet another exploitation of natural resources. This is inevitable and some objections may well be valid, but if we want to continue to live a reasonably civilized existence in an increasingly overcrowded world, we shall have to

The most endangered bird in Europe, the Spanish race of the imperial eagle, which formerly bred in at least four countries, is now reduced to a population of *c.* 100 birds and only breeds in Spain, where Eric Hosking took this photograph in the great Coto Doñana international reserve.

21

accept certain restrictions and make special – and expensive – alternative arrangements.

Time is fast running out and it remains to be seen whether those in political authority can shoulder their responsibilities in time and act quickly enough to relieve a situation which grows more serious every day. It is totally useless for a lot of well-meaning people to wring their hands in conference and to point out the dangers of pollution or destruction of the countryside, if no one is willing to take or capable of taking any action. It will be a waste of time and effort to establish even the most brilliant advisory body if there is no way of putting its advice into effect.

Life and Wildlife

H.R.H. The Prince Philip, Duke of Edinburgh

Life and Wildlife

by H.R.H. The Prince Philip, Duke of Edinburgh

Discovery

The conventional beginning to an interest in nature and conservation is the picture of a small tousle-haired boy roaming the country lanes and fields, pockets crawling with insects and small reptiles. Dedicated to animals from an early age, a despair to tidy-minded parents and teachers, dirty, absent-minded and frequently truant, the budding naturalist scrapes unwillingly through school and college.

Forty years later, the picture of the early days of the distinguished naturalist becomes even more romantic and embellished with prophetic details.

I am not a distinguished naturalist; in fact, I'm not really a naturalist at all. I have merely developed or acquired an interest in conservation. Far from having a passion for spiders and toads as a small boy, I can remember not the faintest interest in them or anything else to do with "nature," for that matter.

To me the world was there; I accepted it. Wild animals were as much a part of the scenery as railway trains or street lamps. It's true I once kept some guinea-pigs with the help of the gardener, but very soon their breeding ability defeated our combined efforts at birth control and the swarming colony was quietly disposed of. I don't remember even shedding a tear.

I think I was fortunate in being born into a very matter-of-fact family. There was no sloppy sentimentality about "darling furry creatures" of "our feathered friends" and no anthropomorphic attachment to dogs or other pets. Animals were simply animals to be treated with consideration, but not with gushing adoration. I suppose that living partly in the country, frequently in large family houses, surrounded by pets of all kinds and being on fairly intimate terms with the usual farm animals, I never consciously segregated human from animal existence!

Anyway, I made my way through school totally oblivious to the call of nature or whatever it is that captures the imagination of the budding naturalist. Even a fairly elementary course in biology failed to arouse any enthusiasm and the internal arrangements of a frog left me cold.

Stalking roe deer and red deer and shooting game birds was so much a part of the life of many of my relations that it has never become a moral problem as far as I am concerned, although I realize it can raise strong emotions in others. The sight of blood had nothing of the mystical significance which it seems to hold for those who grow up shielded from the facts of life. But I very soon learnt the basic rules and traditions of those who for generations have gone after game animals and birds: the rigid observance of close seasons, the need for special care in hard weather, the overriding concern to avoid unnecessary suffering, and the need to understand the whole life-cycle and habits of particular game animals and their predators.

I certainly learnt the fundamental lesson of conservation that if you want any game animals the following year you have to ensure a proper breeding stock and a suitable habitat. Looking back now, I realize that this was my real introduction to natural history and it doesn't surprise me to find how many amateur naturalists came into it through shooting, stalking or fishing. I am always amazed that so many townspeople seem to be incapable of understanding that hunting and conservation are now entirely compatible so far as conservation is concerned. They simply will not, or do not wish to recognize that in most parts of the world the leadership in conservation has come from experienced hunting sportsmen.

This early introduction was brought to a rather sudden halt when I joined the Navy in 1939, just in time to be swept into six years of war. Again, if I had had any particular interest in nature I would be able to record that I had kept notes of observations of seabirds during those days. In fact, I have to admit that I don't consciously remember seeing any birds at all in the whole period I spent at sea in the North Sea, Indian Ocean and Pacific. To the sailor there are anyway only three types of birds: sparrows, seagulls and ducks – but I have omitted the traditional descriptive adjectives.

Discovery, in the sense that I became aware of the fact that there were more than these three types of bird other than game birds, came rather slowly, and then only because I had bought a rather expensive camera and a telescopic lens.

In 1956 I went to Melbourne in the Royal Yacht *Britannia* for the Olympic Games. Following a short visit to New Zealand, we sailed across the South Pacific to visit what were then called the Bases of the Falkland Islands Dependencies on the Grahamland Peninsula of the Antarctic Continent. From the Chatham Islands off the coast of New Zealand to Grahamland is 3,800 miles of open sea in the roaring forties. The old wind-jammers used that route across the South Pacific from Australia round Cape Horn to England. They crashed across, driven by a succession of depressions which caught them in a series of westerly gales. The passage took us thirteen days and by a stroke of luck we picked a gap between two depressions and crossed in relative comfort. We soon got used to the long, heaving swell but our only company were the seabirds of the southern oceans.

Simply as a pastime I tried to take photographs of them. That did it; from then on I was hooked. I had to know what each species was called. I had to try and get a reasonable picture of every species that came anywhere near the Yacht, and in no time at all I had exposed the first of several miles of film and started a hobby and an interest which has grown with the years.

Three years later I made another long voyage but this time it was across the Central Pacific. Strangely enough it was on Christmas Island, which was then being used to test nuclear devices, that I managed to take the photographs of some of the best-known tropical seabirds. Needless to say, it never occurred to me that any of these pictures would be published, but one thing led to another. Some time later I showed the best of the pictures to a friend who, I was somewhat surprised to discover, was a very knowledgeable ornithologist. To me they were rather inadequate

A white-capped noddy, photographed on Christmas Island.

snapshots of some birds I had seen in the course of that journey. From him I discovered that many of the birds had not been photographed all that frequently. This led to a little book, *Birds from Britannia*, which I had hoped would include the maximum number of pictures and the minimum text. Unfortunately, the publishers refused to do anything unless I wrote what I considered to be an immense number of words. When the book came out I was amazed to discover that all my work amounted to no more than an overgrown pamphlet.

Other journeys followed, to Africa for independence ceremonies, the Galápagos, Iceland, South America, Canada and Australia, and most recently to Ethiopia. Each time, I must confess, the planning included some provision to do a bit of bird watching and sometimes some photography. Even if a proper expedition were not possible, I soon discovered that the grounds and gardens of Government Houses invariably held a store of new and fascinating birds.

In Canada I managed to squeeze a few days out of a busy programme to escape into the Laurentians, and I returned with eyes red-rimmed by binoculars and a well-thumbed copy of Roger Tory Peterson's *Field Guide to Birds*. After the Independence of Tanzania I managed a few days in the Serengeti National Park with some friends and we were able to add half a dozen names to the Park's checklist of birds. It was there that I came across my favourite bird name, the "Barefaced Go Away Bird." If you don't believe it, look it up.

In Iceland it was the famous Lake Mývatn and in Kenya the remote and fascinating Lake Rudolf. In Australia I gave the citizens of Perth a faint shock by getting up before dawn to watch and photograph birds on the Swan River. In Canberra I again got away before dawn on the day of the capital's fiftieth birthday celebrations to watch some mist settling on the shores of Lake George. If I wasn't all ears and appreciation at the speeches and ceremonies later that day, this supplies the explanation. In South America bird watching is almost too much of a good thing, everywhere there is something new to be seen, and expeditions with knowledgeable ornithologists such as I managed in Chile and Argentina produced an indigestion of new forms.

This makes it look as if all my contact with the natural environment took place away from home. In fact, not many years after the war a combination of fortunate circumstances made it possible for me to resume some of the country pursuits. Indeed, one thing led to another. It is quite impossible to spend a day on a Scottish river or loch, or up on the high hills, and fail to notice the life of birds and other animals. One day it might be the dramatic sight of a golden eagle floating watchfully over the heather, or perhaps a wild cat or fox about its business, golden plover, ptarmigan, black cock or perhaps an adder just a bit too close for comfort; on the river it might be an otter or the screaming oyster catcher or the silent, flitting flight of the dipper, or some small wader.

It is the incidental happenings of a dawn or dusk wildfowling

H.R.H. The Prince Philip in Serengeti National Park.

A passenger pigeon.

expedition to some remote marsh in East Anglia which make the whole experience so fascinating. The sights and sounds and the mysterious movements of birds create a very special atmosphere and state of mind. Without an interest in these pursuits I would never have seen the Norfolk Broads in the grip of an icy winter, or watched the dawn come up over the St Lawrence marshes, or witnessed the spectacular collections of wildfowl in the swamps of India, Pakistan, Persia and Greece.

In fact, I have been wet and frozen, and fried in the sun. I have walked for miles through fields and over hills; I have frightened myself silly climbing to the top of rickety pigeon platforms, and I have sat shivering on the edge of a kale field in a blizzard. I once sat in what North Americans call a "blind" with a chap who prided himself on being able to call duck. Unfortunately, he was just getting over an attack of whooping cough. Every time he started to quack it brought on a bout of whooping.

To anyone with a conventional view of pleasure, to the town-living, comfort-loving commuter, the idea that there might be any thrill in wildfowling or rough shooting must seem too painfully ludicrous to be considered. Yet this is the stuff of natural history, this is a certain way to arouse an enthusiasm for conservation. Without this introduction I would never have learned about the sights and sounds of the country and the wilderness or taken my camera to places like Hilbre Island, off the northwest coast of England, the nature reserves in the Outer Hebrides, or to Lake Rudolf. Perhaps the most fascinating expedition of all was a four-day visit to the Galápagos Islands, forever associated with Darwin's great work, the Mecca of naturalists and a veritable paradise for bird- and animal-photographers. It is here above all that the whole problem of conservation becomes most obvious.

I came to conservation through shooting and bird watching, but that is only a very limited sector of natural history. Others arrive at the dilemma of conservation through animals and zoology, or through a delight in flowers and botany, or through the study and practice of forestry, or again through fish and marine biology. Sooner or later, it becomes only too apparent that every branch of natural history is a part of the whole. It is only a matter of a short time of innocent bird watching and photography before the question of survival of species begins to dawn on the mind. It was made to dawn on my mind pretty forcefully when I agreed to attend and speak at the inauguration of the United States World Wildlife Fund National Appeal in New York in 1962.

There is nothing like having to make a speech about a subject to concentrate the mind upon its problems. I don't know what effect, if any, my speech had on the audience, but it certainly had an effect on me. I was suddenly brought face to face with the fact that there was a grave and growing threat to the very existence of a large number of wild animals and that wild places and populations of all kinds were in considerable danger. I put it like this:

"Since the time of Our Lord and that, you will recall, is 1962 years, about a hundred animals and the same number of birds have become extinct. Species that took at least two and a half million years to develop wiped out forever. Just in case you're still feeling a bit smug, let me remind you that the passenger pigeon which

Left, a Darwin finch and right, a hawk-tailed gull pinching a booby's egg, both photographed in the Galápagos.

used to darken the skies of North America was exterminated not as a pest but just for fun in one human generation within the last hundred years. Today there are two hundred and fifty species of animals and birds in danger of extermination by the sheer callousness of mankind. Ironically, the national symbol of the world's greatest nation, the bald eagle, proud emblem of the mighty United States of America, is itself on the list. 'Father, what's that funny bird on the dollar – have you ever seen one?' 'No, my boy, we killed them off in a fit of absent-mindedness.'"

The figures I quoted at that time were not entirely accurate and anyway they only tell part of the story. The International Union for Conservation of Nature and Natural Resources (IUCN) has taken the year 1600 as the point at which reasonably exact records begin. At that date there were approximately 4,226 species of mammals living. Since then 40 species are believed to have become extinct and at least 120 are presently in danger of dying out. In 1600 there were about 8,648 living species of birds. Since then 93 have almost certainly become extinct and a further 187 are in great danger.

This means that in the last 400 years alone the world has lost about a hundred species of its higher animals. What is more important still is that the extinction of three-quarters of this total is more or less directly due to the activities of mankind.

Purists would also question the statement that the species took at least $2\frac{1}{2}$ million years to develop. The only generalization that would be permitted is that all but a tiny handful first developed as their present species during the Pleistocene period, which started well over 1 million years ago and "passed" about 10,000 years ago, and that most of them have existed for less than a million years.

That speech in New York was the first of many on this subject. Later that same year I said at the launching of the British National Appeal for the World Wildlife Fund:

"All appeals for money have an uphill struggle, but this one has even more formidable problems to overcome. In the first place, it has got to batter its way through the barrier of ignorance, indifference and emotion to get the facts of the situation understood and appreciated far and wide. In the second place, this situation is not brought about by any natural disaster which crashes down on people and animals without distinction. The unpalatable fact about the wildlife crisis is that it is brought about by man. There is no getting away from it; in this disaster man, and man only, is responsible."

As I said, one thing has led to another. There have been more speeches and I have become an International Trustee of the World Wildlife Fund. There have been meetings, conferences and attempts at bringing pressure, but from my own point of view the most satisfactory part of it has been meeting the true naturalists and experts. It's like belonging to some secret society. Word gets about among those interested that you are one of them and it is an immediate introduction. Like all enthusiasms it cuts across the conventional barriers of occupation, nationality, class or anything else.

Indeed, natural history forms one of the main bridges between science and the humanities. Our natural surroundings and our fellow creatures are as much a matter of fascination to poets, painters and musicians as they are to ethologists, zoologists, botanists and ecologists. Even lack of knowledge is no barrier. Enthusiasm is recognized and encouraged by the experts and I have yet to meet one who felt it below his dignity to help and to explain to the beginner. The brotherhood of naturalists is very real and membership in it is immensely rewarding.

Exploration

There must be literally hundreds of millions of people all over the world who are as ignorant, even oblivious, of the problems of conservation as I was only a few years ago. This, strangely enough, is probably the most important factor in the whole realm of conservation. Using the term "nature" to embrace everything on this earth which was not created by man, it very soon becomes apparent that this "nature" is being rapidly destroyed, not maliciously, but by sheer ignorance, lack of consideration and neglect. To this must be added misunderstanding. Love of animals, in the sense of lavishing affection and care on domestic pets, or in the sense of tender care for individual animals, has virtually nothing to do with conservation. The morality of killing animals and the argument about cruelty have equally no direct relevance to conservation. These are side issues, and their pursuit to the exclusion of the wider and, in my opinion, more important aspects merely leads to confusion.

Conservation is an immensely complicated problem, and people who leap to the apparently obvious conclusion that it means complete protection of all wild things, or loving care for individual animals, are guilty of gross oversimplification. They have merely allowed their emotions to overrun their reason, and their intuition to overrule the results of rational and painstaking collection of facts.

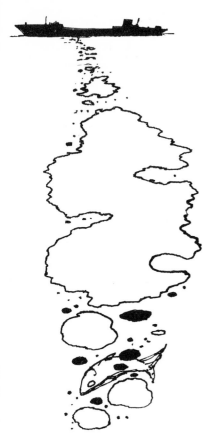

The very first fact is that man's relationship to the rest of the world has changed completely over the years.

For hundreds of thousands of years people have been living in a more or less hostile environment. Life was a constant struggle against what seemed to be the blind forces of nature. The greatest successes and achievements of mankind barely made any impression. Today all that has changed. We have got to get used to the idea that mankind is now dominant. It may have come as a great surprise, it may have been quite unintentional, but the fact remains that there is hardly a remote corner of this earth which is not subject to man's interference or control. Deep freeze, canned goods, airconditioning and modern transport, refuse collection and sewage disposal, have made life easier and relatively free from the influence of climate and season. Synthetic materials, space travel and spare-part surgery have made it seem that we are independent of nature and God.

This may sound rather arrogant. It may suggest that God's power has somehow been limited. This is not arrogance, it is realism. Indeed, it might well be argued, from verse 28 of the first chapter of the Book of Genesis, that this is what God intended: "And God said unto them, Be fruitful, and multiply, and replenish the earth, and subdue it; and have dominion over the fish of the sea, and over the fowl of the air, and over every living thing that moveth upon the earth." Dominion means power, but power means responsibility.

Industrial development, increasing population, pollution, exploitation of natural resources; these are the works of men. The power of God to influence mankind and to give direction to his activities is as great as ever, but it is no use behaving like spoilt children and blaming others when something goes wrong. We simply must get this straight; we are responsible for the things we do. We are responsible for the direct results of our actions, and we must also take the blame for any indirect results.

At one time we could plead ignorance. When industrial methods began to be used on a large scale for the first time, there was no way of knowing what effects they would have in the long term, and people did things which we now know to have been wrong and destructive. Today we ought to know that any ill-considered development may easily have disastrous results, not because of some outside malevolent influence but due entirely to our decisions. This is why we are now confronted with a polluted environment.

One of the very first things which primitive hunting man discovered was that if he wiped out his food supply there would be nothing left to eat the following year. The one important lesson which had to be learnt before man could succeed as a cultivator was that the best seed must be kept back for sowing if he was to reap a good harvest in the following year.

Several animals, and certainly the ants, have also learnt these lessons long ago. Yet here we are in the second half of the twentieth century, the century of reason, knowledge and science, and in many respects this fundamental lesson continues to be ignored. Sea-fishing is a typical example of the free-for-all exploitation of wild populations. The same applies to taking wild crocodiles or leopards for their skins. This is nothing less than a primitive scramble to cash in while the going is good in the boneheaded belief that there is an inexhaustible supply. What makes one despair is that even with all the international agencies we have so carefully created, we are wholly powerless and incapable of enforcing the obvious and sensible controls.

The concept of "cropping" is so old and so basic to the whole existence and development of man that I am astounded to find that it is not being applied in so many critical situations.

At one time it seemed that the only hope of keeping the human species from extinction was to breed as many children as possible. Today, the wastage through premature death and disease has been so much reduced that the same level of breeding is producing a population explosion. Whatever may be the moral arguments, the fact remains that the total number of human inhabitants of this earth is growing at a most alarming rate.

Before anyone can begin to apply moral judgments or to make any attempt to reach a philosophy about conservation, it is essential to make some effort to discover the facts. By that I do not mean that you should first decide your attitude and then select only those facts which appear to prove your original hypothesis. The only way to collect facts is to clear your mind of all theories and prejudices and to let the facts speak for themselves. That, in essence, is the point of this book. It may not contain all the facts but at least there should be enough to make it possible for any reasonable person to come to an objective assessment of the whole issue of conservation.

There are three basic factors from which all the problems of conservation follow. They are: first, the size and immensely rapid growth of the human population of this earth; second, the fact that *Homo* is *sapiens* and through his knowledge and technical ability is creating his own environment beyond and outside the traditional natural restrictions; third (and I have mentioned this already), the sublime ignorance of the major proportion of the human population, who are utterly oblivious to the first and most important fact of all, namely that they are a part of nature's network – that complex web of life on this speck of matter whirling through the infinities of space.

Let me elaborate a bit on each of these factors. First, the human population. The phenomenon now widely described as the "population explosion" means that the human race has reached plague proportions, and there is every indication that it is going to get worse. Indeed, a simple mathematical calculation will show that if we don't do something about it, in 500 years from now there will be standing room only on the land areas of this earth. Five hundred years may seem a long time but just look back. The year 1470 is not so very long ago. It's well into recorded history, and many things survive from that time. Indeed, the span is equivalent to only twenty generations.

The fact is that the evolutionary process, which is the interaction of the environment on the genetical inheritance of the species, finally produced man, a creature who became capable of speech and thought and construction. In all other animals the body has to adapt to the environment. Man turned this upside down and has

set about adapting the environment to suit his body. He has succeeded so well that he has made it practicable for far more people to exist on this earth than would have been possible under the traditional laws of nature. Moreover, the force of the evolutionary process is that any life form which does not adapt to circumstances becomes extinct. In that sense every life form is permanently in danger of extinction. As far as man is concerned, the danger is very obvious, but with this difference: if man becomes extinct it will be through his own carelessness, either by blowing the earth to bits or simply by breeding to destruction. Both are very real dangers!

The direct result of this increase in the population is that more space is taken up by housing. Those houses have got to be serviced by roads, sewage and refuse disposal, water and power supplies and facilities for recreation and amenity. Furthermore, these services will have to be supplied at a considerably higher standard than they are at present. The indirect result of this increase in the population and the improved standards which will be provided is that industry must expand, and agriculture must become more efficient. There will have to be bigger industrial areas, more power stations, more transport, more reclamation of marginal land, more water supply and the whole operation will be conducted under the relentless pressure of competition. This competition will inevitably demand, as well as justify, scientific, technological and industrial innovation, and the long-term influence of any innovation is bound to be a matter of speculation.

In any event, all this makes demands on the earth's surface, and as every demand is met, so it follows that space is denied to its previous wild inhabitants.

This is the second factor, our ability to make things. Not surprisingly, we make things for our own benefit. We manage things in our own interests. Natural resources are exploited for our own purposes. Rivers are dammed, marshes are drained, forests are cut down, cities are built, the land is cultivated, animals are domesticated, so that we can live and increase in numbers. The fact that all these activities are destroying the places where wild populations previously existed is inclined to be completely and conveniently ignored. Provided, of course, we don't detectably poison ourselves, who cares how much pollution of the air, of the land or of the waters and seas takes place? Yet this pollution, this quite incidental, even unintentional side effect of human progress is playing havoc with the natural environment of many animals, particularly fish. Indeed, even the experts are unable to measure the full effects of pollution or determine whether they are actually measuring all its effects.

The fact is that, for the first time in history, man has achieved virtually complete control over his habitat. We can, if we so wish, let this control operate by default, and just let things happen. If we do that, we shall grossly over-populate the earth, we shall pollute the air, the land and the water, we shall exterminate all animals and plants which get in the way of our farms, cities and industries, we shall convert all the jungles, swamps and deserts into usefully productive land. If we can do all these things, surely it is not beyond our capability to decide what sort of habitat we

34

would like to live in and then make the necessary plans and arrangements to achieve it.

The first thing, therefore, is to care for the present environment, the next step is to care about the future. I don't pretend to be able to forecast what is going to happen. The future has always been full of surprises ever since man discovered how to think about it. However, this world has been going for quite a long time and, barring accidents, it may continue to go on for quite a long time. So far one generation has succeeded another and, again barring accidents, there is every reason to believe that this process will continue. Something totally different may well happen, but going entirely on past experience I think it would be reasonable to conclude that a hundred years from now this world will be inhabited by people not substantially different from ourselves. Many things about them may be different, but it seems reasonable to guess that they too will want to enjoy the best achievements of previous generations, natural loveliness and the companionship of wild creatures. If this is the case, then the best we can do is to draw up plans so that they get what we believe they will enjoy.

In fact, the most important responsibility of conservation is planning. The plans may well be wrong but at least we will have tried, which is far better than leaving things to chance. Practically everything we enjoy today in the environment of the advanced or heavily populated areas of the world was quite deliberately planned by previous generations. Almost everything we deplore happened by chance or neglect. This may be an oversimplification, but as an illustration I think it would be fair to say that for every slag heap that disfigures the countryside there must be a hundred parks and gardens that were deliberately created by people concerned about beauty.

This concern for beauty is just as great, if not greater, today and the purpose of conservation is to mobilize this concern; to extend it from an individual attitude to a group consciousness; to create a wide public involvement, so that each generation grows up aware of its responsibilities and so that public opinion is informed and active on all aspects of conservation.

Conservation is not simply a matter of preservation or an active concern for beauty. It must also take into account all the other activities, particularly in the open country. It is concerned with sports and games and recreation in general; it is concerned with the use of water for all purposes; it is concerned with the use of land for agriculture and forestry; and it is concerned with amateur and scientific study of wild animals and plants. The reconciliation of all these conflicting interests in plans for the future is an immensely complicated and challenging task.

Wildlife in nature, and that includes everything from microbes to blue whales, from the spore of a fungus to the giant redwood tree, has been so much part of life on earth that we are inclined to take its continued existence for granted.

We may not want to destroy this natural heritage but we are doing it anyway. This is the third factor. To a large extent the wildlife of the world is disappearing not because of a malicious and deliberate policy of slaughter and extermination but simply through a general and widespread ignorance and neglect. In some

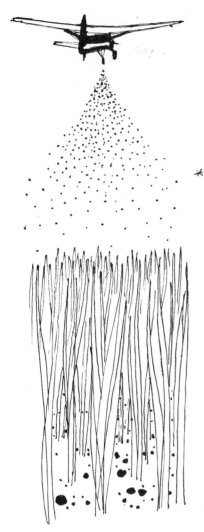

cases, of course, slaughter plays an important part. The blue whale, for instance, had been brought to near extinction by commercial exploitation and this has happened to the largest animal the world has ever known. In the case of the North American passenger pigeon, the species was wiped out by indiscriminate shooting. To be fair, this has more to do with the absence of proper control than any malicious intent. I don't imagine for one moment that the fishermen and hunters individually, or as groups, actually set out to exterminate these particular species. They were simply oblivious to the effects of their actions.

In other cases killing plays no part at all. The destruction of a habitat, the interruption of a food chain, the interference with an environment can have equally devastating results and there is no conveniently obvious culprit to take the blame. Where there is direct competition for land use between humans and wild animals, the animals inevitably lose, but I doubt whether the developers and reclaimers have ever thought of themselves as exterminators of wildlife.

Destruction by pollution is well known and was vividly described by Rachel Carson in *Silent Spring*, but I doubt whether even now individual chemists or producers of noxious effluents fully appreciate the importance of the part they can play in the conservation, or the destruction, of nature. No one denies for one moment that the chemists are all making immensely valuable contributions to human welfare, by feeding the hungry and giving employment. Too often, however, they are simply ignorant of the whole issue of conservation and I suspect that many would much rather *not* know about it. In any event they certainly have no monopoly of humanitarian and social consciousness.

Conservation of nature poses quite a number of moral problems but these are as nothing compared to the problems posed by the remaining groups and tribes of extremely primitive people. It is easy enough to say, in all righteousness, that they must be given the advantages or the so-called benefits of modern civilization. They are bound to be happier if they are healthier in body and freed from the drudgery of scratching a bare existence. But this ignores the very serious practical difficulty that when these people are exposed to modern civilization, two things usually happen. First, they tend to contract and die of a number of diseases to which they are not accustomed, and second, the change from a tribal hierarchy and subsistence economy to an impersonal bureaucratic government and a money economy destroys the whole moral basis of their existence. There are many cases of this happening to South American Indians, and similar situations exist in every other continent of the world.

Knowing what we do, it might be tempting to conclude that these people should be protected from any outside interference so that they can continue to exist successfully in conditions which suit them. The objection, of course, is that this would be much the same as treating them like animals. This is the dilemma – whether to go to them in an attempt to integrate them into modern civilization, in the almost certain knowledge that this will destroy them utterly as a distinctive tribe or group, or whether to protect them in isolation, in their own interests.

We have been long accustomed to making decisions based on high moral principles. This is probably as it should be, but every now and then it can lead to very awkward situations. I think on the whole it is better to start by taking a factual and realistic view of any given problem, because it is worse than useless to apply moral principles from a position of ignorance or with a complete disregard for the practical consequences.

Attitudes

I have tried to discuss in very broad terms the salient features of the problem of conservation. The question now arises as to what attitude we should adopt. What is the philosophy of conservation? Painting a landscape of what is happening doesn't really decide whether the scene is good or bad, or what, if anything, ought to be done about it. It doesn't even suggest why we *should* do anything about it.

It would be quite easy to argue that all the real problems are concerned with people, their relationship to one another, war and peace, the structure of society, employment, education and poverty. From this it follows that the important issue is the brave new world of machines and gadgets, houses and roads, and all the paraphernalia of what is termed "civilized" existence.

How, then, does conservation fit into this? Why all this fuss suddenly about nature and wildlife? For all practical purposes conservation is just a nuisance, the cause of pests and diseases. Farmers don't like it when weeds or insects, birds or mammals, interfere with something which they are growing for a living. Birds get in the way of aircraft, deer damage the forester's trees and so on down an endless list of disadvantages. People might well be forgiven for feeling that we would be much better off if humans and their domestic animals and pets were the only living creatures on the face of the earth.

Unfortunately, I have no obvious, comprehensive and demolishing answer to this rather doubtful logic. Once upon a time it might have been possible to sweep this argument aside by saying that all living things were created by God and that His intention was that we should all exist together, and it was our responsibility, as His special creation, to care for all His other creatures. The particular merit of this traditional view is that it encourages a certain humility in the individual, it makes him look at himself and his surroundings and his fellow creatures in relation to the power and timelessness of God. The Creator is the only important being, everything else is incidental. We are part of His creation, which has both immediate and present substance as well as a continuous existence in time. From this it follows that the problems of our own limited moment of existence are both the outcome of events that have gone before and the cause of events that will happen after we have gone. No philosophy or approach to life based on the idea of God is complete or makes any sense unless it sees value in the record of previous events and unless it makes its own commitment for the sake of future generations.

In this sense we are at a point of crisis in the world. We are capable of realizing that if things go on as they are, there is grave danger that much of God's creation will be destroyed. We are equally capable of realizing that by deliberate action we have the power and the capacity to prevent it. Furthermore, we know that when the record of our times is studied, all the generations who come after us will realize that we had this choice and that we either succeeded or failed to make the right decision.

I say it is a point of crisis because the destruction by extinction of the continuing existence of any life form is irreversible. The dodo cannot be re-created. Once all the living creatures of a particular kind have been killed, or at any rate prevented from living, that kind will never be seen again. It is this very special circumstance which gives such urgency to the whole issue of conservation.

To many, this traditional approach to the problem is still utterly convincing, but there is a growing number of people who find it difficult to accept this simple and direct answer. So many facts and scientific explanations have been discovered which suggest that God's power is somehow less comprehensive than was at one time believed. This implies a rather simple, mechanistic view of God and the influence which He has exerted on human development, but it is none the less real and many people are looking round for some other more satisfactory inspiration.

For them there is what might be termed the "scientific" answer. All life is part of the evolutionary process and every living thing is in some way related to every other living thing. The justification for maintaining the living things of this world is that they exist, that they are interesting products of the whole process of existence on this planet. This process includes mankind, and in order to understand the scientific answer it is necessary to get the broad system of living organisms into the right perspective.

Although a vast number of life forms have become extinct in the course of evolutionary time, there are a great many still surviving whose evolutionary development came to a halt – forms of life at every stage from single-celled organisms right through inter-mediate beings such as worms or insects to the advanced creatures represented in particular by the mammals. In addition, apart from what might be called "Modern Man," there are groups of humans still existing in remote jungles and deserts in various stages of primitive social development. This means, in effect, that we have living around us, if not a direct ancestral evolutionary line, at least a whole series of collateral relations stretching right back, almost to the very origin of life itself. Darwin held that evolution was the result of the blind process of Natural Selection. In other words, those species which were able to breed and reproduce their kinds successfully continued to exist while those which for some reason or other failed to do so simply died out.

The pattern of evolution is in no sense deliberate, no animal deliberately sets about changing its internal arrangements or the colour of its fur or feathers in order to have a better chance of survival. The steps in evolution are due to a long succession of small variations in a species. If they were beneficial, it resulted in better breeding success; if they were malignant, that branch died out. The significant thing about natural selection is that it does not only operate on the physical make-up of animals – their claws and fur, feathers and wings, skeletons and digestive systems – it includes the whole social organization and behaviour patterns of each species. The things which animals have to do control their physical evolution: successful methods of finding food, escaping from predators, mating, and bringing up their young are the criteria for natural selection. These successful methods are inherited, though in some cases improved by learning or imprinting, and they form the basis of all behaviour patterns. To do all these things, animals must go through a more or less complicated but stereotyped series of actions which are dictated in much the same way as physical growth and development.

This particular study of the life-cycle behaviour and organization of animal species has been the subject of inquiry for many years and has recently been brought into sharper focus by the relatively new science of ethology. This has already filled in some blank areas in the picture of the animal life around us, and, provided we approach the subject with care it is also giving us a new perspective on many patterns of human behaviour. The reason for care is that to the casual observer it is very easy to assume that when an animal behaves in a way which looks similar to human behaviour in similar circumstances, the reasoning which led to the particular action is the same in both cases. The observer is naturally tempted to invest the animal with human powers of reasoning and consecutive thought.

Ethology should not be an attempt to relate animal and human behaviour. What it seeks to do is to understand why animals behave and react in particular ways. However, whether it can be proved scientifically or not, it is difficult, I think, to avoid the conclusion that the major forces which underlie certain general patterns of behaviour in animals may also lie behind similar human actions. For example, it is now fairly well established that the controlling factor in the behaviour of all advanced animals is the need for some form of territory or property in order to gain a supply of food, and to sustain a family or breeding group, and this property is owned either individually or in groups. It is the acquisition and defence of territory which causes intraspecific conflict and it is also the ownership of territory which is the essential prelude to mating and rearing young. In areas of dense population competition is naturally much keener than in areas where pairs, or groups, are widely dispersed.

From this arises the theory that the conflict which takes place between animals of the same species in the acquisition and defence of a territory is the basis of aggression, and that the combination of pairs, or groups, in mutual defence of territory and their young is at the base of affection. In other words, the clue to the answer to the great question "Why are we here?" lies to some extent in the whole structure of the living organisms all around us.

In the end, or rather at the beginning, the religious and scientific answers are, therefore, concerned with the same problem. One of the very first questions asked by thinking man must have been about his origins and how it all started. The very first book of the Bible is concerned with the beginning. The question is still being asked, but we have learnt enough to know that no geocentric earth and man-centred explanation is satisfactory. The basic elements of life are common throughout the known universe, the idea that there is a sudden and complete jump from non-life to life is no longer tenable in the face of discoveries about the properties and interactions of nucleic acids and proteins.

The history of all life is natural history and the present complex of life is the result of an immensely long and complicated process. Conservation, therefore, is both a religious and a scientific concern for living matter in all its forms.

But the scientific argument is not entirely satisfying. For one thing, it makes no allowance whatever for emotion. It wholly ignores the function of the human spirit and the pleasure and inspiration which nature has given to mankind for so long.

There are, in fact, two sides to human evolution. First, the purely physical, where natural selection operates by favouring the strong, the disease-resistant, the capacity to breed and the total behavioural suitability of the species to its environment. Second, with the development of man's ability to communicate and exchange ideas, came the evolution of his power of thought, and his whole psycho-social-cultural ecology which results from it. As reflective thought developed, so the instinctive and imprinted patterns of behaviour became modified or controlled by the results of communicated experience, by the ability to think ahead, and above all by the development of abstract ideas. Mankind had entered into a wholly new dimension of existence. The intellect was born.

This is the basis of what might be called the "human" answer. Man is certainly a part of the whole natural process but he also has a soul. The pleasure and satisfaction and inspiration which mankind derives from natural surroundings is the justification for keeping these natural surroundings as unchanged as possible. People need to commune with nature; it is as much part of us as we are part of it.

It doesn't need a great stretch of the imagination to find examples of man's intellectual dependence upon his natural surroundings. Some of the finest and most moving poetry ever written was sparked off by glimpses of natural beauty, or by the song of birds. Generations of painters have been challenged by the abstract and shifting patterns of the earth and sky. The responses of Turner and Constable among many others have given pleasure and wonder to millions of people. In music there is no end of choice, from Beethoven's "Pastoral" Symphony to simple folk-songs.

Indeed, natural history had its beginnings among intellectuals and today the naturalist pursues his interest as much as an art form as a science. Conservation as a necessity is a concept derived from the study of natural history, and the appeal of the idea of conservation is as strong to the emotions and to the artistic appreciation as it is to the material and scientific interest.

This is a very powerful argument for some, but it suffers slightly from the fact that it is fundamentally selfish. It suggests that if we practise conservation, it is entirely for the benefits we derive from it. After all, it might be said, the plants and the animals are themselves wholly unconcerned whether their species lives or dies. Their only concern is their own individual survival; they are

40

totally unaware of how they came to be born and they are equally oblivious to what happens after they die.

This argument suffers from a further disadvantage. If it is accepted without reservation, it might easily lead to the view that there is no need to be concerned with that part of nature which appears to be noxious, dangerous or ugly. If conservation is for people, then it is quite justifiable to destroy anything which is felt to be anti-people.

In the end, I cannot really believe that any reasonable person would actively condone the destruction of nature once they became aware of the facts of the situation. In spite of all the arguments, philosophies and theories, I still believe that we would cast round to find any excuse to continue the battle for conservation, and for coexistence with all our fellow beings on this troubled earth.

In the Field

Wild animal photography has become big business. Miles of film are exposed for those natural history television programmes, for magazines, and for the glossy "coffee-table" books. The quality of the photographs is superb and every intimate detail of every phase of existence of every bird and animal is recorded in glorious colour with matching biological description.

With the appearance of the professionals in a field which had previously been the preserve of amateurs and pretty way-out amateurs at that, techniques changed dramatically. Straightforward "portraits" of birds and animals were no longer enough. Even the more competent amateurs had discovered how to cope with exposures and focus. The professionals, as usual, wanted something different and by every kind of trick and contortion in camera angles and exposures, using all sorts of developing and printing gimmicks, the world of nature took on an entirely new look. It went from a form of stamp-collecting to Art with a capital A.

It might well be asked what possible point can there be for an amateur to direct his wobbling lens at wild animals? Whenever this thought begins to worry me – and it does every time I look at one of those programmes or books – I remind myself of that comforting saying: "If a thing is worth doing, it's worth doing badly!" I enjoy bird watching, I enjoy taking pictures of birds, to me it's worthwhile and therefore I don't mind doing it badly, and I am frequently reminded how easy it is to do it badly.

There are two basic problems about bird photography. You have to get to where the birds are, and you have to take the photographs without being seen or heard. The most obvious place to go is as near the bird's nest as possible. A bird with a nest full of eggs has to incubate them, so it remains fairly stationary for longish periods. When the eggs hatch, you have a bonus in the form of the young birds in the nest being fed. Furthermore, the adults come and go, and with cunning it should be possible to get them in various situations as well as in flight. But first you have to find the nest, then set up a "hide" or some form of cover. Unfortunately,

41

not all birds are so considerate as to nest on a piece of accessible, open, level ground with the sun conveniently behind the hide.

There are, of course, other opportunities. Birds may be known to feed or rest in certain places, or tides and storms may drive them to some particular sheltered area. In any event a hide must first be built. This can either be a tent type of thing, only much smaller and usually square, or it can be a more permanent structure made of rush mats, reeds or something of that kind. All need observation openings so constructed that the birds cannot see any movement inside the hide.

Most birds are relatively small creatures and even if it is possible to get a hide very close to a nest, there is a prudent limit because the slightest sound or movement will be detected. Even the click of the shutter is enough to make birds jump. Changing lenses or reloading film can be done quietly, but it takes a lot of time and patience. The obvious solution is to use the biggest possible telescopic lens. But there is a snag. The bigger the lens, the more sensitive it is to the slightest wobble or vibration; even the shutter can produce enough wobble to blur the picture and if the negative is to be enlarged it must be very sharp. A big lens also means a big tripod and preferably a monopod under the lens as well. By the time all this stuff is set up inside a tent four feet by four feet, and perhaps five feet high, there isn't much room for manœuvre. Needless to say, no matter how the hide is set up, inevitably there will be certain blind spots which the lens cannot cover. Just as inevitably, these are the precise and only places where the birds stand still.

Passably good photographs can be taken from a car or boat, but as the camera is probably hand held, it means using a smaller lens. It is possible, of course, to attach some form of lens-holder, but the whole thing soon gets fairly complicated if a big lens is used. In some places and circumstances the birds may be relatively tame and a careful approach may produce excellent results. These are usually found only on remote islands or in the Arctic or Antarctic area. Unique are the Galápagos Islands where the birds are so trusting, and the light so good, that even the cheapest box camera could get marvellous results.

Considering the amount of equipment needed – cameras, lenses, tripods, portable hides and so on – and the difficulty of getting all this stuff to the right place, it's not altogether surprising that only professionals and a few crazy but lucky amateurs can attempt to take photographs of the less common birds.

There is, of course, one fundamental difference between the amateur and the professional in this business. The professional hopes and expects to see his pictures published. The amateur is well advised to keep his efforts entirely to himself. Home movies or albums of photographs of the family at the seaside are capable of straining the firmest friendships, Natural history films or pictures are guaranteed to shatter them for ever.

You may well wonder why I have not followed that advice in this book. In Peter Scott's foreword there is a note to the effect that a share of the proceeds from the sale of this book are to be given to the World Wildlife Fund – a charity. What should not be done in the name of friendship may safely be done in the name of charity.

The World Wildlife Fund was established in 1961 as a means of raising money to finance the operations of the International Union for Conservation of Nature and Natural Resources. The Union is recognized by the United Nations Organization as the official international conservation agency, but the United Nations does not provide any cash for it. Maybe it should and maybe it shouldn't, but rather than waste time in fruitless argument the organizers of the WWF decided to try to raise some money by voluntary subscription. No one pretends for one moment that the sums raised are even remotely adequate for what needs to be done, but it is a start, and some very valuable projects have been undertaken or supported by the WWF. Anyway, if you happen to have paid for this book, you will have made a contribution to the WWF and can feel appropriately righteous.

To anyone interested in the conservation of wildlife the attitudes of other people towards wild animals and plants are distinctly puzzling. Pets and domestic animals are almost smothered with love and affection, yet at the same time outrageously high prices are paid for the skins of wild animals to make coats, shoes or handbags. Factory farming methods are condemned, and in the same breath there are complaints about the price of food. Intelligent cropping of abundant populations is hysterically attacked as vicious blood sport. The exploitation for commercial gain of wild populations in the sea or in the jungles is excused as legitimate business.

So long as these people have their food and their pets, they remain happily and self-righteously oblivious to the fact that life for wild animals and plants is becoming daily more and more difficult until one by one they disappear. There is no drama in their disappearance, no slaughter, no malice, no pleasure. They are simply squeezed out of existence by the ignorance, selfishness and greed of mankind.

Drained marshes, cut forests, fur coats, aphrodisiacs from rhino horn, margarine from whale blubber, agricultural pesticides, mechanical farming practices, raw sewage in rivers or the sea, and the reclamation of wild land do more damage to wild populations by the exploitation and destruction of their places of living than any of the more obvious causes of death.

Loving one pet is not the same thing as feeling concerned about nature and wild animals. Feeding the animals in the zoo is no substitute for letting wild animals live in freedom, and they cannot live in freedom if their source of food is destroyed and if the space for existence is denied to them.

The resources of the WWF and the IUCN are stretched to the utmost in protecting nesting areas, flyways and feeding places of migrating birds, in buying up or helping to control the few remaining wild areas of the world and, above all, by trying to establish which species are in danger of extinction and for which reasons. It is a task far beyond the capacity of a fund dependent upon private subscription. It is a task which needs to be tackled by an official international agency with sufficient money and effective power. I dare say that something like that will be set up eventually, but it will fail because it will be given too little money and power and it will be set up too late to do much good.

It simply is not possible to reverse the process of the destruction of nature. Once all the individuals of a particular species of plant or animal are dead they cannot be re-created, at least not by man – and there is no guarantee that God is going to correct our mistakes. I suppose, to be safe, I should say that it is not yet possible to re-create a particular species of plant or animal. It is conceivably possible that scientific knowledge of the process of life might eventually be able to do it, but it wouldn't do any good if there was nowhere for these re-creations to live.

If this sounds rather bitter, it is really only a reflection of the intense pleasure and satisfaction I get from watching and taking photographs of birds. You cannot do this for long without learning something about their way of life and their requirements for food and space for living and breeding. It doesn't take long or a very deep study to discover what is happening to the natural world, and no one can sit by and passively accept the ruthless destruction of something they love and enjoy.

I am prejudiced and I admit it, but even so I can see that there are immense and practical difficulties about any programme to protect the world's heritage of living organisms. Can you really deny more food to the starving millions by controlling the use of agricultural chemicals? Can you really prevent governments from reclaiming land and marsh in order to settle the poor and feed hungry people? Can you really stop cities expanding, or control where people go and what people do with their leisure? Can you really demand that domestic fresh water should be manufactured, instead of using and polluting the natural supply? I am not blind to the difficulties in the conservation of nature, but that doesn't stop me from feeling strongly that if we destroy our natural environment we shall be destroying a most important part of human existence. We shall be destroying a part of ourselves.

My concern may be selfish. I may well feel like this because I have discovered something to love and to cherish, but I am not alone in this and I don't think my generation will be the last one to feel this way. What started as a personal concern has grown into a fear that my generation will go down in history as the one which could have done something to save the natural environment and which failed to do so. My fear is that future historians will review the conditions and events of the twentieth century and conclude that the people who lived in this time cared so little for the world, or for future generations, that they blindly and ruthlessly exploited all the natural resources. They might well conclude that we cared more for the barren moon and outer space than for our fellow creatures. If we allow ourselves to destroy and devour the place where we exist we shall only be following one of the oldest natural laws. Whenever any animal or plant population reached plague proportions, it destroyed its own living space and supply of food and died. If it did not die out entirely, at least the population was drastically reduced. This could happen to mankind.

We know that we are capable of taking thought and, unlike animal populations, we can foresee what is going to happen. We are told that we have a divine soul and that we are a special creation. Well, now is our chance to prove it, to prove that we can save the world and save ourselves by our own intelligence.

Observing with Camera

The king penguins from the Antarctic (left) and the jackass penguins from the Falkland Islands (lower right) are only two of the fifteen living species of penguin, all of which live in the Southern Hemisphere. The word "penguin" was first applied to the flightless great auk of the northern Atlantic, which were reduced to a tiny population by sealers and fishermen who rendered them down for their oil, and were finally exterminated by collectors in Iceland on June 4 1844.

The largest of the penguins is the emperor which stands over three feet high, can weigh 90 lb., and lives deep in the Antarctic. One of the smallest penguins lives around the Galápagos Islands on the Equator. This illustrates the rule that all animals of the same group tend to have larger forms living towards the poles and smaller ones towards the Equator.

The wandering albatross (top right) is also a Southern Hemisphere bird, but in direct contrast to the flightless penguins, these birds can keep the air for hours on end in any weather.

The blue (locally called purple) heron (top left) was taken in the Galápagos. In the normal course of events herons are amongst the shyest and most suspicious birds. This one calmly went on fishing while I took its portrait from a few yards away.

The cormorant and Caspian terns (lower left) were taken on the Swan River in Perth, Western Australia. My excursion to watch and photograph birds early one morning was reported in the local newspapers. I am not sure what the residents of Perth thought about this strange behaviour.

The fish eagle (right) is a relatively common sight in East Africa. This one is from Lake Rudolf in northern Kenya, an area still fairly undisturbed. The lake is one of the chain stretching along the Great Rift Valley and therefore an important stopping-place for migratory birds of all kinds.

The fur seal (lower left) occurs in most parts of the southern oceans and, as it was much sought after for its fur, it very nearly became extinct. This one was taken in the Galápagos Islands, and of all the birds and mammals which live on those islands it is the only one to show any anxiety when approached by humans. Even so it makes little attempt to escape and it is obvious what an easy prey it must have been for the hunters.

The other photographs show sea lions, two young, and a female (upper left), all taken in the Galápagos. The bull sea lion is quite an impressive creature and he has no hesitation in showing his displeasure if you try to bathe from his section of the beach. I was lucky enough to find two sea lion pups, about the size of labrador dogs, in a pool cut off from the sea at low tide. Moving very slowly and with a lot of patience, I eventually managed to gain their confidence and touch them. They didn't mind having their hind flippers held but they didn't appreciate any attempt to hold their "hands." They seemed to enjoy being patted and stroked and their mother showed no concern about the weird creature which was playing with them. In fact she spent most of the time lying on her back in the water with arms folded across her chest and only the tip of her nose above the water. I am sure I heard an occasional bubbly snore.

On the next page is a picture of a marine iguana, another resident of the Galápagos Islands. These curious prehistoric-looking creatures live on shore but feed on seaweed on the sea bottom. They swim with their tails only and they appear to be able to stay under water for quite long periods. In some parts of the islands the lava rocks close to the sea are one swarming mass of these miniature dragons.

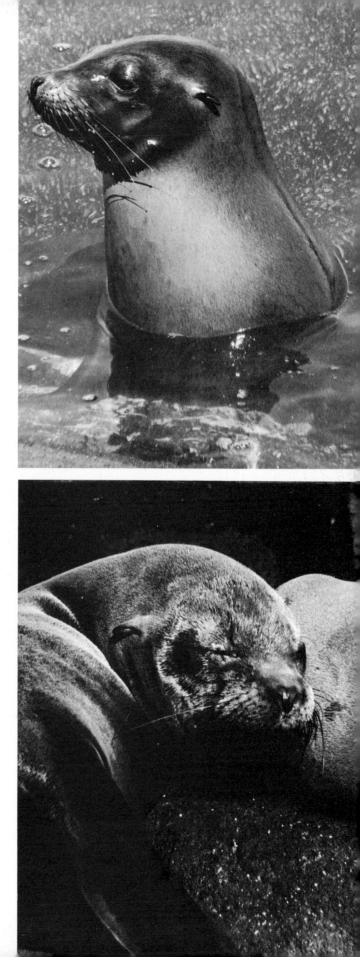

The flightless cormorant (left) is another inhabitant of the Galápagos, and it demonstrates the remarkable natural peace of these islands. The cormorants have lost the use of their wings because they have no need to fly. They can fish close inshore and there is no need to escape from anything. It was this sort of modification which gave Darwin the clue to his theory of natural selection, although he used the different-shaped beaks of the finches he found on the Galápagos to illustrate his point. The finches are now called Darwin's finches.

The two marine iguanas (right) seem to be thoroughly integrated. This must be one of my favourite photographs. Anyone who has ever tried to take photographs of birds or other animals knows how much depends on luck. This was the luckiest chance I ever had.

More Galápagos inhabitants. The Galápagos hawks (left) remained on their perch while I moved slowly closer to their tree. In the end I got right up to the tree and photographed them almost directly overhead. The reason they look a bit ruffled – and it may also be part of the reason why they were reluctant to be disturbed – is that they were engaged in making passionate love as I approached their tree. That scene is not illustrated simply because at the time I was negotiating a particularly awkward bit of lava and thick bush. I have always thought that hawks had particularly inscrutable expressions but there seems to be a little something in the look of these two. The Galápagos hawk is registered as an endangered species.

Those who have learnt to fly know about "circuits and bumps;" this brown pelican (right) is doing circuits and splashes. When a suitable shoal of fish has been found, pelicans plummet down on them with wings closed from about forty to fifty feet in the air. Having made a catch they surface, take off, fly round in a circuit and repeat the performance. In this case the circuit took the birds past the edge of a cliff just before their final dive. I think most birds should be photographed in flight; they look their best on the wing and after all the most important part of their construction is adapted for flying. The only snag is that it isn't all that easy. The birds move quite quickly and as far as I am concerned, even with gun attachments and rapid-focusing devices, it takes an awful lot of exposures to get a picture which is reasonably in focus.

In contrast to problems of photographing birds in flight, those of taking birds in the nest are relatively simple – once you've found the nest. The golden eagle chick (left) was born in an eyrie on a low cliff in the Outer Hebrides, off the west coast of Scotland. It was not particularly difficult to edge my way along the ledge, but holding the camera and large lens far enough out to be able to see into the eyrie had some interesting moments. Cameras need two hands and balancing on a ledge of even a low cliff without holding on can be quite dramatic.

In most cases golden eagles hatch off two chicks but before long one of them gets bigger and stronger than the other, and it eventually gets rid of its weaker brother or sister out of the eyrie.

The golden eagle, in company with all other raptors, is a predator in that it lives on other animals. With the widespread use of various kinds of persistent pesticides these chemicals find their way into insects and then into smaller animals, then into bigger animals and eventually into the predators which are at the end of the food chain and, therefore, get the biggest dose of the chemical. Even an accumulation of doses is seldom fatal but unfortunately it has an even more dangerous effect in that it makes the eggs infertile. No eggs – no replacements – and before long the population, or even the species, no longer exists.

By the time the effect is noticed it is usually too late to do anything about it. This is the particular worry of conservationists, that we may be doing things now which will only prove to be disastrous sometime in the future. Even non-persistent and highly specific chemicals can have unexpected effects. A chemical may be directed at one particular weed but if this weed harbours a particular insect which forms an indispensable part of the diet of a bird or animal, that animal is doomed.

The chick of the common gull (right) was in a nest on a small island in a little bay on the west coast of Scotland. The hide was within a few feet of the nest and I took this picture while the parent bird was away.

The fulmar (left) and the razor bill (right)
are relatively common seabirds on the west
coast of Scotland and nest on the ledges of
the towering cliffs of the islands and head-
lands which brood over the restless sea.

The fulmar derives its name from the fact
that it uses a particularly evil-smelling
oily liquid to spit at attackers, of which
there are plenty. The fulmar was an important part of the economy in old times at St
Kilda; after 12 August the young birds were
taken for food and their fat was used in
oil-lamps. The fulmar is one of a large
number of petrels, which range in size from
the giant petrel of the southern oceans,
commonly called a "stinker," to the very
small storm petrels or "Mother Carey's
chickens." All petrels are distinguished
by a pair of nostrils looking rather like
small tubes at the base of the upper beak.

The activity on the ledges of cliffs during
the breeding season is never-ending. There
is a constant to-ing and fro-ing, discussion
and argument between razor bills, guillemots,
puffins and kittiwakes. The noise of shrill
squawking rises above the crash and
grumble of the surf, and the smell can be
quite powerful also.

The interesting thing about seabirds is that
they are mostly black and white; only a few of
them display any colour. There are some
obvious exceptions. The puffin's beak looks
like a miniature rainbow and the frigate bird
has an extraordinary bright red pouch under
his beak which he blows up like a balloon in
mating display. The rock hopper and macaroni
penguins have straggly red and yellow
feathers on the tops of their heads which
make them look like rather solemn clowns.
Both king and emperor penguins display a
restrained but very smart pattern of colour
about their heads.

I find it fascinating to speculate on the
circumstances which have produced the
variety of shapes, colours and behaviour in
birds. Food-getting, camouflage, intraspecific
rivalry and the selection of mates by females
all play a part in this process.

The glossy ibis is well named because although it is black, its feathers are iridescent; depending on the way the light strikes them, they can look green or bronze, purple or even copper-coloured. So many birds with long spindly legs tend to look rather awkward, but the glossy ibis is better proportioned. In flight ibises have a light feathery quality and when a whole lot of them are flying together the long line seems to float up and down and drift about, tracing delicate patterns in the sky.

White-faced whistling tree duck in a marsh by Lake Rudolf in Kenya. The lake got its name from the Austrian explorer, Count Teleki, whose expedition discovered the lake in 1888. He named it after the Austrian Crown Prince Rudolf.

Lake Rudolf is unusual in that there are rivers running into it but none running out of it; evaporation takes the place of an outflow. The rate of evaporation is more or less constant, but the inflow from the oddly named Omo River, which drains the Ethiopian mountains, varies according to the season. This means that the water-level in Lake Rudolf can vary as much as sixty feet over a period of ten years. There are other lakes in desert areas which behave in much the same way and some of them, particularly in Australia, can disappear altogether for years at a time.

The water in Lake Rudolf is not salty but on the other hand it cannot be described as fresh. It has a faintly slimy feel about it and a taste not unlike those medicinal salts which are so freely advertised for various digestive complaints. The water is cloudy at all times and looks pale grey except in certain lights when it goes a palish greeny-blue. Most of the area surrounding the lake is arid and the only green patches are on the swampy and low-lying places. It is uninhabited except for some very primitive tribes, one of which, the Molo, lives off the lake fish, principally Nile perch. These fish reach a good size; 200 lb. and 300 lb. are not unknown.

The other inhabitants of the lake are crocodiles in fairly large numbers. Central Island, with its crater lakes, is a very popular breeding resort for these enormous reptiles as it is quiet and undisturbed. The lake is quickly whipped up by the wind into a short steep sea which can be most unpleasant for a small boat. This effectively isolates the island from all except the most determined naturalists.

Some birds are prepared to tolerate the approach of motor cars when they would become anxious and restive about people on foot. A slow and gentle approach in a Land-rover, advancing about twenty feet at a time, can often bring you to within good photography distance. Both the egret (left) and the brown eagle (right) were taken in this way on the shores of Lake Abyata in Ethiopia. The secret, of course, is not to get out of the car and to push out only the minimum amount of lens. The only difficulty is that the "arc of fire" – as it were – is somewhat limited and it is only a matter of time before the photographer starts to perform the most intricate contortions in the process of trying to get his bird into the viewfinder and then into focus. I realize, of course, that cars are designed for sitting in, but I now know how extremely difficult it is to get into any other position in them. An afternoon spent driving around in the hope of getting a few chance shots can be just as energetic and almost as painful as a game of hockey.

Lake Abyata is another of the string of Great Rift Valley lakes and its shores are a paradise for any bird watcher. It is particularly fascinating for a European to see so many familiar waterbirds such a long way from home. Shoveler and pintail duck, ruffs, avocets, sandpipers, little stints and even coots are to be seen everywhere mixed in with the indigenous species. Pink pelicans, flamingoes, painted storks and hammerkops, as well as herons and egrets of various kinds, are the more obvious large birds on the lake. On the grassy meadows along its shores there is another population of such birds as sand-grouse, crowned plovers, kingfishers, various birds of prey such as the brown eagle and the lanner falcon and many others. It would be a major tragedy if the peace of this lake were to be disturbed by any kind of development.

Spoonbills (right) figure prominently among the shore birds of Lake Abyata. They usually feed in groups of about eight or ten and the proceedings are conducted with great energy. The party advances at a brisk walk, sweeping their bills from side to side like a man using a scythe. This action presumably stirs up small creatures on the bottom which are then caught and tossed back into the throat by throwing the head up in the air followed by a lot of bill smacking and swallowing. You can hear a party of spoonbills on a feeding expedition quite some distance away as they advance, splashing and swishing through the shallows.

Not very far from Lake Abyata is Lake Shala but its character is totally different. Instead of flat shores and marshy patches, Shala is more like an enormous crater with steep cliffs and rocks almost all the way round. There are two islands in the lake which are particularly interesting; one supports a breeding colony of pink pelicans, which go over to Abyata to feed, and the other has a colony of Abdim's storks (left). I imagine they felt so secure on their rocky island that they were quite undisturbed as we crawled slowly towards them until we were only a matter of thirty feet away.

These pink pelicans (right) have selected an island in the middle of Lake Shala as their nesting site. I didn't count them, but at a guess I would say there were about 200 pairs. The remarkable part about it is that the adults had to fly some five miles to Lake Abyata to feed, Shala apparently being unable to meet their demands. The birds display considerable aeronautical skill as they wait until the day's thermal up-currents of air are formed at a particular point on the shore before they attempt to set off for their feeding grounds. They fly low across the lake and then into the thermals which carry them high enough for them to glide all the way to their destination. The returning birds appear about 500 feet above the island when they go into a spectacular descent to the island or land on the water beside it.

While all this traffic is going on, the young pelicans gather together in groups and gasp for air as the day heats up. The island makes these birds safe from ground predators, but the Egyptian vultures know all about the chance of picking up an un-attended egg or sickly chick as they patrol the suburbs of the nesting site.

The white heron (left) and the black-winged stilt (right) are two more quite common birds on Lake Abyata. The stilt is a most delicate-looking bird with its pointed beak and spindly legs, yet it is an accomplished flyer and covers long distances on migration. It looks a bit peculiar in the air, something like a pencil with wings.

Herons on the lookout for food can be fascinating. They will stand absolutely immobile for ages before making a sudden lightning dart at their prey. They have a way of stepping with immense care and hesitation from one foot to the other and then all at once making a dash and a stab. Judging by its extended neck, I suspect that this particular bird had either seen some movement in my hide or its naturally suspicious nature felt there was something wrong.

Taking birds in flight poses some very
difficult problems and I should imagine that
more film has been wasted in the attempt
than in any other form of bird photography.

In this montage, there is a blue-footed
booby (centre right) and a blue-faced booby
(top left and right) from the Galápagos.
The brown booby is from the southern
Atlantic.

We Healdath

Anglo-Saxon

by James Fisher

A System for Paradise

by James Fisher

The vanishing of wildlife at an accelerated rate is but one marker of the mess man has made of his environment. It is a measurable phenomenon; in the phrases used by Max Nicholson in his stimulating new book (*The Environmental Revolution*, 1970 January), the technosphere – the industrial environment that has evolved since about A.D. 1600 – could overwhelm the biosphere.

The real trouble lies much deeper. Thousands of animal species, including hundreds of the higher vertebrates, are now in danger of global extinction. In the course of evolution, extinction is a natural process; and the fossil record, deeply studied as it has been for well over a century, can give us some measurements of its natural rate. It is safe to say that the present extinction-rate of wild living things has been quadrupled by man since he has, with his industry and machinery, imposed the technosphere upon our planet. This is a fact, and it is the simplest bit of arithmetic we can offer to show that something dreadfully wrong is happening to the world's environment as a whole.

Of all the animals man is the dirtiest. He is the most powerful pollutant, destroyer, eroder and exploiter that the biosphere has ever encountered. Of the biosphere man is himself a product; an ape promoted by evolution's natural selection process from a stock of omnivorous, intelligent, experimental-minded, not over-specialized, probably African apes, to be the master of a planet. Man's keys to masterdom: tools – tools to make tools, tools to make those tools, language with which to teach, writing with which to store information, lately electronic tools which can themselves speak and write and remember – and the athletic strength, stamina, endurance and versatility, which make him at home from the poles to the tropics, from ocean to sea and undersea, on the highest mountains and the lowest deserts, and in the air and space above. Even naked, man is one of the finest runners, climbers, jumpers and swimmers the land mammals have ever produced.

This book, written by two citizens of the United Kingdom, which originated the idea of European Conservation Year 1970, takes as global a view of the issues as the writers can embrace.

Conservationists do not deserve an international image of being enemies of development; but they insist that they must enter development, or be entered there, at the planning stage. They are planners, not "abominable *no* men." Only a rich world can afford to spend money on environmental conservation, and only from industry and mechanized husbandry (which is farm industry) can the world become rich. The conservation struggle is to steer development, not to stop it, and to plan a happy harmony between man – who may have doubled his population during the lifetime of some of the younger readers of this book – and his environment.

The plans are not going to be easy to make. Vast areas of the

Reticulated giraffe photographed in the Northern Frontier District, Kenya.

world, particularly in the tropics and subtropics, are already in desperate degradation and some present human populations are starving. Research, analysis and action are being deployed, though not widely enough.

Nevertheless, the world servants of the United Nations, UNESCO, IUCN (the International Union for Conservation of Nature and Natural Resources), IBP (International Biological Program) and WWF (the World Wildlife Fund) all play huge parts. The first two of these are international-statutory, paid for by governments; the rest are international-private, paid for by foundations and non-government groups and private people the world over. They work well together, irrespective of the political or religious faiths of the countries and people concerned; for conservation can – and does – unite us all. We share one environment; we are all part of nature.

It is not many years since, on becoming closely connected with UNESCO, the world's senior wildlife body changed its name. It is now the International Union for Conservation of Nature and Natural Resources. Previously it stood, by its title, simply for the protection of nature.

Nature of course must be protected, but the switch from the somewhat negativist protective aim to the wider and far deeper conservationist aim shows which way the wind is blowing. At least the leaders of thought in the world realize that nature is one, that it forms a living, evolving and changing network over the face of our planet and that man is, practically everywhere, at the top of nature's pyramid.

In the length of his life as a species, about 200,000 years, man has become by far the most abundant large animal on the face of the earth and has made more radical changes to the natural communities of plants and animals on its surface than have been made by any other agency in the 3 billion or so years of life on earth – even more than the succession of the dozen or more disturbing glaciations of the Ice Ages of the last million years.

If percipient beings of man's calibre could have watched earth from the moon in the last few centuries, they could have seen with the naked eye man's dust bowls and forest slashes creeping over the continents. Percipient beings on Mars with optical instruments of no great sophistication could have seen the same. Man has become the lord and master of the earth, with prodigious power, pride and possibilities. As master of the earth he has shown himself capable of global lunacy, but capable too of high altruism and thoughtfulness.

Ecologically, the world is now faced with two alternatives: either a return to the muddle, misery and international malice of medieval times, or an advance to new adventures in forestry, farming, food-raising, the rational exploitation of wild resources, the tender preservation of natural communities for nature's sake, a new régime of mutual aid and, through responsibility for wildlife, self-education and re-education. Ecology is a new science which has borne its name for scarcely 100 years, but from earliest times the battle between the conservationist thinkers and the rash and greedy exploiters and disturbers of nature has been an ecological battle, even if they did not always call it that.

A System for Paradise

In some hundreds of thousands of years of Stone Age life man learned the art and tradition of food-gathering techniques and skills which enabled him to hunt all manner of living things of the land and shallow waters from shellfish to honey, from tubers to fruit, from sparrows to moas, from rodents to elephants. It is thought that by late prehistoric times the carrying capacity of the Old World provided enough wild food to support about 7 to 10 million humans. Now there are over 3 billion humans and before all of these are dead, there will be twice as many.

Rise of Power

The swift evolution of man's power over animals and plants began simply with the taming and domestication of animals. As that great zoologist and palaeontologist the late F. E. Zeuner put it, the habits of man on the one hand and of certain animal species on the other made the appearance of domestication almost inevitable.

Through symbiosis, scavenging, the dawn of agriculture and its effect on guest/host relations, social parasitism and true parasitism, the climate of systematic domestication emerged. From the master of domestic animals of the pre-agricultural phase – fowl, geese, pigeons and some other birds, the dog, members of the cattle family and pigs – man became a farmer. In due course he became the proprietor of later animals of domestication, pest-destroyers (cat, ferret, mongoose), transport animals (elephants, horses, asses, camels, llamas), special servants (bees and silk worms), and the organizer of experimental domestications, such as zoological gardens and avicultural establishments.

Giant panda; the symbol of the World Wildlife Fund; a rare and protected animal of China.

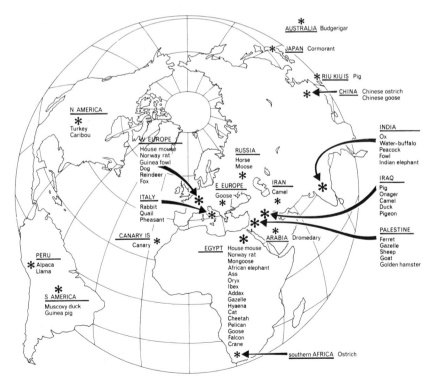

Some domestic animals, with the possible theatres of their early domestication.

79

Wildlife Crisis

After the stabilization of sophisticated domestication and agriculture came the great movements westward into the new continents and oceans; and the rise of exploitive agriculture, forestry, fishery and whalery in the last two or three centuries. As a global problem an assessment of the world's biological resources in terms of soil, water, forest potential and (in the sea) plankton, has now become imperative.

What is the carrying capacity of the world? Can we find out, and adjust our human world deployment – without destroying human rights and dignity – before it is too late?

Cropping Nature

Despite undoubted overkill in Old (Palaeolithic) and Middle (Mesolithic) Stone Age times and, in certain special cases, also in medieval times and indeed up to the present day, groups and tribes of humans became the special predators of special animals and often entered into a good ecological relationship with them. It was a relationship unconsciously ecological, conducted under rules hallowed by long tradition and sharpened by trial and error.

Under such rules, for instance, the seabird-fowlers of the Hebrides, the Faeroe Islands and Iceland have for centuries been able to harvest a crop of the eggs of certain seabirds and the young of others that amounts to half the actual production of these eggs and young birds on their great island cliffs. The birds

World distribution of rhinoceroses, showing that today's distribution is relict compared with that of the family in the Pleistocene period which ended 10,000 years ago.

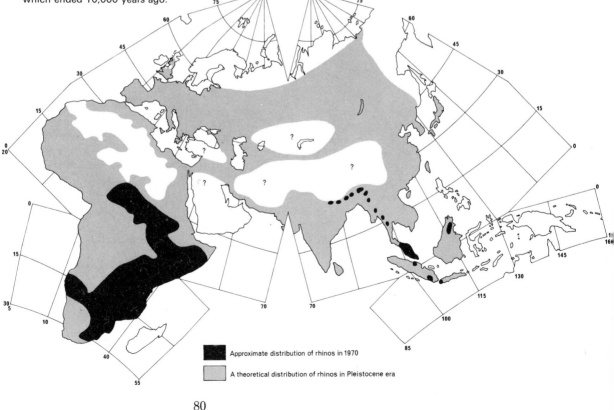

■ Approximate distribution of rhinos in 1970

▒ A theoretical distribution of rhinos in Pleistocene era

80

The giant race of the sable antelope which now has relict populations, in all *c.* 500–700 animals in the Luando and the Cangadala Reserves of Angola.

A chronology of the full species of birds and mammals believed extinct since 1600.

	Birds	Mammals
1600–49	3	1
1650–99	9	0
1700–49	9	0
1750–99	11	6
1800–29	4	1
1830–39	7	1
1840–49	2	1
1850–59	2	1
1860–69	3	1
1870–79	5	2
1880–89	5	2
1890–99	11	5
1900–09	10	10
1910–19	5	2
1920–29	2	1
1930–39	3	3
1940–49	4	2
1950–59	0	1
TOTAL	95	40

From this table it can be seen that extinction was at its greatest around the turn of the nineteenth–twentieth centuries. The period of greatest extinction was 1887 to 1908, a period of twenty-two years in which no fewer than twenty-four birds and fourteen mammals became extinct. IUCN records since 1600 have the earliest bird extinction date as 1638 (the broad-billed Mauritian parrot, p. 223) and mammal extinction date as 1627 (the aurochs, p. 246); and the latest extinction date for a bird as 1945 (the Wake Island rail, p. 221) and for a mammal as 1956 (the Assam rabbit, p. 234).

have remained at a fairly stable population, which shows that, in the biological sense, this was, and still is, a legitimate crop.

In the days of the shotgun a similar but less stable "balance" seems to have been achieved between hunters and game birds and wild fowl, at least in Russia, Europe and North America. In the old days there was the same kind of relationship between some, though not all, tribal Africans and their primarily antelope prey, and perhaps (though they overkilled for some considerable time after discovering Australia) between tribal Australians and their marsupial prey.

Not all tribal and traditional peoples mastered the secret of balanced predation. It has been proved, however, that the balanced predation of wild animals is a possibility. That it is also a desirability is abundantly manifest in today's Africa. Here many of the greatest minds in conservation are now convinced that the conservation of the veldt and its carrying capacity can only be assured by a return to the conservation of stocks of wild antelope and other wild mammals, and to their rational cropping – in preference to the encouragement of domestic animals which can ruin the soil and are, from other points of view, notably that of disease, often less fitted to the environment.

Survival

Although I began by accentuating the transition of modern thinking from preservation to conservation, there remain many acute problems over the preservation of particular species. Since the dodo became extinct in about 1681, at least eighty-five other bird species have followed it into oblivion. About a quarter of these may have become extinct naturally; the rest were extinguished as a consequence of human activity. The difference is unquestionably due to the harsh pressure of man on rare and vulnerable species. Since 1600 this has obliterated about three or four times as many as have become extinct naturally.

A similar story with similar figures can be told for the mammals. Ancient vertebrate animal communities have been particularly vulnerable in Australia, New Zealand and Hawaii where ancient and relatively primitive communities have been invaded first by Stone Age man and next by Western man and a very high element of his introduced wild species, not to mention his domestic stock.

More than 120 species of birds, for instance, have been successfully introduced into parts of the world entirely foreign to their original distribution. Nearly 200 species of birds are now so rare that they are in danger of extinction and a large proportion (over two-thirds) of these owe their rarity to direct predation by man or his associated animals, to the destruction of their habitat by man, or to man's introduction of exotic species and their diseases which have usurped their ecological niches.

Such concern does this state of affairs give the IUCN and the World Wildlife Fund that a special Survival Service Commission of the former has been established to keep a careful eye on all endangered species. Only one of the five living rhinoceros species in the world has a population greater than 2,000 and the Javan rhinoceros may number only a couple of score.

81

Birds (full species) extinct since 1600, plotted at the places where they were last seen wild. Four species were last recorded alive in captivity (nos. 9, 36, 45 and 53).

1 Great elephant bird *Aepyornis maximus*
2 Tokoweka (a moa) *Megalapteryx didinus*
3 Burly lesser moa *Euryapteryx gravis*
4 Brawny great moa *Dinornis torosus*
5 Guadalupe storm petrel *Oceanodroma macro-dactyla*
6 Spectacled cormorant *Phalacrocorax perspicillatus*
7 Flightless night heron *Nycticorax megacephalus*
8 Poua (a swan) *Cygnus sumnerensis*
9 Pink-headed duck *Rhodonessa caryophyllacea* (last in captivity in England)
10 Labrador duck *Camptorhynchus labradorium*
11 Auckland Island merganser *Mergus australis*
12 Guadalupe caracara *Caracara lutosa*
13 Kermadec megapode *Megapodius* species
13a Himalayan mountain quail *Ophrysia superciliosa*
14 Chatham Island banded rail *Rallus dieffenbachi*
15 Wake Island rail *Rallus wakensis*
16 Tahiti red-billed rail *Rallus ecaudata*
17 Chatham Island rail *Rallus modestus*
18 New Caledonian wood rail *Tricholimnas lafres-nayanus*
19 Fiji bar-winged rail *Nesoclopeus poecilopterus*
20 Van den Broecke's red rail *Aphanapteryx bonasia*
21 Flightless blue rail *Aphanapteryx leguati*
22 Ascension flightless crake *Crecopsis* species
23 Laysan rail *Porzanula palmeri*
24 Hawaiian rail *Pennula sandwichensis*
25 Kusaie rail *Aphanolimnas monasa*
26 Samoan wood rail *Pareudiastes pacificus*
27 Tahiti sandpiper *Prosobonia leucoptera*
28 Cooper's sandpiper *Calidris cooperi*
29 Jerdon's courser *Cursorius bitorquatus*
30 Great auk *Pinguinus impennis*
31 St Helena blue dove *?Columba* species
32 Mauritius blue pigeon *Alectroenas nitidissima*
33 Rodriguez blue pigeon *Alectroenas rodericana*
34 Bonin wood pigeon *Columba versicolor*
35 Bourbon pink pigeon *Columba duboisi*
36 Passenger pigeon *Ectopistes migratorius*
37 Tana ground dove *Gallicolumba ferruginea*
38 Crested Choiseul pigeon *Microgoura meeki*
39 Dodo *Raphus cucullatus*
40 Solitaire *Raphus solitarius*
41 Rodriguez solitaire *Pezophaps solitaria*
42 New Caledonian lorikeet *Vini diadema*
43 Tahiti kakariki *Cyanoramphus zealandicus*
44 Raiatea kakariki *Cyanoramphus ulietanus*
45 Mascarene parrot *Mascarinus mascarinus*
46 Broad-billed Mauritian parrot *Lophopsittacus mauritianus*
47 Rodriguez parakeet *Necropsittacus rodricanus*
48 Bourbon parakeet *Necropsittacus borbonicus*
49 Rodriguez ring-necked parakeet *Psittacula exsul*
50 Guadeloupe parrot *Amazona violacea*
51 Martinique parrot *Amazona martinica*
52 Guadeloupe conure *Aratinga labati*
53 Carolina parakeet *Conuropsis carolinensis*
54 Cuban red macaw *Ara tricolor*
55 Jamaican red macaw *Ara gossei*
56 Jamaican green-and-yellow macaw *Ara erythrocephala*
57 Guadeloupe red macaw *Ara guadeloupensis*
58 Dominican green-and-yellow macaw *Ara atwoodi*
59 Martinique macaw *Ara martinica*
60 Delalande's Madagascar coucal *Coua delalandei*
61 Commerson's scops owl *Otus commersoni*
62 Rodriguez little owl *Athene murivora*
63 Forest spotted owlet *Athene blewitti*
64 New Caledonian frogmouth *Aegotheles savesi*
65 Ryu Kyu kingfisher *Halcyon miyakoensis*
66 Stephen Island wren *Xenicus lyalli*
67 Kusaie starling *Aplonis corvina*
68 Mysterious starling *Aplonis mavornata*
69 Leguat's starling *Fregilupus rodericanus*
70 Bourbon crested starling *Fregilupus varius*
71 Huia *Heteralocha acutirostris*
72 Kittlitz's ground thrush *Zoothera terrestris*
73 Grand Cayman thrush *Turdus ravidus*
74 Raiatea thrush *Turdus ulietensis*

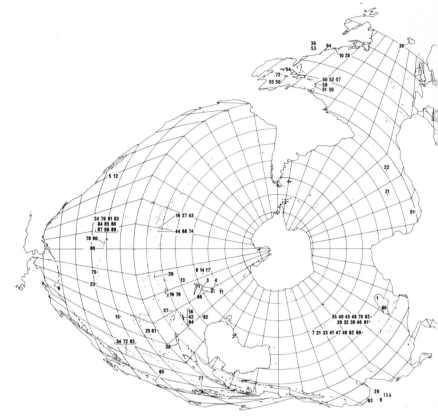

The animals on IUCN's survival list are in many ways the litmus paper of man's conservation agency. It is true that by removing danger from their future we will not solve all the problems of our overcrowded planet. Protection laws and their most difficult enforcement may indeed save the Javan rhinoceros and the ivory-billed woodpecker and scores of other animals. The fact that no bird appears to have become extinct since 1945 may be a measure of awakening conscience, for twenty-four species disappeared between 1860 and 1899 and the same number between 1900 and 1945. (See table on p. 81.) This conscience of course is old, but only lately has it become powerful.

To relate its history and rise to power is difficult. Where and when, in the depths of history, can we first identify the conservationist conscience, find the beginning of the procession of forward-looking minds, the influences that have warned, acted, prophesied, and lobbied parliaments and heads of state? Such minds might date from the ornithologist Holy Roman Emperor Frederick of the fifteenth century. They came into their own after the Renaissance. They were partly scholars, partly enthusiasts, partly poets and partly artists. They were opponents of greed and futility, and most of them were good, down-to-earth, practical naturalists, the real nature-lovers, like the Englishmen White, Bewick and Clare, or the American Audubon, representing thinkers who inherited the idea of the picturesque and turned it into a more radical kind of romanticism. The establishment in 1872 of the world's first national park, in what is now Wyoming, can, as we shall see, be directly traced back from the influence of Rousseau and Goethe, Wordsworth and Coleridge, to the Emersonian intellectuals of New England and Harvard. Where are the intellectuals and the poets now in conservation, who must be benignly mixed with the scientists and wardens, the ecologists and land-management practitioners? Increasing cadres of them can be now identified. There is some hope for the world's conservation, but as we shall prove, it depends on the campuses of the universities of the world, old and new, in five continents.

The Tangled Bank

"It is interesting," wrote Darwin in 1859, in the last paragraph of the greatest of all books of natural history, "to contemplate a tangled bank, clothed with many plants of many kinds, with birds singing on the bushes, with various insects flitting about, and with worms crawling through the damp earth, and to reflect that these elaborately constructed forms, so different from each other, and dependent upon each other in so complex a manner, have all been produced by laws acting around us."

Not often did Charles Darwin reach such literary heights, or such scientific economy, in the promulgation of his ideas that shook the world. He never quite attained poetry; but then no poet has ever achieved such truth, although through all the centuries

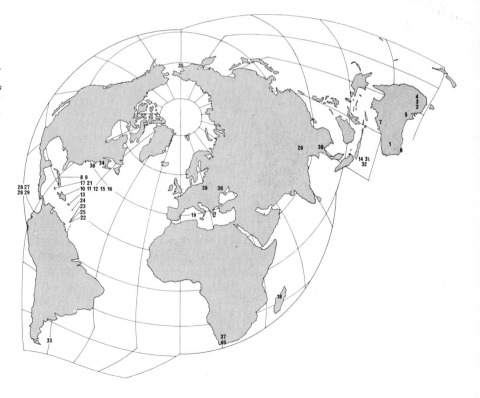

Karl von Linné (Carolus Linnaeus)
when Professor of Botany at
Uppsala in Sweden, painted by
A. Roslin.

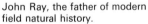

John Ray, the father of modern
field natural history.

Facing:
The great Indian rhinoceros now
has a world population of *c.*
740 in a dozen groups in India,
Nepal and Pakistan mostly living
in official sanctuaries under strict
protection.

of language, poets have contemplated tangled banks. Come to
that, men have contemplated tangled banks ever since men were
men. The first men were naturalists; they had to be.

By analogies with the primitive peoples of today and by the
study of the cave-paintings and other artistic remains of the Stone
Age peoples of the past, it is possible to guess to a certain extent
how human understanding of the bank's tangle grew through
the ages.

Some Stone Age naturalists were brilliant hunters and artists,
and some Stone Age primitive peoples of recent years have been
clever enough to discover for themselves, and hand down without
the benefit of writing, such complicated truths as the transmission
of disease from wild animals to humans and their domestic stock,
or the link between unusual animal movements and conditions of
drought or famine.

The Mesopotamians, and more particularly the Greeks, had a
vast knowledge of animal and plant lore. In the Dark Ages nature-
study flourished where much other culture almost perished. Yet
modern natural history's true foundations were no more than a
blueprint at the time of the Renaissance, and indeed afterwards.
The scaffolding did not really get lashed up until the middle of the
eighteenth century, with the publication of the first edition of
Carolus Linnaeus's *Species Plantarum* in 1753 and the tenth
edition of his *Systema Naturae* in 1758. These two books by the
great Swedish naturalist have been adopted as the starting points
for modern botanical and zoological naming.

Without sound naming, natural history cannot exist. Based on
the method proposed by Linnaeus, and his "binomial" system of
noun and adjective (the noun being the genus name and the two
together the species name), proper descriptions and names,
internationally acceptable, spread rapidly through the civilized
world, and were adopted by scientists and literate amateurs
wherever they flourished. Where not adequate, the nomenclature
was revised, refined and most copiously added to.

Linnaeus, like all great scholars, built upon the past; in
particular upon the work of one towering genius of botany and
zoology, John Ray (1628–1705), who is rightly known as the father
of modern natural history. Ray's and Linnaeus's works, which
enjoyed a wide circulation, inspired many amateurs of the
eighteenth and early nineteenth centuries. These men were
amateurs in the strict sense of the word (i.e. enthusiasts), gentle-
men of education and more-or-less leisure, who travelled and
marvelled and wrote of the world around them. As early as the
time of Linnaeus there was a recognizable division into two
streams: field men and museum men. Linnaeus himself, an
indefatigable field man, was almost the exception that proved
the rule.

It was the museum men, on the whole, who dug the quarry from
which Darwin (another fine field man, incidentally) excavated his
noble hypotheses, which gave men a new, searing, and at the time
they were first proposed, a frightening understanding of nature.
But it was the other stream, the field men and poets and artists,
who aroused the world's *love* for nature, whose golden words
and pictures created the sense of what we sometimes now call

"wilderness values," and urged the literate not only into enthusiasm but into activity.

I would like to give the members of these two streams safe names: which is not an easy thing to do, for through our last two centuries of dynamic and hurrying history these streams have flowed now apart, now together, now slowly, now fast, now full of silt, now clear and deep. A few notable naturalists have belonged to both. At present, as we shall see, the streams flow together, and if they do not continue to do so, the world will become a sorry, perhaps even an impossible, place.

I will call one stream the "academics." In the main these are the university and museum men with a scientific background, dedicated to the tidying of knowledge into some form of intellectual order, and to promulgating new hypotheses as a consequence of the systematic treatment of the facts of life, in so far as they could discover them.

We will call the other stream the "enthusiasts." Often without the help of science, the enthusiasts have always seen nature in some way as a whole, romantically, mystically, with love, sometimes with hatred, often humbly and with worship. Insofar as they were analytical, the enthusiasts were inclined to "take things up," to busy themselves here and there as the fancy took them, benignly obsessed with the solving of circumscribed problems. They had no campaign for the systematic dissection of nature, far less the subsequent reassembly that alone would bring fundamental understandings. They were quite happy to let most fundamentals remain mysteries for, after all, many of them were poets of mystery. Let us examine first, then, some enthusiasts.

The Enthusiasts

The love of nature, to the extent that it has possessed our present civilization, has its roots in Western Europe and North America, and has had its chief prophets among the Hungarians, Russians, Scandinavians, the people of the Low Countries, the Germans, the Swiss, the French, the Lowland Scots and the English; and in North America largely among descendants of these peoples. Everybody has his own list; and if my favourite enthusiasts are almost wholly English-speaking it is because I am English, and because (if the others will forgive me for mentioning it) the English had the greatest share of all.

Gilbert White (1720–93)

White, the father of field natural history, was born in Selborne, in the county of Southampton (now Hampshire) in England and educated at the local grammar school at Basingstoke and Oriel College, Oxford.

From the age of seven until he died White lived in The Wakes, the rambling house below the chalk downs and beechwoods of Selborne to which naturalists from the world over have made pilgrimages ever since. His career was entirely in the Church of England. Officially vicar, for most of his life, of a parish in Northamptonshire, he entrusted this living to a succession of curates, and himself worked as curate, for a long time, of

The Mikado pheasant, a rare and declining bird of the mountains of Formosa (Taiwan).

Gilbert White, sketched at the age of twenty-seven by his friend T. Chapman.

Wildlife Crisis

Faringdon, the parish next-door to Selborne. For several spells, including the last nine years of his life, he served as curate of his own parish of Selborne.

White would never leave Selborne for long: he performed his ecclesiastical duties there conscientiously. In middle age he began to compile field records of botany, zoology – and particularly ornithology – which showed a tender accuracy and thoughtfulness far in advance of his time.

As a poet White was far from contemptible. He was emphatically in the main Augustan stream of Dryden and Pope, and inspired by the classics.

White's original contribution to natural history is almost entirely embraced in 100,000 words of most beautiful and careful prose, published late in 1788, four and a half years before his death, as *The Natural History and Antiquities of Selborne*.

In essence White's *Selborne* consists of letters that the parson wrote to two distinguished zoological academics, Thomas Pennant and Daines Barrington, both Fellows of the Royal Society. He approached his problems gently, slowly, contemplatively, indeed almost lazily. His discoveries were such as could be made only by a scholar who was also a field man.

For instance, he found the difference between the three common species of leaf-warbler of the British countryside; the difference between the two whitethroats; the noctule (the largest British bat); and the harvest-mouse (the smallest British rodent). He gave one of the earliest reasoned accounts of the principles of protective coloration; anticipated modern theories of the meaning and use of birds' territories; forestalled Darwin's views on the origin of the domestic pigeon and the economies of earthworms; published life-history studies (some first printed in the Royal Society's *Transactions*) of nightjars, swifts, swallows and martins; and studied the field cricket so thoroughly that many of his observations do not appear to have been extended, or even confirmed, for over a century and a half.

To all readers of White, these discoveries reflect the solid inquiring spirit of the devoted, humorous and talented parson. But they find far more than these in the book. Though White's appreciation of scenery was in the Gothic, pastoral style of an age which, for the landed classes at least, was one of considerable elegance, his readers are left with a vision of the benign, green, unerodable, immortal English countryside as acute as that which any sensitive farmer, emigrant when young, carries in his dreams. White described what the dying Falstaff babbled of, with intelligence, wit and above all humanity and tolerance.

Thomas Bewick (1753–1828)

Thomas Bewick of Cherry Burn, and Ovingham, and Newcastle-upon-Tyne in the county of Northumberland in England, called himself "Bewick, Restorer of the Art of Engraving on Wood." Most people today call him "the bird man," because of his most famous book: but in truth he was a better artist than naturalist, even if he did inspire more naturalists than artists.

A farmer's son, Bewick spent an ordinary boyhood with many stolen hours of bird's-nesting, damming the burn, hunting foxes and hares with other truants, tracking polecats in the snow, digging badgers at night; or filling the margins of his slate and his Latin exercise book with pictures, and doggerel verse to fit them.

Bewick had some difficulty in persuading his parents to let him embrace art as a career; but they gave in, and at fourteen he was apprenticed to Ralph Beilby, a skilled enameller, engraver, etcher and seal cutter in Newcastle. Bewick never had a drawing lesson in his life, but so skilled at woodcuts did he prove, that Beilby soon was passing most of this work to him – and by the end of his seven years' apprenticeship Bewick was cutting wood blocks for children's books and books of fables, bar-bills for pubs, illustrations for broadsheets; he had also won a prize from the Royal Society for the Encouragement of the Arts.

After his apprenticeship Thomas Bewick went home to the farm. After eighteen months of moderate boredom there, he sewed three guineas into the waistband of his breeches and walked out on a "wild goose chase," as he himself called it, going where fancy took him through the Highlands of Scotland, with the determination not to visit any town or even inn.

He was overwhelmed by the kindness and hospitality of the people of the hills; and much distressed by the dreadful evictions of the tenant crofters that were then taking place. To develop and enclose land for sheep farming many landlords were forcing tenants out of Scotland, many of whom emigrated to the U.S. and Canada. "In exchange for men," Bewick wrote bitterly, "they have filled the country with sheep." This sentiment is echoed by all good naturalists today, to whom the "over-sheepifying" of the Highlands was one of the cruellest and, from the point of view of ecology, most senseless greedy acts of history.

Bewick's attitude to nature was in the Augustan tradition. Like Dr Johnson, he felt little emotion for mountains: while he admired the "great projecting rocks," he felt that "it was a pity they could not be converted to some use." The particular use he suggested was that illustrious names should be inscribed upon them (starting with Alfred the Great), as well as quotations and texts and poems, "to put the passing stranger in mind of some religious, moral or patriotic sentiment."

Bewick's view of nature was intimate and miniature, not broad and grand. His little woodcuts have such scenes as the corners of streams with overhanging boughs, or woody glades, or rocks by the seashore, or dooryards: and into this tiny compass he could put as much as Hogarth. The cuts which illustrate his *Quadrupeds*, his *Land* and *Water Birds*, and his *Fables* show a broad humanity, some pity and horror, much humour, and occasionally a little earthy coarseness.

Horrified by a brutal hare hunt he saw when young, Bewick could not afterwards kill any mammal or bird. Even when working on his most famous book, the *British Birds*, he never killed any himself. He had not much use for stuffed or dead birds as subjects; and when he had to use them they have a stuffed look in his pictures. With the wild birds he watched with affection he is at his best: his famous blackbird woodcut, with his old home at Cherry Burn in the background, may well have been sketched many times at the very spot on which it appears in the cut.

Thomas Bewick by the banks of the Tyne engraved by F. Bacon after the picture by James Ramsay.

John Clare, painted at the age of twenty-seven by W. Hilton.

When Bewick died at the age of seventy-five he had done for art what Burns did for poetry – put a little honest humanity into it. To naturalists he gave the inspiration of a new, gentle, tender view of the homely and familiar.

John Clare (1793–1864)

Of all the enthusiasts in our chosen band John Clare is the least known and therefore the least influential. He was not quite one of the mute, inglorious Miltons lamented by the poet Thomas Gray. As a young rural poet he was taken up by the society of his day, published as a nine days' (or rather about nine years') wonder, then dropped and forgotten when he fell into a mental illness from which he never recovered.

Much of Clare's prose, but less than half of his nearly 2,000 poems have been published. His works have never enjoyed the fame they deserve. Perhaps one of the reasons for this was the fact that he completely broke the literary rule first promulgated by the influential Dr Johnson in 1759, and carried by Keats and others into the Romantic period. As stated by Johnson "the business of a poet is to examine, not the individual but the species; to remark general properties and large appearances: he does not number the streaks of the tulip, or describe the different shades of the verdure of the forest."

Clare – who described in loving detail tiny insects climbing "the totter-grass and blossom's stem" as "huge in size as mighty oaks to them," and skylarks' nests in wheat and barley, by a clod, in a horse print, in a cart rut, in a grass tuft, in a rush tuft, by a thistle, made of twitch, grass, stubble-straw and lined with roots, hay and horsehair, with four eggs of dusky blotched brown with a purplish zone round the large end – saw all these things minutely, and recorded them with accuracy and passion. He was a country boy with a background of poverty and slender education, who lived most of his active life in the Soke of Peterborough – that part of England where the wooded, rolling limestone country of the south Midlands merges into the Fenland of East Anglia.

Clare's poems were practically all nature poems, and rural village poems. He wrote in bouts of scribbling that lasted, sometimes, for several days; when he stopped he seldom had to alter a word. He wrote of the spinneys and fields, and the places that in those days were heaths, and the old limestone quarries, and the great parks and lakes, and the rivers Nene and Welland. The scholars who have investigated the sum of his works – which were neglected by the scientific naturalists of his day – believe that he knew more about animals and plants than any important English poet before or since, and than any naturalist in his county at the time.

Clare's works, for instance, contain such fine descriptions of flowering plants that no less than 135 are recognizable species, even though he did not name them scientifically. He added as much as 10 per cent to the number of plants reliably reported for Northamptonshire and the Soke of Peterborough. A great county botanist of later years, George Claridge Druce, who knew and loved Clare's work, tried to catch him out, but gladly failed; he visited Clare's old haunts a century and a half later, and found the

John James Laforest Audubon at the age of *c.* forty-eight, engraved by H. B. Hall after the portrait by Henry Inman in 1833.

right kind (the rarer kind) of bryony in the right place, the proper orchid in the proper marsh, exactly where Clare said it was.

By Clare's time (and he was working at his best between 1820 and 1837) only about 70 kinds of birds had been recorded in print for Northamptonshire and the Soke of Peterborough. He nearly doubled the list. Lovely descriptions, or accurate notes, exist in his published works of no less than 119 bird species, of which 65 had never been previously recorded for the area.

We learn from him that in the early 1830s all sorts of birds nested in the farmland and fens around his home that with felling and draining and keepering have since departed. He gave us, indeed, the last, or almost the last, local records of nesting black-necked (eared) grebe, bittern, grey-lag goose, kite, Montagu's harrier, spotted crake, black-tailed godwit and ruff. Since his time a wilderness has retreated before the advancing agriculture of a lovely part of England; and it is a moving thing that the most passionate poet of nature should have written so humbly and well of a community of wild things that will never return.

Clare's world, like that of the famous French naturalist J. H. Fabre, was a world of detail. Keats criticized him in that "the description too much prevailed over the sentiment" in his poems – to which Clare's riposte was that "as is the case with the inhabitants of great cities [Keats] often described nature as she appeared to his fancies, not as he would have described her had he witnessed the things he described."

In 1946 two great ornithological scholars of Oxford University were bird watching in a local wood in a frost. They watched how robins followed them and dropped to feed as soon as their feet had broken the hard topsoil. Soon afterwards one of them published his hypothesis, that the confiding behaviour of woodland robins might derive from the fact that through generations the birds had come to regard man, or indeed any earth-kicking animal, as an agent for breaking through the frost layer.

Dr Lack believed that he had been the first to notice the robin's interest in trampling feet. But here, 120 years earlier, is Clare:

> Yet all, save robin, will retreat
> And shun rude man's forbidding sight
> Who seemly welcomes trampling feet
> And ruffs its feathers in delight,
> Brisk hopping from its shielding thorn
> As one who would our steps detain
> Then droops its wing and sits forlorn
> When left to solitude again.

Not his best poem by any means: but a typical piece from the greatest enthusiast of all, the forgotten parish poet who knew the flowers, the insects, the beasts and the birds better than he knew himself.

John James Laforest Audubon (*c.* 1785–1851)
The present value of the original and published works of the world's most famous nature artist doubtless exceeds £1 million sterling ($2.5 million). Audubon's name has perhaps even greater public importance in North America than that of White in

David Henry Thoreau from a portrait in the Concord Public Library in Massachusetts.

Europe. Audubon has become the symbol of natural history and of the conservation movement in a great continent.

The artist himself believed that he was the lost Dauphin, the small son of Louis XVI and Marie Antoinette who was believed to have been spirited out of prison at the time of the French Revolution. But it seems more probable that he was the illegitimate son born in 1785 April to a Mademoiselle Rabin in what is now Haiti in the West Indies, and that his father was the French naval captain and planter, Jean Audubon, who legally adopted him in 1794.

Audubon's formative years were spent partly in France and partly in Pennsylvania, on his father's farm at Mill Grove near Philadelphia. Compared with those of Clare, for instance, they were extremely protected. He had every encouragement to develop as an artist, and to learn nature in the woods and by hunting. But with a decline in his father's fortunes he sought his own as a merchant in the Middle West. It was primarily by the encouragement of his wife Lucy Bakewell, the niece of an early employer, that he risked (and endured) insecurity by devoting himself to his amazing *The Birds of America* (1827–38) in which 1,052 birds, belonging to over 450 species, were depicted, life-size, on 435 hand-coloured engravings of "double-elephant" size. This was his first and greatest, but by no means his only, work.

Audubon reached security and honour late in life, and with the help of his wife, herself no mean artist, and two sons, who collected material for him from all over North America and looked after his business affairs; one of them was a good artist, too. Until he finally settled in New York in 1840 Audubon was a phenomenal traveller, crossing the Atlantic many times to arrange for the engraving and sale of his plates in Edinburgh and London; collecting subscriptions himself by toting his portfolios around the principal cities of the United States; exploring the Ohio and Mississippi rivers and Florida in his search for bird material. He boasted, probably correctly, that he could outwalk a horse.

As Robert Cushman Murphy says, "As regards the star to which he hitched his wagon in early manhood, namely, the reproduction in munificent form of his paintings of *The Birds of America*, no trial was sufficient to make him swerve a half-point from his course. For that cause he not only suffered cold, homelessness, raggedness, hunger, and their attendant despondency, but even the far sharper punishment of the contempt of men for his condition, and for his apparent disregard for the welfare of his wife and children." Disregard, indeed not: but his family had a slender time until his rewards began to come.

Untrained in science, Audubon gradually became a competent zoologist, describing and naming new species, conducting important field experiments (for instance, on the alleged sense of smell of American "vultures"); and he was unassuming in his relations with other men.

His friends were as far apart as Daniel Boone, Thomas Bewick and Sir Walter Scott. He happily collaborated with other naturalists, such as the great ornithologist William MacGillivray of Scotland, and the mammalogist John Bachman, whose daughters married Audubon's sons.

Audubon died among elms and beeches on the Hudson's bank after a few tired years with failing eyesight at the end of a lifetime (equivalent to three normal lifetimes) of fantastic vigour. While he lived he inspired two continents, through his work and his lively presence, with the romance of the great American wilderness. In his later years he became deeply anxious about the effect of man's greedy exploitation of the wild. His image comes down to us more as a frontiersman in buckskins and coonskin cap, than as a dedicated artist with a life's obsession to capture America's birds and mammals in art and works forever. In fact, he was both.

His art can be criticized in detail for he had perforce to work much from dead specimens or on animals he never saw in life. But he swept through the American natural history lighting many beacons, the embers of which glow now. No day passes that thousands do not speak his name.

David Henry ("Henry D.") Thoreau (1817–62)

Thoreau, even more than Audubon, was a man of the American wilderness. He published but two books in his lifetime – *A Week on the Concord and Merrimack Rivers* (1849) which sold less than 300 copies in four years; and *Walden: or Life in the Woods* (1854), his masterpiece.

Thoreau's wilderness, unlike Audubon's but like Clare's, was the world around his home. Like Clare's world, it was a wilder world then. Today Walden Pond is preserved with some difficulty, though, fortunately, the area around Concord, Massachusetts, where Thoreau was born has – apart from its town and village centres – suffered no great increase in human population in a century. It is an historic region, settled as early as 1635, and the wooded New England country around is low with small hills and many waters and watermeadows. Thoreau early showed an interest in nature which was encouraged at his unusually progressive school, and by the age of twelve was collecting specimens for the great Harvard zoologist, Louis Agassiz. In due course, Thoreau himself entered the University, and after graduating he became a surveyor by trade. But soon left all for life in the woods, writing and lecturing.

Harvard in Thoreau's time was as heavily imbued as any American community with the new revolutionary philosophies of Europe and North America; and Thoreau early came under the influence of the poet and philosopher Ralph Waldo Emerson, who was fourteen years his senior. Unlike Emerson, he sought transcendental truth in the field by observation rather than in the mind by inspiration: and the difference between them, which after many years together became intolerable, was strictly comparable to the gulf that separated the poets Keats and Clare.

In 1845 Thoreau built with his own hands a hut by the shore of Walden Pond; there he lived "off the country," keeping a wonderful journal of wildlife, and wandering afoot with as much vigour, and to as much purpose as Audubon.

Of this period in his life he later said: "For more than five years I maintained myself thus solely by the labor of my hands, and I found, that by working about six weeks in a year, I could meet all the expenses of living."

Ralph Waldo Emerson from a portrait in the Concord Public Library.

Through his friendship with Agassiz and his knowledge of the Harvard collections he was able to do fine and accurate natural history work, particularly in botany. Thoreau does not appear to have had Clare's bright sensitivity to birds, though he made many "first records" for the Concord area. Even though he had a crude optical glass he made a number of mistakes in identification, and he never learned many songs. But in other spheres of nature he was a pioneer observer and thinker.

His biographer H. S. Canby rates him an ecologist, before the word "ecology" came into use. "It was in the relations of plant, bird or animal to its environment, including its relations with man, that his contributions to knowledge of wild life were outstanding," says Canby, and adds, "The dead bird, as he often said, did not interest him. Its proper name was not enough. It is its relation to the scheme of life that is important."

Thoreau died young, like others of his family a victim of tuberculosis. His voice speaks to present generations perhaps most strongly of human liberty and civil rights, and into this sphere fall such ever-quotable sayings as: "Wherever a man goes, men will pursue him and paw him with their dirty institutions, and if they can, constrain him to belong to their desperate odd-fellow society."

But to the naturalist his message was sure and inspiring, and full of humility and wonder: Get to grips with nature and find nature and man out. "It is true," he once said, "I never assisted the sun materially in his rising, but, doubt not, it was of the last importance only to be present at it."

Facing:
Przewalski's horse, an ancestor of the domestic horse, is now represented by a captive breeding population in zoos and animal parks of over 150, and a wild population – probably smaller – under protection and scientific investigation in Mongolia where it seems to be confined to the Takhin Shar-nuru highlands in the southwest.

Overleaf: The polar bear may now number under 10,000 living individuals and is under protection or harvest control in all the Arctic countries of the world, whose conservation scientists meet regularly to plan its future. WWF funds have helped research lately.

WWF funds have also helped research on the addax, a desert antelope confined to the Sahara which now has a relict distribution, surviving in probably not more than ten herds in six countries; formerly it inhabited at least nine. The decline is due to human over-hunting.

So much then for a sampling of the enthusiasts. We could argue, facilely, that such heroes of nature-literature were compelled into their attitudes by the social forces of their day; and that their inner fire could never have burned without fuel from their times and mores and surroundings. Are the inspiring writers but labels on the stages of our social progress? Surely not. At least they are the seeds, which must be sown in a bath of solution before the crystal can grow. The seeds of our enthusiasm.

The enthusiasts, as I have presented them, in contradistinction to the academics, are the schoolboys of natural history: schoolboys sometimes turned teachers, but at heart eternal youths, with all the love and wonder, terror and joy, the sense of amazing discovery and amazing mystery that we grow up with, and maybe lose when we have grown. We will meet some academics later. I have kept them apart rather artificially, in fact, for there are few academics, at least nowadays, who dwell in ivory towers beyond the poets and dreamers, and fewer still who forget their youth. Beneath the skin of nearly every academic specialist is an amateur, an enthusiast, trying to get out. Often, praise be, they do.

My thesis, then, is that, by the middle of the nineteenth century, a tremendous amount of enthusiasm for nature – mystical, realistic, earthy, elemental, transcendental, intellectual, the lot – had been aroused, and had created a climate for action. The action consisted of the conscious, deliberate striving of civilized communities to regain paradise.

Paradise

> The meanest flowret of the vale
> The simplest note that swells the gale,
> The common sun, the air, the skies,
> To him are opening paradise.

Thomas Gray, who wrote this, was another eighteenth-century Augustan rural poet, who lived not far from the edge of the city among the tidy tilth and pastures of the county of Buckingham. I wonder how "paradise" came to him – surely as a vision of a heaven? Yet this was not the original meaning of the word which, though it sounds Greek, is not. It is Persian – *pardes*. The "paradises" of the Persian kings were unruffled hunting estates, situated within an easy ride of their lodges or palaces. They were what we would call "hunting parks," just like the first parks in England, which were laid out by the Norman conquerors, with their holiday lodges for royalty and nobility. The Normans called them *parcs*, and the English *parks* to this day.

The park concept, of wild property or wild estate, owned or managed by virtue of its very wildness, has been with us ever since Norman times. It provided, not unnaturally, the springboard for the recapture of wilderness by the broader public, just so soon as the democratic revolutions began to succeed in Europe, and scenery ceased to be considered merely "picturesque."

In the liberal climate surrounding the French Revolution, the view of nature, and within it the park idea, began to assume new dimensions. The artistic eye focused on broader horizons. We can trace the succession of poets and writers from the last of the Augustans: Gray – Collins – Goldsmith – Horace Walpole – White – Cowper, then on to the first of the romantics and radicals: Rousseau – Goethe – Crabbe – Wordsworth – Coleridge – Scott – Byron – Shelley – Keats – Emerson – Thoreau.

From the political wings the social voices of de Chateaubriand, Fourier, Robert Owen and Victor Hugo added their yeast to the ferment of intellectual thinking. New notions, new ideas, even new morals surged across Europe, and across the Atlantic. And perhaps the poets and the writers of that time saw the truth sooner than the academics and scientists: that withal man's new-found freedom, nature stood (at least for a while) serene, with more layers of mystery than an onion has skins, as the ultimate challenge of men.

Each in his own way, Byron and Thoreau faced nature in the spirit, the very essence, of their times.

> There is a pleasure in the pathless woods,
> There is a rapture on the lonely shore,
> There is society, where none intrudes,
> By the deep sea, and music in its roar:
> I love not Man the less, but Nature more,
> From these our interviews, in which I steal
> From all I may be, or have been before,
> To mingle with the Universe, and feel
> What I can ne'er express, yet cannot all conceal.
> Byron, *Childe Harold*, 1812

The monkey-eating eagle of the Philippines now has a population probably of under 100 living birds, surviving on two islands only. It is protected by law but still suffers from illegal hunting.

"Terrace Mound" of Minerva Hot Springs in the Yellowstone National Park; one of the galaxy of scenic wonders that started the international process of national park dedication.

"We need the tonic of wildness – to wade sometimes in marshes where the bittern and meadow-hen lurk, and hear the booming of the snipe, to smell the whispering sedge where only some wilder and more solitary fowl builds her nest, and the mink crawls with its belly close to the ground. At the same time that we are earnest to explore and learn all things, we require that all things be mysterious and unexplorable, that land and sea be infinitely wild, unsurveyed, and unfathomed by us because unfathomable. We can never have enough of Nature."

Thoreau, *Walden*, 1854

Mysterious: Yes; Unexplorable: No; Wild: Yes, but not infinitely; Unsurveyed: No; Unfathomed: No; Unfathomable: Ultimately, yes.
We can never have enough of nature: No; but can nature have enough of us?
Such is the fruit of another century of progress.

> The inhabitants of Terra
> Have enjoyed a period of error.
> On Earth, Nature's scars
> Are visible from Mars.*

as the first man on Mars will be equipped to confirm for himself as he sights his telescope on the dust bowls of China, Australia, Africa and the southern Middle West, and on the slashes in earth's forests.

Before our generation mingles with the universe our prayer for nature must be: For what we once beheld in awe, make us truly responsible.

* With apologies to Mr E. Clerihew Bentley.

100

But I am anticipating: we are still with the good prophets, and not yet facing the Furies; and one good early prophet felt a good early responsibility. Wordsworth was not in any strict sense a conservationist, of course. Scarcely did anybody suspect in those rather spacious days that the rape of our planet had begun. But the English Lake District was to him a land of such beauty and history and serenity that he felt compelled to share it with everybody. It should, he said, be deemed a sort of national property, in which every man had a right and interest who had an eye to perceive and a heart to enjoy. The late John Dower, whose one-man Government Report of 1945 brought the National Parks of England and Wales into being at long, long, last, said that this statement might "justly be counted the first shot in the campaign" for them. It was a long time a-flying, in that case, for Wordsworth wrote what he wrote in 1810, when he was forty, at the height of his powers.

The first deliberate custodians of wilderness in the world were not in fact Europeans, but North Americans.

The First National Park

Consider the United States of America just after the Civil War. Four million men had been involved, with terrible casualties. Yet within five years of its ending vast new areas of the Middle and Pacific West had been colonized. Lively and daring pioneers, not all of them young, were exploring quite unknown country, bringing along with them the morals and values and institutions of an older society; and reshaping or selecting these values and institutions in the school of necessity and survival. It was in this raw, fast developing land that the expression "national park" seems to have been used for the first time, in the sense in which we understand it today.

In the northwest corner of what is now the state of Wyoming, and was then part of the territory of Montana, Jim Bridger, a tough pioneer of the old West, had since 1846 trapped and prospected and explored virgin land in what became known as the tract of the Yellowstone. He brought back unbelievable stories of burning plains, and boiling springs, and great lakes and canyons. In 1859 Bridger guided the first Government expedition into the area, under Captain Raynolds of the Corps of Topographical Engineers, U.S. Army, with F. V. Hayden as geologist. Other expeditions followed, which gradually built up a picture of the incredible wonders and beauties of the Yellowstone.

In 1869, at considerable risk, three explorers went in: David E. Folsom, S. W. Cook and William Peterson. Without military escort they reached the heartland of the tract, and came back so astonished at the marvels they had seen that they were rather loath to expound upon them to their friends for fear of being disbelieved. However, Folsom wrote an article which was published in the Chicago *Western Monthly* the following year.

The article was considerably cut by the editor of the *Western Monthly*, though this editor evidently did not share Folsom's apprehension of disbelief to the extent of pruning any of his descriptions of natural wonders. What he did prune, however, was

101

the first overt suggestion that Yellowstone was a suitable area for a "national park."

Fortunately, Folsom showed his uncut article to Nathaniel Pitt Langford and discussed his idea with General Henry D. Washburn, Surveyor-General of Montana; and both Washburn and Langford were members of the famous expedition of 1870, which started the active conscious conservation movement throughout the world.

What is now generally known as the Washburn–Langford–Doane expedition set out from Fort Ellis on 1870 August 21. Led by Washburn, and guided by Gustavus C. Doane, a highly intelligent lieutenant in the U.S. Second Cavalry, its members included Judge Cornelius Hedges (aged thirty-eight) and Samuel Hauser, who at the age of thirty-seven was President of the First National Bank of Helena, Montana. With the soldiers' escort the party consisted of nineteen in all, one of whom (Truman C. Everts, who had been the U.S. Assessor for Montana and ought to have known better than to stray) got lost but eventually turned up all right after five painful weeks in the wilderness.

Apart from losing Everts, by September 19 the party had covered an amazing amount of ground. They had seen and mapped many of the known wonders of the Yellowstone, and discovered many more – the Tower Falls, the Grand Canyon of the Yellowstone River, the hot springs at the East Fork, the Crystal Falls, and, above all, new geysers: geysers like Beehive, which spouts 220 feet every 20 hours; Castle which spouts 100 feet for 25 minutes once a day; Fen, some 60 feet high, which spouts for 10 minutes every 8 hours; Giant, which only went off once while they were there, to 200 feet; Giantess, the highest at 250 feet; Grotto; Mad Geyser; and the most famous of all, Old Faithful. Not the highest (though it spouts 150 feet) Old Faithful was – and is – the most regular geyser, spouting every 65 minutes, on the average, for $4\frac{1}{2}$ minutes exactly.

Round the camp-fire that September night the party discussed the wonderful place. Doane and Washburn worked over their military and surveyor's reports. Hauser would have been a poor banker, and we know he was not, if he had not pondered about real estate, and profitable speculation and his business associates and clients. Indeed, that was the way the talk went. What a pleasure resort this paradise could be! How risky would it be to take up land around the marvels and beauty-spots? Langford maybe dug out Folsom's article, if he had brought it along: Langford and Washburn certainly referred to it later.

And then Judge Cornelius Hedges, as that excellent chronicler of Yellowstone, H. M. Chittenden, relates,

"interposed and said that private ownership of that region, or any part of it, ought never to be countenanced, but that it ought to be set apart by the government and forever held to the unrestricted use of the people.

"This higher view of the subject found immediate acceptance with the other members of the party. It was agreed that the project should be at once set afoot and pushed vigorously to a finish."

On their return several members of the expedition wrote of their Yellowstone experiences in a spate of distinguished and accurate journalism. General Henry Washburn published valuable notes; a

Vernal and Nevada Falls from Sierra Point in the Yosemite National Park; two of the fantastic hanging waterfalls of this prodigious ice-gouged valley.

writer named Walter Trumbull wrote a full account in the *Overland Monthly*; Judge Cornelius Hedges wrote in the local Montana papers; Sam Hauser, who later became Governor of Montana, saw to it that the *Helena Herald* had something to say; Nathaniel Langford wrote in *Scribner's Magazine* and lectured in Helena, Minneapolis, New York and Washington, carrying the expression "national park" all over the continent.

But best of all was young Gustavus Doane's masterly *official* report. It passed through the customary military channels and reached Congress early in the following year, 1871; and in this year another official Government expedition went into the Yellowstone and saw new marvels.

Congressman Clagett of Montana introduced his famous Park Bill in the House before 1871 was out. It was voted in, after one of the most formidable and altruistic lobbying campaigns in U.S. history, by 115 votes to 60, with 60 abstaining, and was signed by President Ulysses S. Grant on 1872 March 1.

"Be it enacted by the Senate and House of Representatives of the United States of America in Congress assembled, that the tract of land in the territories of Montana and Wyoming, lying near the headwaters of the Yellowstone River . . . is hereby reserved and withdrawn from settlement, occupancy, or sale under the laws of the United States, and dedicated and set apart as a public park or pleasuring ground for the benefit and enjoyment of the people; and all persons who shall locate or settle upon or occupy the same or any part thereof, shall be considered trespassers and be moved therefrom."

Incidentally, Nathaniel Langford, who wrote so well about the expedition in *Scribner's*, became the first Superintendent of Yellowstone National Park.

A footnote must be forgiven. In a book with a moral, the moral of human responsibility for nature, it is our duty to investigate how such a sense of responsibility could have arisen and spread in Western society, at a time when free enterprise was acute, not always altruistic, never quite blind but seldom far-seeing. Considering that now we must come to terms with nature to survive —

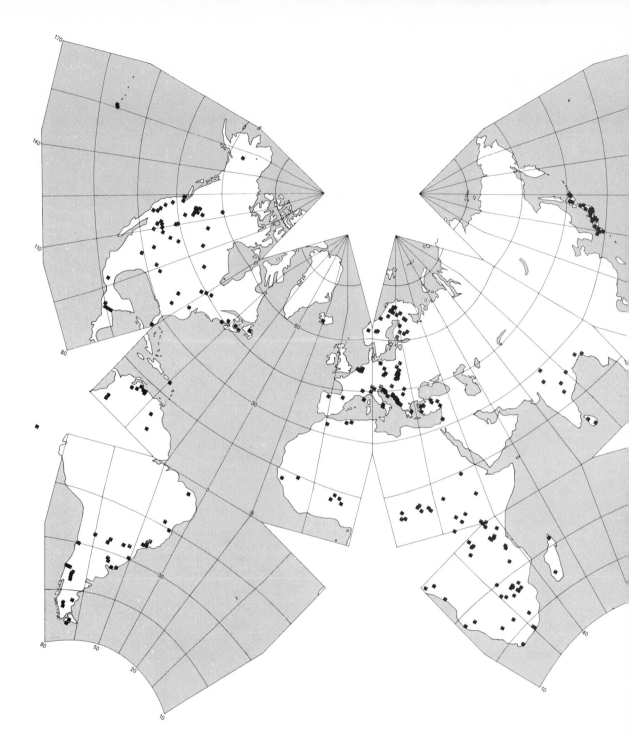

supposing that we manage to avoid blowing our planet's surface to
bits, and nature along with it – it is good to dwell a moment on
that first great act of conservation legislation. It is easy to say that
it was easy to dedicate land that was newly discovered and
scarcely belonged even to the Indians (they seldom hunted in the
Yellowstone). But it would have been still easier to let the
Yellowstone go, to the prospectors and the squatters and the
ranchers and the lumbermen. Grant's enactment was an overt act
of idealism; and, as we shall shortly see, it was the thin end of a

104

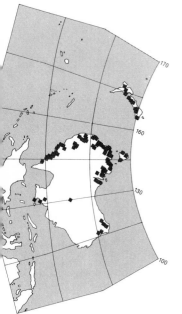

benign wedge of conservation acts and deeds that gradually
spread the world over.

Why could such ideals prevail, around a camp-fire in the
Yellowstone absolutely, in Congress overwhelmingly? That they
prevailed I am not so surprised, after many years of field study of
the North Americans and their way of life. But the chain of
circumstances is a very interesting one.

The protagonists were youngish, tough, responsible-minded
pioneers of the Wild West. Such enthusiasts did they become for
the national park idea that they gave up much to propagandize,
and passed up opportunities of acquiring wealth and property.
They were far from New England, where the new idealism (and in
particular the Emersonian-Longfellowian brand of peculiarly
American idealism) was still fast growing in the hotbeds of the
universities of Connecticut and Massachusetts. But were they
really so far away?

I looked up the biographies of Cornelius Hedges, the judge, and
of Samuel Hauser, the banker. Hedges went to school at Westfield,
in Hampden County, Massachusetts; graduated from Yale
University in 1853; taught at the Academy in Easton, Connecticut
for a year; and then studied law with the Honourable Edward B.
Gillette in 1855 at Harvard Law School before being admitted to
the Bar. Hauser's education was not so advanced; but he was
carefully tutored by his cousin Henry Hill, a Yale graduate.

The United States of America, then, got off to a fine start in
1872, with every advantage – vast areas of amazing wilderness,
owned by Indians or by nobody. What of the United Kingdom?

Progress slow, but inclining to be sure

The *idea* was there; but how difficult the situation! Not an acre to
which deeds of some sort (of which many survived) had not been
written back to Norman times. Not a public acre, in the legal sense
apart from surviving common land and the zone below high tide mark.
Public opinion in England, Wales and Scotland was thinking in
terms not of public *ownership* of wilderness, but of public *access*.

A lone voice was raised in Parliament in 1884. It was that of James
Bryce, a distinguished politician who reached Cabinet rank and
eventually the House of Lords, and once served as Ambassador to the
U.S. Bryce introduced his first "access to mountains" Bill in 1884.

By 1890 he had tried six times more; and in that year the Americans
dedicated their second national park, Sequoia; and their third,
Yosemite; both of these in the Sierra Mountains of California.

In the U.K. they were still debating in the Commons. James
Bryce waxed eloquent about the "exclusion of people from the
right to enjoy the scenery of their own country, and to seek
healthy recreation and exercise on their own mountains and
moors" in a debate in 1892 on the motion "That in the opinion of
this House, legislation is needed for the purpose of securing the
right of the public to enjoy the free access to uncultivated mountains and moorlands, especially in Scotland, subject to proper
provisions for preventing any abuse of such right."

They talked for hours, before the Bill was withdrawn. Bryce and
his friends introduced half a dozen more Bills in the next decade or

The world's national parks
recognized by the International
Union for Conservation of
Nature and Natural Resources.
IUCN does not admit a national
park to its mainstream list unless
it is primarily a nature conservation
park and wholly or mainly
wilderness with a light human
population. Though the ten national
parks of England and Wales are
very helpful to nature conservation
and contain many natural reserves,
they are too heavily farmed and
inhabited and have too much
recreational traffic for IUCN's
present standards.

so. All were withdrawn, even though Bryce was now in the Government.

Meanwhile the U.S. pressed on with the dedication of other vast national parks: Mount Rainier in Washington, 1899; Crater Lake in Oregon, 1902; Wind Cave in South Dakota, 1903; in 1906, Mesa Verde in Colorado, and Platt in what was then the territory of Oklahoma.

By 1907 there were eight national parks in the United States and its Federal Territories; and there was one also in the Republic of Argentina. Bryce, now a peer, was sent to the U.S. as Ambassador that year, and back home his brother, Annan Bryce, and Charles Trevelyan actually got another "access to mountains" Bill through its second reading. It disappeared permanently, however, at the Committee stage.

The first successful national parks legislation in Europe was passed in Sweden in 1909, in a country where wilderness space was, admittedly, in the U.S. rather than the U.K. style of supply. By 1920 there were sixteen parks in the United States, and parks also in Canada, New Zealand, Australia, Yugoslavia and Switzerland.

In the 1920s began a movement to redevelop existing national game reserves in countries large enough to have such broad, open territory. From this came the first national parks of Russia, Morocco, Tunis, Ethiopia, British East and Central Africa, the Congo and South Africa.

By 1930 there were also national parks in Madagascar, Japan, Greece and Hungary; and four more mountain Bills had been talked out of the Parliament of the United Kingdom. By the beginning of the Second World War three more European countries, one even more crowded than the U.K. (the Netherlands) had their proper parks; and after three more tries Royal Assent *was* given in 1939 to the "Access to Mountains Act" of that year. Ironically, it was never put into effect because of the war.

Anglo-Saxon Attitudes

Instead of a tedious analysis of the reasons for the delays in Britain, I would like to offer the reader three peculiarly Anglo-Saxon qualities. One is good will: the essential and almost permanent urge in our Parliament to debate what are known as "good causes:" usually voting is free and according to conscience rather than on party lines. This is the case with causes such as animal protection and preservation, and this was the case with access to mountains. The administrative machine was what blocked Bryce and company in their many tries. Good will alone was not enough.

The second Anglo-Saxon attitude I shall demonstrate by a quotation from W. H. Hudson, the famous nature writer. It was first published in 1909 in the early days of motoring.

Facing:
The Travancore race of the large-spotted civet, now very rare and endangered in south India.

Pygmy hog, which may survive in the Terai district of Nepal, but has not been recorded since 1959.

"The stream invites us to follow: the impulse is so common that it might be set down as instinct; and certainly there is no more fascinating pastime than to keep company with a river from its source to the sea. Unfortunately this is not easy in a country where running waters have been enclosed, which should be free as the rain and sunshine to all, and

were once free, when England was England still, before landowners annexed them, even as they annexed or stole the commons and shut up the footpaths and made it an offence for a man to go aside from the road to feel God's grass under his feet. Well, they have also got the road now, and cover and blind and choke us with its dust and insolently hoot-hoot at us. Out of the way, miserable crawlers, if you don't want to be smashed! They have got the roads and have a Parliament of motorists to maintain them in possession, but it yet remains to be seen whether or not they will be able to keep them.

"Sometimes the way is cut off by huge thorny hedges and fences of barbed wire – man's devilish improvement on the bramble – brought down to the water's edge. The river-follower must force his way through these obstacles in most cases greatly to the detriment of his clothes and temper; or, should they prove impossible, he must undress and go into the water. Worst of all is the thought that he is a trespasser. The pheasants crow loudly lest he should forget it. Occasionally, too, in these private places he encounters men in velveteens with guns under their arms, and other men in tweeds and knickerbockers, with or without guns, and they all stare at him with amazement in their eyes, like disturbed cattle in a pasture; and sometimes they challenge him. And I must say that, although I have been smartly spoken to on several occasions, always, after a few words, I have been permitted to keep on my way. And on that way I intend to keep until I have no more strength to climb over fences and force my way through hedges, but like a blind and worn-out old badger must take to my earth and die."

Hudson's success as a writer and propagandist for nature was in my opinion due to the fact that he made scarcely any realistic analysis of it at all. That was not what his devotees liked or wanted. He was blessed with traditional and true enthusiasm, but his enthusiasm was out of date. He believed in that still fashionable illusion, the balance of nature. He also believed that only emotions could teach; that material progress was nature's certain enemy.

His was a common Anglo-Saxon attitude – and indeed a European and American attitude also – that I wish I could find a name for: a brand of sentimentality, of twisted idealism, in fact, which had at base a deep awareness of natural beauty, a deep loathing of change, and a deep indifference to the real problems of the use and misuse of a countryside at the mercy of a multiplying population. I have often wondered how Hudson would have written after a couple of years trying to make a decent farm pay its way.

So far, then, two attitudes, good will and sentimentality. The third contributor to Britain's fiscal sloth, through three-quarters of a century, was complacency. Here is a quotation from a Lakeland writer, W. G. Collingwood,* contemporary with Hudson, which seems to contain elements of all three:

Aye-aye, the last surviving member of the lemur family Daubentoniidae, may have a world population no greater than fifty.

* *The Lake Counties.* (Quoted from revised edition, Dent, London, 1953.)

"Thousands of town-dwellers are Lake-folk at heart. They have every right to call the Lakes theirs, if affection and adoption count for anything. It needs no Act of Parliament or Land Nationalisation to make the district into a People's Park. That is what it is already – the garden of the towns. You will find wherever you go in it, how little of the whole is forbidden ground; how rarely private ownership interferes. There have been footpath squabbles, and now and then a new landlord has tried to be selfish; but the tradition of the place is against exclusiveness. Also there have been mischievous visitors; but I have often heard the owners of some

most frequented 'beauty spots' say that they have never had any trouble
with the tourists. A smile (for the people) and a stick (for the path) will
take you anywhere. And in return for this welcome the public, far and
wide, loves the Lake country as its own. When there is any fear that a
corner of it is likely to be spoiled, high and low cry out. People of
influence protest: they have spent many happy summers there. Working
men and women send their shillings: they have had glorious days among
the heather and among the ferns."

After years of painful battles with complacency Britain
eventually got its national parks, and its Nature Conservancy. The
social shakeup of the Second World War at least produced a
climate of opinion which admitted that in the areas of greatest
beauty landowners were not inevitably rich enough, or unselfish;
and that businessmen were not inevitably altruistic; and that the
Government was not inevitably far-seeing; and that the tourist
was not inevitably wise, tidy and thoroughly versed in country
ways; and that to stop an outrage to nature it was not enough to
write a public letter to *The Times*, or a private letter to one's
Member of Parliament or to the Cabinet Minister who married
one's brother-in-law's niece.

The ten national parks of the United Kingdom occupy nearly
one-tenth of the total area of England and Wales. There is none in
Scotland or Northern Ireland. They were all established in the
1950s, and are run by groups of administrators from the counties
concerned on quite different lines from those of the U.S. which are
Federally owned and administered, and occupy about 0.55 per cent
of the country's total area. The Countryside Commission, which is
the central Government agency, has a mainly advisory capacity.

The difference between park and non-park in Britain is often
quite undetectable to the traveller, and the small percentage of
British citizens who understand what, and roughly where, their
national parks are, often complain that they "do not know
whether they are in one;" the boundaries are not everywhere
posted. But from the point of view of nature the parks have great
virtues, as a consequence of the much stricter planning control
operated within the park areas. "Frozen user" is as good a way of
describing the British national park rule as any; and the chances
of any changes being permitted which could damage vast tracts of
natural plant and animal communities, or the balanced agricultural economies, within the park boundaries, are remote.

The British national parks are not very spectacular innovations,
and from some points of view are more or less "on paper." But
from the point of view of nature protection they are a sound
insurance.

Nature Reserves

"Nature is the oldest thing on earth," wrote E. M. Nicholson,
when Director-General of Britain's Nature Conservancy, "but
Nature Reserves are among the youngest." This is only fairly true;
for there is a good case for recognizing the regulated hunting-
grounds of the ancient kings and lords of Europe and Asia as true
nature reserves. The idea of keeping largish areas as inviolate
wilderness is, in fact, as old as hunting; and to the love of hunting,

up to and including the days of the gun, the world owes many a wilderness that would otherwise have been felled or farmed or built upon.

There is a lot of public confusion between national parks and nature reserves. Modern national parks are in the strict sense areas set apart for public recreation, and guarded from any sort of change or exploitation by strict management. This management must of course extend to the wild life of the park: in general the living community (including the human community) is the thing-to-be-preserved, not the status of each and every member of it.

In nature reserves in the strict modern sense, the thing-to-be-preserved may also be the plant and animal community, but if so the community is a much more rare, special and precious one than the broad community of a national park. More often the nature reserve is dedicated to the preservation of a few rare species of plant or animal that are in danger of extinction, or even one species.

There are obviously, by this definition, many areas which are on the borderline of the park and the reserve. The Swiss National Park, for instance, would (as Nicholson points out) be regarded by the British as a National Nature Reserve, so strict is the attention of its managers to the living community, and so strict their rules for human control. In the British sense a national park is free to all who wish to wander on public footpaths and negotiated access areas (plenty); access is usually controlled where (as may happen) a nature reserve happens to lie within it.

In most national parks there are more rules than in the U.K.; visitors may fish, but not hunt, and are rather carefully encouraged to keep to well-marked roads and trails. On the other hand the great Cairngorms Nature Reserve in Scotland is so big, and so free to visitors, that one feels it has been called a nature reserve simply to give it status in law, because Scotland has not yet got round to making legislation for national parks. Many of what were originally game reserves in Africa, and are now known as national parks, also have this hybrid status.

The great network of nature reserves in Britain began to be dedicated some eighty years ago in East Anglia, by the private efforts of nature societies. At first the protection movement was a local one, but it soon became national under the care of such bodies as the Royal Society for the Protection of Birds, the National Trusts for England-Wales-Northern Ireland and for Scotland, and the Society for the Promotion of Nature Reserves. Since the Second World War the Government has created the Nature Conservancy while on the private side is the Council for Nature, which co-ordinates the preservation activity of all national and many local societies and acts as watchdog, pressure group and intelligence agent, like the National Audubon Society or the Wilderness Society in the United States.

In North America the history of private nature protection and conservation societies is nearly as old as it is in England. The Pennsylvania Audubon Society was started as early as 1886. The term "Audubon Society" was coined by George Bird Grinnell in that year. Today forty-five out of the fifty states have at least one Audubon society or powerful natural history society that has

U.S. Government agencies concerned with conservation, with years of origin:

1879 Geological Survey
1885 Biological Survey (became Bureau 1905)
1891 Commission of Fish and Fisheries (became Bureau 1903)
1891 President given power to establish forest reserves
1902 Bureau of Reclamation
1906 Forest Service
1911 Forest Service responsibilities extended
1916 National Park Service
1924 Forest Service powers further extended
1928 Forest Service Research Program
1933 Tennessee Valley Authority
1933 National Park Service responsibilities extended
1935 Soil Conservation Service
1937 Soil Conservation Service responsibilities extended
1940 Bureaus of Biological Survey and Fish and Fisheries united as Fish and Wildlife Service with new responsibilities

The appropriation for these agencies is less than 1 per cent of the U.S. national annual budget.

influence upon state legislation. The principal Government agencies and their years of origin are listed opposite.

In most of the more northerly countries of Western Europe the situation was, and is, much the same: a nineteenth-century rise in local and national natural history societies; the private acquisition of threatened areas towards the end of the century and their dedication and management as sanctuaries; early in the present century, an extension and co-ordination of conservation activity, an increase in the number and variety of reserves; and around mid-century the "capitulation" of governments, to the extent that they assumed at least some degree of responsibility for wildernesses, special communities or threatened species.

This responsibility varies very much from one country to another; but most advanced countries now have something like the U.S. Fish and Wildlife Service or the British Nature Conservancy. Their governments have come to own or at least manage national nature reserves, wildfowl refuges, geological monuments and all sorts of areas of special scientific interest; to provide or pay for researchers on conservation problems; to control and licence the exploitation of game and other natural resources; and to advise other government departments (e.g. agriculture and health) on farm pest control, water conservation, sewage disposal, river pollution and other problems.

All this sounds very fine, for it means that in some form or other most of the older countries have their conservation corps. So do many colonial countries; and the scores of these that have won their freedom in recent years have often inherited a sound attitude to nature and at least the wherewithal to administer their own conservation problems.

Yet all this fiscal and social dedication, all over the world, may be as ineffective as were the bucket-passers at the Great Fire of London if the rape and plunder of our planet continues at its present rate.

The Plundered Planet

On 1934 May 12, as Fairfield Osborn reports it,* "the sun was darkened from the Rocky Mountains to the Atlantic by vast clouds of soil particles borne by the wind from the Great Plains lying in Western Kansas, Texas, Oklahoma and Eastern New Mexico and Colorado – once an area of fertile grasslands but now denuded by misuse, much of it to the point of permanent desolation."

It took an eclipse of the sun over Washington's Capitol, by dust clouds from a thousand miles away or more, to establish the U.S. Soil Conservation Service.

All over the world, through ancient and modern misuse of nature, our topsoil has been blown away by the wind, washed away by the rains, poured away into the sea. At the present time about $5\frac{1}{2}$ billion tons of U.S. soil go down the drain each year, at an annual estimated (and irrecoverable) cost of nearly $4 billion. Since man settled in the Middle West 57 million acres (an area equivalent to the states of New York and Pennsylvania combined) have become worthless for further farming.

* *Our Plundered Planet*. Faber and Faber, London, 1948.

A System for Paradise

From the dust bowl round the Yellow River in Central China, that river carries away $2\frac{1}{4}$ million tons of soil a year. In Turkey the Menderes River has been stealing farmed off soil for 2,000 years, so much so that Tarsus, which was a port in the time of St Paul, now lies ten miles inland, with an apron of silt between it and the sea. Only 2 per cent of Greece has its original topsoil.

When the world was a fairly stable natural garden, and man a rare animal, the ordinary processes of nature were, in general, accumulative. That is to say, wherever soil could grow, it grew. Except in the polar regions, in mountain areas where rock outcropped, or desert areas too far from water, the succession of natural plants moved harmoniously and with the rhythms of the changing climate to form "climax forests" which lasted for thousands of years in essence unchanged. These forests were dominated by characteristic species of plants and inhabited by stable communities of animals. They changed only with the slow march of evolution, assisted and indeed promoted by the geological shifts of the earth's crust and the major, long-term swings of the weather.

And while each plant community flourished, whether it was grassland, scrub, light woodland or dense forest, it made humus of its decayed dead, trapped nitrogen from the atmosphere, drew salts from the bedrock, drank water from the air and soil, and fertilized its own soil. Stable soil, full of organic nourishment, can deepen in a stable plant community under good conditions by an inch in anything from 300 to 1,000 years, depending on the circumstances – and allowing for natural erosion, for wind and

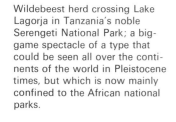

Wildebeest herd crossing Lake Lagorja in Tanzania's noble Serengeti National Park; a big-game spectacle of a type that could be seen all over the continents of the world in Pleistocene times, but which is now mainly confined to the African national parks.

rain can wash very, very little away from a stable climax plant community.

All the work of a thousand years of nature can be destroyed and spent in a few months, or even by one violent storm, if man's husbandry destroys the plant community and attempts to substitute the wrong one for it. England is a lucky country, for it is practically unerodable, and blessed with the kind of climate that has permitted the substitution of a mixed farming community for about 90 per cent of its ancient forests. This was done without the loss of precious soil – and can and has been done in many countries where conditions are as benign.

But elsewhere in the world where the land surface is far more brittle the urgent and unscientific plough has brought ruin. During the Second World War, and shortly after it, to fulfil national policy, 40 million acres of virgin or near-virgin land took the plough for the first time in the United States. Only long time will bring it back to fertile life, for it is now nearly all eroded beyond recovery.

Our Plundered Planet, Fairfield Osborn called his harrowing book; and earth's plundering by multiplying man is the concern of this book. All kinds of horrors will come our way, as we visit the major "habitats" of the world in turn. Can we stop extermination? Ninety-five full species of birds have been altogether wiped out since 1600 – twenty-four of them in the twenty-two years 1887–1908, which just about coincides with the period when, as an earth-developer, man was at his greediest.

In the early days of the European exploitation of Africa the herds of wild mammal game stretched to the horizon across the great fertile plains. Today such sights are to be observed, to all intents and purposes, only in the national parks. And only in these national parks – nowhere else in the world – are we, as Julian Huxley puts it, "able to see and study a slice of the Pleistocene, before man had discovered how to modify and even control his natural environment, before he had destroyed most of the large animal inhabitants of the habitats he was so ruthlessly and short-sightedly exploiting."

Control our natural environment we can, or at least we are learning to. But because we can, it does not follow that we do. Ask the man in the street what IUCN* stands for? Or FAO†? Or how many peoples of the world are still living at, or below, starvation level?

Nature's Network

Those who have conservation at heart strive to deploy those fundamentals of nature which must be understood before we can conserve anything. Every exercise in practical conservation involves a contemplation of its own version of Darwin's tangled bank, or an aquatic version of it. Time must be devoted to the investigation of the lives of its living things, however simple or elaborate they may be, and their place in nature, and their interdependence, and the rules and laws that govern these things; and to the study of the lattice of life and the place of man in it; and to mixing history, geography, geology, meteorology and biology

* International Union for Conservation of Nature and Natural Resources.
† Food and Agriculture Organization of the United Nations.

together to make the most inspiring of all disciplines: scientific natural history.

In 1859, the year of Darwin's *Origin of Species*, which I quoted from earlier in this chapter, the French biologist Isidore Geoffroy Saint-Hilaire coined a good word from the Greek for scientific natural history – ethology. Λογος (logos) means a thought in Greek, or the word or words by which a thought is expressed. ηθος (ethos) means an accustomed place or lair or haunt; or custom or disposition or manners. Nowadays ethology is generally applied to animals in the second of these senses, and describes the study of their behaviour.

For the study of animals and plants in relation to one another and to their surroundings, logos is now fitted with another prefix, applied to it, of course again from Greek, by the evolutionist E. H. Haeckel in 1868. *Oikos* (œcos or oicos) means a house or home; and Haeckel's *Oecology*, afterwards simplified to *ecology*, is now generally used to describe the study of animals at home, from every aspect. Conservation, then, can be rather grandly called "an experiment in ecological synthesis:" or more simply, an analysis of, and a programme based on the natural *history* of the main zones of the earth's surface and the communities of plants and animals that inhabit them.

The Academics

Those who come to our aid in this study are the scientific academics. As I tried to explain earlier, they are not so different from the enthusiasts; indeed, most of them are, or were, enthusiasts. But for them the love of nature was not, or is not enough. Come to that, love alone is not going to save nature: but applied ecology could. It is one of the youngest of sciences, and most sciences are young; and it is developing so fast that to distil and summarize its discoveries to make rules and laws and generalizations is very difficult.

We have already shown that the word *ecology* itself did not come into general use until 1868. Most of the other words we use in general biology are also young. Even *comparative anatomy* (1617) and *cell* (in the sense of an animal or plant cell, 1665) are fairly young. *Embryology* dates from as late as 1772, *taxonomy* from 1813, *chlorophyll* from 1817, *nucleus* from 1823, and the first use of *evolution* in the modern sense from 1831. *Palaeontology* dates from 1836, *protoplasm* from 1839, *biocenosis* from 1877, *enzyme* from 1878, *symbiosis* from 1879, *plankton* from 1888, *mutation* from 1894, *autecology* and *synecology* from 1896.

The first ecological work was surely T. R. Malthus's *Essay on the Principle of Population* in 1798. Many works of the nineteenth century, notably Darwin's, are full of implied ecology. But as far as I can find the first book with "ecology" in its title was E. Warning's *Oecological Plant Geography*, as late as 1896. F. E. Clements's pioneer *Research Methods in Ecology* dates from 1905, and the first book on strict animal ecology was C. C. Adams's *Guide to the Study of Animal Ecology* of 1913. The *Journal of Ecology* was established in the same year; *Ecology*, another fine journal, in 1920, the *Journal of Animal Ecology* in 1932.

Wildlife Crisis

We conservationists are fully conscious that new wings of ecology are still being planned, and that the scaffolding still stands and the builders are still at work with drills and wire and paint. And let us take as our guide some lines from an old enthusiast of nature, hoping that the title of the work in which he wrote them will not deter us.

> Accuse not Nature, she hath done her part;
> Do thou but thine, and be not diffident
> Of wisdom, she deserts thee not, if thou
> Dismiss not her.
>
> Milton, *Paradise Lost*, VIII, ll. 561–64

British Paradise

"We healdath" could be the family motto of all English-speaking conservationists, though the English word "heald" went out of use nearly a thousand years ago.

Ic healde, I am proud to say. I conserve. The heald is an Old English word for sanctuary management and the altruistic tending of land, homes and people. I make no apology to the Celtic fringe for suggesting an Anglo-Saxon word for conservation in its broadest sense. The Anglo-Saxons have the English language as their major offering to British, Irish and North American culture. They also have had, as have the Germanic tribes from which they descended, a history of leadership in the study of nature and environment.

If we dig into our slender literature of over a thousand years ago we find startlingly good naturalists, poets with a fine eye for scenery, writers with a passion for the great outdoors whatever the weather, saints like Aldhelm, Cuthbert and Guthlac, who were dedicated to the protection of wildlife and the love of wild animals. There were saints also from the Celtic fringe like Kentigern and Columba, showing that in those Dark Age days the Anglo-Saxons were not the only *healdende* – conservationists – of wild animals.

Man has had a very long history in the British Isles, particularly in England. The Red Crag deposits of East Anglia are now dated as Pleistocene of the latest Villafranchian horizon.* In these levels, formed half a million years ago or very slightly earlier, are eoliths, worked flints whose origin is still controversial but which could have been made by man.

If they were made by man, the man was probably *Homo erectus*, our ancestral or probably ancestral species that used to be placed in the genus *Pithecanthropus*, whose bones were discovered recently in Hungarian deposits more than 300,000 years old. Abbevillian† artifacts of this date in England of human origin are beyond doubt.

The oldest bone in England which can unequivocally be referred to the genus *Homo* is the famous cranium from Swanscombe in Kent, found in a Thames gravel which was laid down at the end of

* The Villafranchian deposits of Europe were laid down between *c.* 3 million and 0.5 million years ago. They were regarded as the uppermost horizons of the Pliocene period (which precedes the Pleistocene) until an International Geological Congress ruled otherwise. In Europe Villafranchian times show marked climatic changes but no important invasions by land ice.

† Abbevillian: an early "hand axe" culture.

the great interglacial, at a time now thought to be just under 200,000 years ago. Most scholars now regard Swanscombe man as belonging to our own species, *Homo sapiens*. The fact that the Swanscombe material resembles, but is not identical with *Homo neanderthalensis* does not bother the modern anthropologists who now mostly regard Neanderthal man as only racially different from modern man. Anthropologists and palaeontologists have to be racialists – though strictly from the systematic point of view, of course.

Adam Swanscombe, then, was a sapient man; so far the oldest sapient man discovered anywhere in the world. England, which at his time was an isthmus of Europe,* has thus had a planning problem longer than any other country we know of.

I make no apology for starting with the Stone Age, for it is in the Ice Age or Pleistocene Stone Age that man's influence on his environment begins.

It began, beyond doubt, when he was a hunter and before he was a farmer. He did not begin to be a farmer until the Late Mesolithic times that followed the last glaciation, in the current interglacial Flandrian period. This has now lasted 10,000 years and is thought by students of solar radiation cycles to be going to last at least another 10,000 years before the ice comes back again.

I have been studying the fossil trend of British and Irish birds and mammals, with special reference to the terminal dates of some of the species in our deposits. An object of the exercise: to find out whether the departure of the various species was natural (i.e. that their extinction was evolutionary; few higher vertebrate species have had a natural geological life of more than a few million years), or man-aided. If extinction appears to accelerate significantly at a certain time, and the presence of hunting man is significantly in evidence through the finding of his bones or artifacts in the deposits concerned, then there is an *a priori* case for man being the agent of at least some of the extinctions, though climate and environmental change and evolutionary senility can, and still provedly do, bring species to an end.

In Britain and Ireland we cannot identify a Pleistocene overkill as sensational as that which took place in the Americas, where man invaded via the Bering Straits 15,000 years ago or more and reached the tip of South America 10,000 years ago or more. What happened in Britain and Ireland, where *Homo sapiens* has so far lived ten times as long as he has lived in the Americas?

Let us begin by following the fortunes of the fauna through the ages. The time of Swanscombe man was at the end of the:

Hoxnian, or *great interglacial*, a period of ice retreat that ended about 170,000 years ago. Five animals have their youngest fossils in the Swanscombe deposits (180,000 years old): a giant beaver and four voles. There is no evidence that Swanscombe man helped them on their way to extinction.

Wolstonian glacial, 170,000–120,000 years ago. This period began and ended with important ice advances, with a warm interval in between. In this interval, known as the Ilford interstadial,† a vole has a terminal date and during the second ice advance a clawless otter is recorded in Devon for the last (and indeed only) time.

* England was an isthmus of Europe until about 7,000 years ago, except for a time in the last interglacial period when a rise in sea-level cut it off.

† Interstadial, geologists' term for a subdivision of a glacial period in which the ice temporarily retreats.

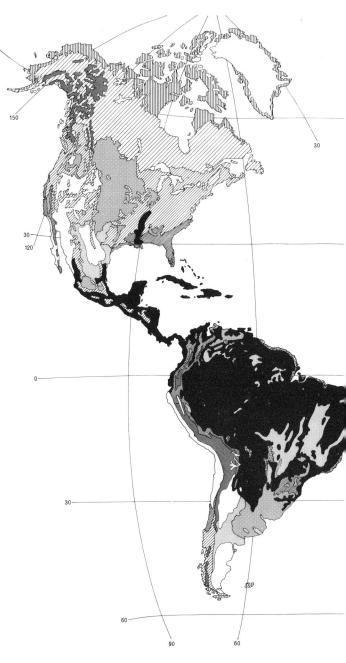

The principal vegetation zones of the world, after Professor D. L. Linton's map on the "Oxford Projection."

Ipswichian interglacial, 120,000–80,000 years ago. This was a period so warm that the sea-level rose (through the melting of ice) enough to break the isthmus to the Continent for a time, but not before the hippopotamus had invaded England for the first time since the Cromerian interglacial, which ended about 270,000 years ago. The hippo became quite common and lived in the rivers of England and Wales as far north as the Tees at Stockton. It disappeared when the late Devensian glacial period set in. Man, though present, was not very common in Ipswichian times and cannot be certainly regarded as an extinguisher.

During this interglacial period the woolly elephant and woolly rhino reached Scotland, perhaps for the only time, though they

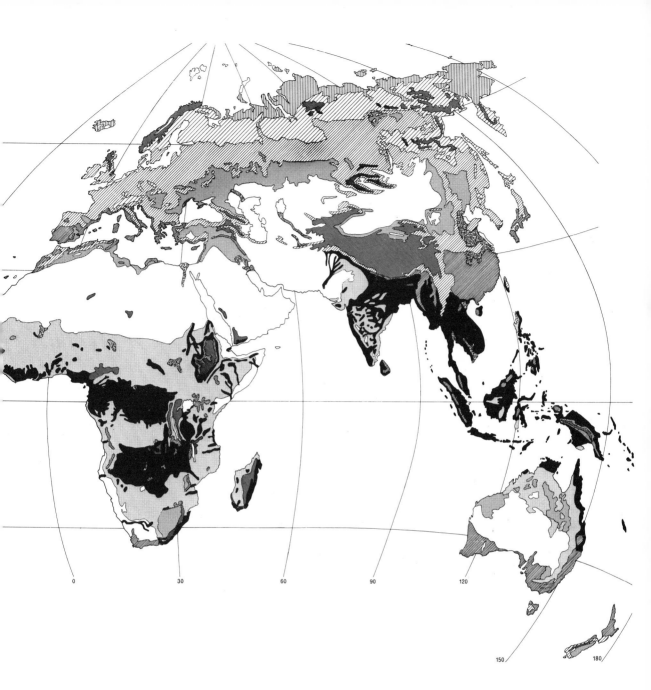

may have survived there during the Devensian glaciation. The forest elephant, steppe rhino, moose and leopard are recorded for the last time in Wales. The Polignac deer, the steppe elephant, the Asiatic wild ass, the ibex and possibly a tapir are recorded for the last time in our fauna, as was the Clacton fallow deer. The steppe elephant and Clacton fallow deer doubtless died natural deaths: they either were, or were little different from, the ancestors of the woolly elephant and modern fallow deer, which took their places in nature. The fallow deer appears in England and Wales in Ipswichian times but not again for certain until the Neolithic period, so it may have departed with the onset of ice and re-appeared just before the Channel break in Mesolithic times.

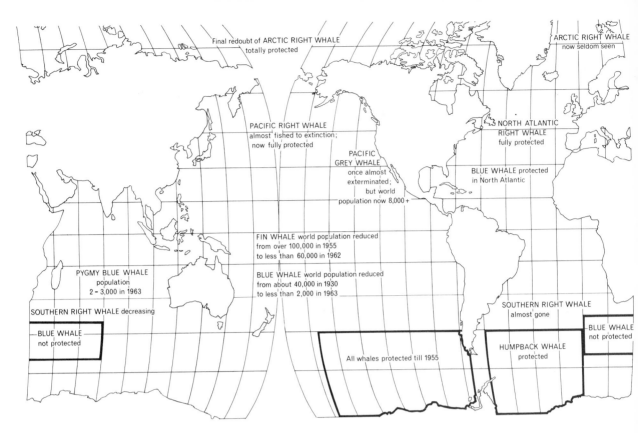

Whale map

Devensian glacial, early phases 80,000–50,000 years ago. This period was heralded by a glacial advance and ended by a glacial advance, with a warmish interstadial – known as the Upton Warren interstadial – between. Muskox and steppe lemming appear for the last time in deposits of the second glacial stadial (advance). Five other rodents and a shrew depart. In the interstadial the forest and steppe rhinos lived in England for the last time; so did that mini-bunny-rabbit the pika, which survives today no nearer to Britain than the southern Urals, and the hazel grouse of Europe.

Devensian glacial, late phases 50,000–10,000 years ago. This was a time marked by rapid improvements in Upper Palaeolithic human culture, and particularly by the evolution of that sophisticated, peculiarly British counterpart of the Continental Magdalenian culture, the Creswellian culture. Named after the Creswell caves in Derbyshire, the culture extended into the caves of Wales and the West Country.

For the first time, now, we can note an acceleration of the extinctions, and entertain an economical hypothesis that this was man-aided. The beginning of this period was an interstadial and warmish; a little over 20,000 years ago the final glacial stadial set in. This third Devensian glacial had periods of retirement, of which the last was the short Allerød interstadial, about 12,000 to 11,000 years ago.

In Wales the cave bear may have survived until Late Devensian times, though the material awaits rechecking. The peculiarly

European and Near Eastern cave bear was never very common in Britain, and was last recorded for certain in England in an Early Devensian horizon at Kent's Cavern in Devon. Other "last records" found in the Late Devensian, though not very accurately datable within the period, are the striped hairy-footed hamster (which is now unknown west of northern Asia), the wolverine, the leopard and the forest elephant. The date of the last sabretooth in Europe is a little over 30,000 years B.P.* – the lesser scimitar cat (the sabretooth *Homotherium latidens*) in Robin Hood's Cave in the Creswell caves in Derbyshire.

A little under 30,000 B.P. we find the last British European souslik (still living in Western Europe), rootvole (still living in Scandinavia), and saiga antelope (now found no nearer than the Lower Volga). About 20,000 B.P. comes the last Norway lemming known in England, and in Wales the last lion, woolly elephant and giant deer. The last collared lemmings and woolly rhinos in England and Wales date from the Allerød interstadial, as do the last spotted hyena, common vole (it survives in Orkney), lion and woolly elephant in England, lynx and steppe bison in Wales, and Norway lemming in Ireland.

Nature may have extinguished the rodents, the smaller mammals in this list; but we can assign the demise of some, perhaps most, of the larger mammals to Creswellian hunters. Doubtless the woolly elephants and rhinos withdrew to the Continent, though I know of no later terminal dates for them in Eurasia; the mammoth survived till the seventh millennium B.P. in Alaska. The sabretooth may have died out because of a decline in the population of its main prey, which is thought to have been young elephants.

Mesolithic, 10,000–5,500 years ago. Two Pleistocene animals survived in England to this time, the lynx and the steppe bison.

Neolithic, 5,500–3,800 years ago. The appearance of the last fossil lynx in Scotland, and Ireland (where radiocarbon date of 2617 ± 150 B.C.), last fossil aurochs in Ireland (same date), last giant deer in Scotland (Orkney).

Bronze Age, 3,800–2,600 years ago. The last collared (snow) or arctic lemming and arctic fox in Ireland, and moose in England. In the Middle Bronze Age the last giant deer in England (Cambridgeshire) and in the Late Bronze Age the European bison in England, probably a post-glacial invader (in Gloucestershire).

Iron Age, 2,600–2,000 years ago, somewhat later in Scotland and Ireland. Possibly the last European bison in Herefordshire; the last reindeer in Wales; the last giant deer in Ireland. This huge animal became globally extinct in the Iron Age, dying out also in Europe by the Danube. It was almost certainly known to the Romans in the time of the Caesars, and to the Germans who invented the *Niebelungenlied* poems with their *schelch*.

Roman, 2000 B.C.–A.D. 450. Last reindeer in England (Worcester after A.D. 161) and Ireland (Early Christian times). Records in need of rechecking include giant deer, County Clare (possibly in

* Before the present; for convenience palaeontologists and archaeologists have, since the advent of radiocarbon dating in that year, adopted the rule of using "present" to mean 1950.

121

c. 1660 the crane in England
1692 the great auk in England (Isle of Man)
Eighteenth century the spoonbill in England and Wales, the grey-lag goose in Ireland
1790 the capercaillie in Ireland
Nineteenth century the marsh harrier in Scotland
Early nineteenth century the golden eagle in England
1834 the great auk in Ireland
1840 the great auk in Scotland (St Kilda, last bred 1812 Orkney)
Twentieth century the wigeon in Ireland, the kite in Scotland
1902 the hawfinch in Ireland
1908 the white-tailed eagle in Scotland
c. 1917 the marsh harrier in Ireland
1925 the wryneck in Wales
1932 the chough in England
1938 the wood warbler in Ireland
1939 the whooper swan in Scotland
1945 or later the marsh harrier in Wales
1947 the kite in England
Early 1950s the red-backed shrike in Wales
1954 the woodlark in Ireland
1956 the Kentish plover in England
1957 the black-necked grebe in Ireland
1960 the golden eagle in Ireland

Here is a list of birds which have "dropped in" as established breeders in historical times in England, Wales, Scotland and Ireland, either naturally, by some provable recolonization(*); by introduction (I); or reintroduction (R):

I	Pheasant, England by 1059
I	Pheasant, Wales, Scotland, Ireland in sixteenth century
I	Canada goose, England 1671
*	Magpie, Ireland 1676
I	Canada goose, Scotland *c.* 1750
I	Red-legged partridge, England 1770
	Mistle thrush, Ireland 1808
	Gannet, Wales *c.* 1820
R	Capercaillie, Scotland 1837
	Stock dove, Wales 1838
	Crossbill, Ireland 1839
*	Starling, Ireland 1850
I	Gadwall, England 1850
I	Red-legged partridge, Wales 1850
	Scoter, Scotland 1855
	Sandwich tern, Ireland 1857
	Turtle dove, Wales 1865

Christian times), European bison (Staffordshire), reindeer in Wales (Pembrokeshire) and moose in Scotland (East Lothian).

Dark Ages, A.D. 450–1066. The reindeer survived in Scotland, as also did the aurochs, to the tenth century. The reindeer was reintroduced in the seventeenth century (died out), again in 1820 (died out) and finally in 1951 (survives). The brown bear survived in England to *c.* 1000, in Wales and Scotland to *c.* 1057.

Medieval, A.D. 1066–1600. The beaver survived in Wales and Scotland to the twelfth century. The wolf survived in Wales to the early thirteenth century and in England to *c.* 1500. The crane last bred in Ireland in the fourteenth century, the great bustard in Scotland in 1526.

Modern, 1600–present. The wolf survived in Scotland until 1743, in Ireland to 1786. On 1864 November 24 a grey whale was found dead on the coast of Devon, since when no member of the Atlantic race of *Eschrichtius gibbosus* has been recorded alive, and the sub-species is considered extinct. It had been fairly heavily fished by the American whalers previously, and was last taken off New England in the early eighteenth century.

Dates (left) indicate when certain birds dropped out of the fauna of Britain and Ireland in modern times (i.e. last bred or were last seen).

These dropouts may sometimes have been due to natural environmental causes, such as climate, but the majority are attributable to man the hunter, collector, habitat-disturber and habitat-destroyer. There is another side to the coin, however; various mammals have been successfully introduced and have spread; birds have also been successfully introduced or have colonized from other countries in Britain and Ireland, or from the Continent.

So we see, then, that man became an agent of ecological change of a serious kind in the Late Palaeolithic times of the last glacial advance. He finished off our big game mostly around then, though some elements survived longer, such as the fabulous giant deer which lasted at least until the Iron Age, and the bear (the same species as the American grizzly bear) which was present up to the end of the Dark Ages.

Once out of the Old Stone Age and armed with polished stone and later with metal, man began to change the floral face of England, Wales, Scotland and Ireland with the axe, and fire.

The Allerød episode towards the end of the last glacial period brought much of Britain and Ireland out of tundra conditions into a phase of temperate forest. For a time, between 11,000 and 10,000 B.P., tundra and semitundra conditions returned during the re-advance of Highland ice, but these conditions disappeared quite rapidly around 10,000 B.P. and Britain had a quick succession from birch to birch and pine in the preboreal Mesolithic times of 10,000 to 9000 B.P. The plant carpet of about threequarters of Britain (bogs, moors and alpine mountain zones alone excluded) became woodland. The woodland evolved; it was basically pine when

Goosander, Scotland 1871
Great crested grebe, Scotland
  1877
Stock dove, Scotland and
  Ireland 1877
Great crested grebe, Wales 1882
Red-throated diver, Ireland 1884
Little owl, England 1889
Great spotted woodpecker,
  Scotland 1900
Hawfinch, Scotland 1903
Scoter, Ireland 1905
Gadwall, Scotland 1906
Slavonian grebe, Scotland 1908
Fulmar, Ireland 1911
Bittern, England 1911
Eider, Ireland 1912
Sandwich tern, Wales 1915
Little owl, Wales 1916
Pintail, Ireland 1917
Marsh tit, Scotland 1920
Fulmar, England 1922
Black redstart, England 1923
Hen harrier, Wales 1924
Hen harrier, England 1925
Mandarin duck, England 1930
Gadwall, Ireland 1933
Wigeon, Wales 1934
Gannet, England 1937
Goshawk, England 1938
Little ringed plover, England 1938
Fulmar, Wales 1940
Goosander, England 1941
Mandarin duck, Wales 1944
Avocet, England 1946
Turtle dove, Scotland 1946
Red-breasted merganser,
  England 1950
Green woodpecker, Scotland 1951
Black-tailed godwit, England 1952
Red-breasted merganser,
  Wales 1953
Redwing, Scotland 1953
Osprey, Scotland 1954
Collared dove, England 1955
Yellow wagtail, Ireland 1956
Collared dove, Scotland 1957
Little owl, Scotland 1958
Wood sandpiper, Scotland 1959
Collared dove, Wales and
  Ireland 1959
Black guillemot, Wales 1962
Firecrest, England 1965
Savi's warbler, England 1965
Buzzard, Ireland 1966
Tree sparrow, Ireland 1966
Snowy owl, Scotland 1967
Serin, England 1967

ately (mostly later 1960s):
  Grey-lag goose, England
  Canada goose, Wales and Ireland
  Ruddy duck, England
  Ruff, England
  Black tern, England
  Mediterranean gull, England

Ireland probably severed from Wales (it is now thought that this, rather than Scotland, was the last connection), and it was pine and hazel with a significant element of oak by the time the ocean's ice-melt rise had broken the Channel bridge around 7000 B.P.

With a quick improvement of climate around 6000 B.P. (probably the best climate Europe has had since the Ipswichian interglacial), the woodland cover settled down to alder, oak and pine, with a tendency for the pine to retreat to Scotland as oak took over the domination of England. By the end of Mesolithic times England and Wales had perhaps the richest jungle of oak, with alder, lime and some elm, that they have ever enjoyed. Beech came in later, in the Iron Age, when for the first time forests began to shrink under the influence of the metal axe.

The forest clearance had, of course, begun earlier, with the sophisticated polished stone axes of the Neolithic pastoralists. But they scarcely affected the area of woodland jungle. Bronze Age axes may possibly have cleared enough woods to push the open land from a quarter to a third of the land area. But the iron axes of the Iron Age, Romano-British and Dark Age farmers were to come.

In early Neolithic times the woodland occupied some 40 million of England, Wales and Scotland's 57 million acres. It was down to between 30 and 35 million at the end of the Bronze Age, about 25 million at the end of the Iron Age (whose farmers could clear 2 million acres of forest in a century), under 20 million by the departure of the Romans in the fifth century A.D., around 10 million by the Norman Conquest, about 3 million by 1688, and not much more than 2 million acres by the middle of the eighteenth century, when woodland clearance had become a national obsession – in Scotland particularly – and was operated far beyond its use for agricultural improvement.

Though the climate has fluctuated it has not in general been so good as it was in Mesolithic times. Birch, that signal tree of sharp conditions, and the dominant member of the most northerly and montane forests, has returned in strength, particularly in Scotland. The climax forest of today is poorer than that of 4000 B.C., in the places where it can still grow. But now it grows only by courtesy of man.

Reafforestation of Britain and Ireland has been the tale of the late nineteenth and particularly the twentieth century. Even so, Britain has recovered woodland only to the extent that it now has nearer 3 than 2 million acres, if we include scrubland: less than a tenth of what it enjoyed in prehistoric times.

So man has been a major influence on ecological, faunal and floral change in these islands for 30,000 years at least. In Ireland he became an active denaturalizer of the environment a little later, perhaps less than 20,000 years ago. Today he is everywhere monarch and disposer of the scene. Presently, in England and Wales, we enjoy, besides our ten national parks, twenty-five areas of outstanding natural beauty which have been designated by the Countryside Commission and duly confirmed by the Secretary of State for Wales or the Minister of Housing and Local Government. During European Conservation Year 1970 we hope that the Minister of Housing and Local Government will confirm six more areas of outstanding natural beauty in England – the Suffolk Coast and Heaths, Dedham Vale, the North Wessex Downs, the Mendips, the Wye Valley and the Lincolnshire Wolds. This would bring within the AONB network a total area that is nearly as large as that of the national parks, which already occupy almost 10 per cent of England and Wales.

The important thing about the AONBs is that their B is not in fact N. It is a beauty which has been primarily made by man, by over 200 generations of farmers since Neolithic times, rather than by nature. Unless you think, as I do, that man is part of nature.

That talented scholar of the English landscape, W. G. Hoskins, has estimated that the English human population may not have been more than 20,000 in Neolithic times, that it rose in Iron Age times to a maximum of 400,000 at the time of the Roman invasion, and that by the end of the second century A.D. it may have risen to around about 900,000, perhaps over 1 million, of whom about 200,000 lived in towns.

The Romano-British epoch was full of planning problems, as the Roman overlords deployed planned towns, and planned roads in a land that had previously known only tribal settlements with a few long trading trails. We know they had brilliant engineers and we suspect they may even have had planning officers. They were powerful water-planners, too, and began claiming (a better word than reclaiming) important units of our wetlands with the fifty-six-mile-long Carr Dyke in the East Anglian fenland, and the Fosse Dyke in Lincolnshire. After the Romans had to leave Britain, the fenland system tended to collapse, though some units were carried forward on a Roman foundation by the Anglo-Saxon invaders in Romney Marsh, in the Selsey area, near Glastonbury and elsewhere in marshy Somerset, and here and there in the Fens.

By the time of the Norman invasion the population of England was of the order of 1.25 million, about 10 per cent in towns (especially London, Norwich, York, Lincoln and Winchester), with big populations in the east in Lincolnshire, Norfolk, Suffolk and Essex, and in the west in Devon and Somerset. Perhaps rural Yorkshire and Nottinghamshire, Northamptonshire and Leicestershire, could have been regarded as underpopulated development areas in those days.

By the first outbreak of the Black Death in 1348 the population in England may have been nearly 4 million, which the plague possibly reduced by 1.5 million in thirty years. By 1500 England had between 2.5 and 3 million people and, it is estimated, 8 million sheep. By the end of the seventeenth century England's present rural personality was essentially deployed, and the systems and physiognomy of farming country were those that we have now learned to love. Over 4 million acres were integrated into the English estate systems by the Enclosure Acts (over 3,000 of them) of the eighteenth and nineteenth centuries. The typical English mosaic of country estates and tenant farms began to be stabilized in Georgian times, which had inherited a land-care attitude from the sixteenth and seventeenth centuries, and a taste and tradition of architecture that went back to Norman times.

J. L. and Barbara Hammond's classic book *The Village Labourer 1760–1832* shows what state England's rural democracy had

Facing:
Seychelles kestrel, confined to, and very rare in the island of Mahé in this Indian Ocean archipelago.

evolved to, when the first tremors of the industrial earthquake began to be felt. "By the end of the eighteenth century, the entire administration of county affairs, as well as the ultimate authority in parish business was in the hands of the Justice of the Peace, the High Sheriff, and the Lord-Lieutenant," they generalize. Today the JP is safely independent of the day-to-day party politics of Britain's rural kingdom, and the High Sheriff and Lord-Lieutenant have necessary, elegant, decent and benign ritual functions as the servants of the electorate. But the electorate before the Reform Bill, at the dawn of the Age of Industry, was miniscule and privileged and the constituencies were rotten boroughs. It was an evolving countryside, but a private unplanned countryside. That England passed into the Industrial Revolution ecologically not unscathed, but at least not highly scathed, reflects the taste of the landowners of the eighteenth century when the aristocracy led a class-ridden society, and when the seats of higher learning, the universities, were the captives of the upper classes and hence the effective centres of taste formation and style evolution. The reforms of the Victorian Age onwards have given us, now, a relatively classless society, but not a wholly conservative attitude, which seems acceptable to our present millions. This is a celebration of the peculiarly English art of evolving systems, discarding injustices, yet somehow keeping some good attitudes of our old feudal and sub-feudal masters and incorporating them in public opinion. Feudal rights disappeared, as the Hammonds point out, with the Wars of the Roses, but feudal attitudes remained incorporated in our local government system and land law until the Reform Bill and beyond it. In the late eighteenth century the aristocracy were paramount both in local government and in Parliament. There were some flecks of humanity in Parliament's procedures under the multitude of Enclosure Bills, yet wide injustices to the voteless cottagers. The poor farmers remained as peasants, at the bottom rung of the ladder of social change and privilege. The machinery of appeal was deployed in a haphazard and unfair manner. The present tidy acres of rural England contain, in their amazing beauty, the invisible scars of peasant suffering at the hands of some venal commissioners and greedy landlords. The British landscape is built on ages of confusion and measurable injustice, and on a luckily almost unerodable soil. But the native taste and imagination of both the oppressors and the oppressed have ensured, until and I believe beyond now, the inheritance of the golden common factor of country love – with a common and now classless image of England's green and pleasant land.

It was a happy moment for U.K. citizens everywhere when the talkative astronauts in Apollo 12 commented from orbit on their way to the Moon, that England was the greenest place they had seen. That green carpet has healed, now, the wounds of undemocratic rural centuries.

Even before the great Reform Bill in 1832 there were educated, loved and respected voices that stated, in simple terms, targets that a democratic society could aim at, and hinted that there could, indeed should, be a plan for rural England. But it took a century, and the trauma of two world wars, for the British people

Bontebok, now conserved at Swellendam in South Africa with a population of *c.* 750.

127

Wolverhampton in 1866, from an engraving in the Mansell Collection, showing how the Industrial Revolution had already captured vast areas of the Staffordshire countryside for the iron industry over a century ago.

to weave their way through the growing wens of industry, through the railway age to the airport-motorway age, to find themselves still with a green and pleasant land round which to build a national heald. It has been improvised, basically, since the Second World War, by the planning acts, and National Parks and Countryside Acts, urged on by private associations of like-minded charitable, little-l liberal folk of all parties, and groups, some of which are now centenarian. Parliament has been kind, on the whole, but exceeding slow. These days, however, there is a sense of national urgency in the great debates on pollution, conservation, amenity, landscape, recreation, natural ecological change, and planning, especially in the planning of new towns, roads, reservoirs, airports, mines and industry.

The public demand for access to the countryside first organized itself with the foundation of the Commons, Open Spaces and Footpaths Preservation Society in 1865. In 1878 the Epping Forest Act made an honest mini-model of a national park in a part of woodland Essex where the Corporation of the City of London had begun to acquire land with a purchase of 200 acres as far back as the 1860s, though the provision of urban parks goes back to the development of London's Royal Parks in and after 1660. Nevertheless, it was not until 1884 that the problem of gaining public access to countryside began to be ventilated in Parliament, and then only inconclusively. The main deployment of the British conservation and planning wing was still private.

The first modern nature reserves came in the 1880s. They were not the first of all, for St Cuthbert may have managed the Inner Farne off the Northumberland coast as a nature reserve for a few years starting about 676, and the Abbotsbury Swannery in Dorset was flourishing as a nature reserve in 1393 and has been managed as such by the Ilchester family ever since. The naturalist Charles Waterton had a private bird reserve in Yorkshire in 1843.

By 1888, however, with the foundation of the Breydon Society, there were group-owned and managed reserves in East Anglia, and in 1891, when what is now the Royal Society for the Protection of Birds was set up, the foundation was laid of what is now the

128

† Dedicated to prolonging the work of the Countryside in 1970 Conference after 1970.

largest nature conservation body in the United Kingdom. The RSPB's membership, which in 1942 was 3,500, has doubled four times since then, and is now more than 50,000. In chronological order of foundation, I list the rest of the major amenity, conservation and rural recreation bodies of the United Kingdom (left). Those marked * are statutory, I have included some scientific societies helpful to the cause.

In addition trusts for nature conservation had been founded by 1969 in all the English and Welsh counties, while Scotland has its own Scottish Wildlife Trust. These County Naturalists' Trusts are co-ordinated and served by the Society for the Promotion of Nature Reserves and supported by the co-ordinating Council for Nature. Conservation in general in the U.K. is strongly supported by the British National Appeal of the international World Wildlife Fund, of which H.R.H. The Duke of Edinburgh is President; he is also Chairman of the Countryside in 1970 Conference, of whose Welsh committee H.R.H. the Prince of Wales has been Chairman since it was set up in 1968.

The present climate of rural planning in England and Wales has been much affected by the appointment of Mr Anthony Crosland as Minister of Local Government and Regional Planning. In 1970 he had firmly on his desk the aftermath of the Redcliffe-Maud Commission, and was designing the new structure of our local government system in England, and we can expect also a simplification of local government in Wales. This will mean a profound redeployment of our country resource planning, and its closer engagement with development planning.

The Countryside Commission, on which I serve, firmly and happily welcomes Lord Redcliffe-Maud's recommendations that our National Parks in England should be singled out for special planning status, and that they should be their own planning authorities. So far only the Peak District National Park is a full planning authority, though the Lake District National Park has a Joint Planning Board which approaches a single planning authority closely. The Countryside Commission, and before it the National Parks Commission, have always thought that the single Planning Board, with its own special planning staff, was best for a national park, whether it was a multi-county national park or not.

The British keep their fingers crossed about the new structure, and await its emergence with much interest. They can expect the great towns to have administrative unity with huge blocks of country. As ruralites, U.K. countrymen mostly view with favour the entering of the urbanites into their rural responsibility. I believe they realize that there is only one countryside in England and Wales. It is all they have got, and they can make it grow only here and there, as they are trying to do, by restoring derelict land or claiming land from the sea. The development planning wing's raids must be mostly into the countryside, into the golden acres as full of beauty and history as the Bible is full of quotations.

The new authorities will rapidly become experts on rural and subrural areas, and could develop the same tender love for their realities that their present administrative masters enjoy. Let them be not armed for the raid, but prepared for peaceful coexistence with the countrymen.

If they want to buy country, and turn it into roads, reservoirs, airports and factories let them count up to a hundred in a slow and statutory way, for development is usually irreversible, and Britain is the most crowded country in Europe save only Malta, the Netherlands, and (just) West Germany. If the population of the U.K. increases too fast, too soon, it will run out of countryside, and overcrowd what survives of it with motor cars which presently are breeding even faster. Only a pessimist can believe that the U.K. is fighting a losing battle, and that its people will tie themselves in chains of urban strip and suffocate in urban wens. Only an optimist believes that Britain will find a planning formula for its lovely rural kingdom by the end of the century; but the deployment of planning skills already in evidence is impressive indeed, and we cannot afford to be pessimists.

Meanwhile, like all those compelled to wait for principles, we have to fall back on praxis. The praxis I offer is mosaic defence. The joint desk atlas map of the Ministry of Housing and Local Government, made with the Welsh Office, shows the statutory protection areas which presently extend to a quarter of England and Wales combined. The oldest protected areas, from the planning point of view, are the green belts of England, which now surround the main urban centres of Bristol-Bath, Bournemouth-Southampton, Portsmouth, London, Oxford, Cambridge, Cheltenham-Gloucester, Birmingham, Coventry, Stoke-on-Trent, Nottingham, Derby, Sheffield-Chesterfield, Leeds-Bradford, Wirral-Chester, Merseyside, Manchester, York, Durham, Easington, Sunderland, South Tyneside and North Tyneside.

Some of the green belts are fully approved, most are formally submitted and under consideration, a few are accepted as sketch plans. Some of them overlap with parts of confirmed Areas of Outstanding Natural Beauty (AONBs). The figures at the end of 1969 are given in the table.

Natural Beauty (AONBs)

Summary of Statutorily protected land, England and Wales, 1969 December 31:

	Square Miles	Square Kilometres	Percentage
Total Land Area	58,349	157,124	100.00
10 National Parks	5,258	13,618	9.02
25 Areas of Outstanding Natural Beauty	4,291	11,114	7.35
19 Green Belts	5,709	14,786	9.78
66 National Nature Reserves	129	334	0.23
	15,387	39,852	26.38
Less areas in more than one category	522	1,353	0.89
TOTAL	14,865	38,499	25.49

Croxley Green near Watford in Hertfordshire, where housing estates tongue into a statutory green belt and approach the official Chilterns Area of Outstanding Natural Beauty.

In addition, approximately 1,000 square miles (2,600 sq. km.) of England and Wales are state forests of the Forestry Commission, some of which lie in national parks or AONBs. Of these the New Forest, the Forest of Dean (including Tintern Forest), and the Border Forest have been designated as "Forest Parks" by the Forestry Commission and special arrangements have been made for public access, recreation and nature conservation therein. Forest parks also lie within the Snowdonia and Lake District national parks. These add some 430 square miles (1,100 sq. km.) to the conservation land in the table. If the Forestry Commission designates Thetford Chase and Salcey Forest in England as forest parks in ECY 1970, this will add nearly 80 square miles (200 sq. km.).

The private conservationists, led by the Royal Society for the Protection of Birds with 30 reserves, have about 400 nature reserves in England and Wales. The majority of these are operated by the County Naturalists' Trusts, and a fair number by the National Trust. This body has charge, in all, of 1,891 places of historic interest or natural beauty in the two countries (only a minority (17) of which are fully managed as nature reserves) totalling about 619 square miles (1,600 sq. km.).

The County Trust and RSPB reserves add another 63 square

The Isle of May (Fife County) at the mouth of Scotland's Firth of Forth; a National Nature Reserve since 1956, and a Bird Observatory for longer.

miles (164 sq. km.). If the six new AONBs are confirmed in ECY 1970, this will add about 1,360 square miles (3,500 sq. km.) to the protected lands and will bring the total, including forest parks, private reserves and National Trust treasures to about a third of England and Wales. This strong mosaic defence is on the planners' desks, because of a combination of statutory and private enterprise that has few parallels in the world. My figures have taken no account of the very large numbers of Nature Conservancy Sites of Special Scientific Interest (about 2,000 in England, Wales and Scotland). These SSSIs are duly filed with the planning authorities, and supplement the National Nature Reserves. There must, now, be something like 2,000 conservation units in England and Wales, and 3,000 or so in the United Kingdom. Some are units within units, for there are many nature reserves, SSSIs and National Trust properties within national parks, AONBs, green belts and other protected zones. But what a mosaic!

ECY 1970's task in the United Kingdom is to tighten and enhance the network, and, under the aegis of the Countryside in 1970 Conference, to show homework to H.R.H. Prince Philip in November. There has been an immense programme of countryside activities, with a highly informative and educational slant, and an award scheme for countryside improvements.

The national system of Nature Trails, so eagerly displayed in the last decade by the Forestry Commission, the National Trust, the National Trust for Scotland, the County Naturalists' Trusts, the Scottish Wildlife Trust, The Royal Society for the Protection of Birds and the developing conservationist groups in Northern Ireland, has been improved and extended. There will be vast programmes of lectures. Displays and demonstrations will tour the country shows. In February 1970 a strong British delegation, with Their Royal Highnesses Prince Philip and the Prince of Wales and the Chairman of the Countryside Commission, John Cripps, took part at the opening conference of ECY 1970 at Strasbourg, called to ventilate and analyse and constructively criticize the ways in which towns, industry, scientific agriculture and forestry, burgeoning leisure and recreation seekers make demands on the mosaic of countryside that we Europeans are looking after, or trying to look after. The conference has already issued a declaration which has gone to each Government and to the public authorities in each of the countries to act upon.

In Britain the network of support extends far beyond the network of those already converted to planned conservation. Scores of captains of industry help rural planning, and scores of captains of labour. Industry's interest in nature is not idle, or dilettante. The Confederation of British Industry is heavily involved with ECY 1970. The great oil companies have sponsored films, guides, maps and books about the countryside. I.C.I. has been a tower of support. The tea trade, notably Brooke Bond, have a conservationist slant in their public relations work. The steel industry, which has a fine record in opencast restoration, is playing the conservation game, as is the Coal Board. And it has been notable that the "pious" Clause of the 1968 Act – and I quote: "In the exercise of their functions relating to land under any enactment every Minister, government department and public

Hawaiian goose or néné.

body shall have regard to the desirability of conserving the natural beauty and amenity of the countryside" – has not been neglected by the powerful public bodies since it was a published enactment. Most of them observed it before it was mandatory, and the liaison between the Countryside Commission and the Forestry Commission, the British Waterways Board, the Water Resources and Conservancy Boards, the Central Electricity Generating Board, the Gas Council, the Sports Council, the Ministry of Agriculture and Fisheries, and the Ministry of Transport – to name but a few – has been deep, frank, helpful and thoughtful. Many of these authorities have taken the Countryside Commission into their confidence very early about their future plans. They accept planning.

Planning was a non-word two centuries ago when the tentacles of industry began their satanic grasp on our tender ruralities. Now it is an in-word, and special in this permissive age, in that it is not any longer a dirty word. Of course a plan is a four-letter word; I *like* some four-letter words. I *like* industry, because it alone can make us rich, and the longer I work in the conservation trade the more I think that good conservation needs wealth, and that the cost of beauty will become calculable, and in many places high, and that we must pay it as soon as we can because our grand-children, if left to foot the bill, may never be able to pay it, be they as rich as Croesus. Beauty is so often irreversible.

Good planning is based on research. The Countryside Commission has combined with professional experts on rural recreation to form the Countryside Recreation Research Advisory Group. This is very busy. The Commission is studying the motor problem in tender landscape areas very closely, and has not hesitated to recommend grants, e.g. to the Peak District National Park Planning Board for a traffic-control experiment in the overcrowded Goyt Valley, which involves the transport of sightseers in buses from car parks to the tender areas.

This is an *experimental* project, and not until it has been tried out for a season can anybody really make the accusation that the motorist is being robbed of his liberty to motor where he likes on the highways he pays for.

The Commission's policy is to try to move country pressures away from tender spots by persuasion and not force. The "Country Park" idea fits this policy. The 1968 Countryside Act gives local authorities power to provide, with the aid of Exchequer grants made on the recommendation of the Countryside Commission, country parks in rural surroundings within easy reach of centres of high population. Already grants have been approved for a dozen, and we can expect, before the end of the century, over a hundred – perhaps eventually several hundred – to be deployed in a mosaic satisfactory to our burgeoning leisured class of day-visitor motorist families, giving them positive scenic, recreational and intellectual rewards without involving them in traffic queues in the tender areas of our national parks. Country parks can, and will be stately home estates, wildlife parks, outdoor sporting parks, recreational parks, marine parks, water parks; stopovers with decent picnic and lavatory accommodation, to make it possible for people to enjoy open-air museums, Dark Age,

133

The St Levan cliffs near Land's End in Cornwall's Area of Outstanding Natural Beauty, traversed by an official coastal Long Distance Path, and acquired by the National Trust during Enterprise Neptune.

Facing:
The Asiatic buffalo, long domesticated, is now very rare as a wild animal and confined to India's Assam (*c.* 1,425 in six groups) and Godavari River area (400–500) and to the Kosi River area in Nepal (*c.* 100). Figures were estimated in 1966.

Overleaf: The Asiatic race of the lion is virtually confined, now, to the Gir Forest in India's Kathiawar; this had an estimated population of only 162 in 1968. A small breeding group has been introduced to the Chandraprabha Sanctuary in Uttar Pradesh. The surviving world population is under official protection and research on it has been aided by WWF.

Medieval, Renaissance and industrial archaeology and architecture, plant and animal ecology, sheer scenery, park zoos and arboreta, botanic gardens, boating, water-skiing, bird watching, butterfly watching, flower watching, bathing, games of all sorts.

When Britain's Anglo-Saxon forefathers gave sanctuary and protection, preserved and conserved, took responsibility for people, places and things, their philosophy as *healdende* was an undercurrent, and by the context of their few surviving words a traditional attitude that was beyond intellectual questioning. Today, as I offer it to you in the language they spoke, our motto is "we healdath," with the same background. We've been long enough in planning to have but one answer to the question "Why do we plan?" Someone's got to do it!

I will give an example of somebody who thought they had to do it. In its fifty years of life the Forestry Commission has resolutely followed its statutory charge of growing timber economically for the benefit of the nation. But very early in its reign as the biggest English landowner, it took a very liberal view of the public's recreational needs, and a very forward-looking attitude to nature conservation. Before the Second World War, when there were no national parks, national nature reserves or areas of outstanding natural beauty, the Forestry Commission designated some of its own areas as virtual models of these categories.

Starting in 1919 with the Forest of Ae in Dumfriesshire, the Forestry Commission took over vast areas of Britain, and by the 1930s was managing an enormous acreage of state forest, most of it in areas of high landscape quality and deep conservation importance.

As early as 1936, when they declared the Argyll Forests a National Forest Park, the FC showed a positive attitude to the recreational needs of the public. In 1938 they gave the same status to the Forest of Dean, and declared Blackcliff and Wyndcliff woods within it as Forest Nature Reserves in the following year. These were models of the AONBs and national nature reserves of the future: brought in when there was no Nature Conservancy or National Parks (now Countryside) Commission.

These were singular acts of conservation and public service, and the management and wardening of these forest parks was found quite compatible with the Commission's statutory charge to maintain economic forestry.

When the war was over, the FC returned energetically to its pioneering role in conservation. Before the National Parks Commission and Nature Conservancy were erected by the Act of 1949, the FC had designated (1948) Glen More as a National Forest Park, and had started (1947) publishing the series of excellent guides to those state forests (the majority) where they encourage public access. There are about two dozen such guides now, cheap, informative and beautifully produced. Moreover, when the present Nature Conservancy – National Parks – Countryside Commission network of statutory conservation got under way the FC gave all the advice they could, particularly in the national parks that embraced state forests.

In 1951 Gwydr and Beddgelert State Forests came into the new Snowdonia National Park; Thornthwaite State Forest and

Hardknott Forest Park into the Lake District National Park. To avoid confusion, the FC now uses "Forest Park," no longer "National Forest Park" for its designations. With these it has proceeded actively. In 1953 Loch Ard and Rowardennan were designated the Queen Elizabeth Forest Park. In 1953 Waterperry in Oxfordshire was designated a Forest Nature Reserve, which now meant a joint management policy with the Nature Conservancy.

The greatest of all the FC forests, the Border Forests in Dumfries, Roxburgh, Cumberland and Northumberland became a forest park in 1955; when the Northumberland National Park was confirmed in the following year only the eastern outliers were incorporated in it. The main mass, which is of national park standard, has been left to the excellent care of the FC, who have provided a most excellent forest museum and information centre in it.

In 1955 the FC also opened to the public the lovely arboretum at Crarae in Argyll, and in 1956 the magnificent arboretum at Westonbirt in Gloucestershire. They have made their own fine aboretum in the Forest of Dean.

In 1961 the FC created new forest nature reserves in England, Wales and Scotland, and in the later 1960s began rental agreements with various county naturalists' trusts for nature reserves, such as that at Brockadale in the North Riding of Yorkshire and the fine acreage of Bedford Purlieus in the Soke of Peterborough.

May I give just one more example of somebody who's had to do it, and has done it. By 1945 the devoted National Trust had acquired no less than 175 miles of unspoiled coastland in England and Wales – and more in Northern Ireland. Then in May 1965, H.R.H. Prince Philip launched the National Trust's Enterprise Neptune: a deliberate campaign to extend the network of coastal conservation. By the end of 1969 no fewer than 110 more properties had been acquired in 17 coastal counties of England and Wales, as well as 11 in Northern Ireland, and 27 more properties are under negotiation in England and Wales and 5 in Northern Ireland. When these are all brought in, the National Trust will have raised its coastal properties by 26,000 acres or 41 square miles (more than 100 sq. km.), and brought the mileage of its protected coast of England and Wales up to 300, or about a third of the remaining unspoilt coast land.

This marvellous campaign has so far cost £1.5 million which has been raised, not without Government and local government help, but primarily by the dedication and generosity of private conservationists.

Parallel with this campaign was a statutory study of the planning of the coastline which was carried out by the National Parks and the Countryside Commission at the request of the Minister of Housing and Local Government and the Secretary of State for Wales. It was based on nine regional conferences held between 1966 May and 1967 March. The first three reports were published in 1967 and the last regional report – the ninth, in 1968. The tenth or pull-together report, just published, recommends a new mosaic defence category, the Heritage Coast area, which will be designated as a guide to local planning authorities. This final report is in two volumes and incorporates three special studies

The tiger, as a species is now in world danger. Of its seven races all but this presently have a sheet in IUCN's Red Data Book; and this, the Bengal tiger, may soon earn one as its status in India is deteriorating under hunting pressure. Conservation research has been aided by WWF.

undertaken by the British Travel Association, the Nature Conservancy and the Sports Council. Somebody had to do it, and including the Countryside Commission there are four statutory bodies who have.

Someone's got to do it! And that somebody is us, the combined forces of trained planners, conservationists, historians, poets, artists, writers, intellectuals, geologists, geographers, biologists, archaeologists, sportsmen, civil servants, farmers, foresters, landowners, landworkers – and housewives.

European Paradise

The earliest tools which can be assigned to man in Europe have been found in Portuguese deposits dating from the beginning of the first major Ice Age, the Pleistocene glaciation, known as the Günzian glaciation. No bones of the man who made these tools have so far been found in European deposits of this age, but we guess that he belonged to the species most anthropologists now assign to *Homo erectus*, formerly known as *Pithecanthropus erectus*, described and named from bones in Java between 250,000 and 300,000 years old. The Portuguese tool deposits are older, about 500,000 years old.

The oldest bones of man so far discovered in Europe are from the *c.* 350,000-year-old level at Mauer near Heidelberg in Germany. They were named *Homo heidelbergensis* by Schoetensack in 1908. The human palaeontologists are now beginning to rate Heidelberg man as being perhaps a race of Java man and to find a line of descent from him to *Homo sapiens* via another form of man also first discovered in Germany, at Neanderthal near Düsseldorf, named *Homo neanderthalensis* by King in 1864. Neanderthal man is close to sapient man, *Homo sapiens* Linnaeus 1758.

In the fossil record many bones have been found which are intermediate between the types of the four forms named; and there is some evidence of hybridization between Neanderthaloids and Sapient men, for instance, in Pleistocene Palestine. What the fossil evidence shows is that the four forms have a common ancestry, but that at times Neanderthaloids and Sapients lived together in Europe without apparent hybridization – thus behaving as different species.

Bones lately discovered at Vértesszöllös in Hungary have been ascribed to *Homo erectus* and are probably between 330,000 and 290,000 years old. Bones found at a *c.* 190,000-year-old deposit at Steinheim in Germany and named *Homo steinheimensis* by Berckhemer in 1933 are of intermediate Java-Neanderthal type. Bones of the quite typical Neanderthal type persist in Europe until under 50,000 years ago, and bones with some Neanderthaloid characters persist until nearly the end of the last glaciation which came to an end 10,000 years ago. There is no evidence of Neanderthaloids surviving into post-Ice Age or what we now call Flandrian times – the period that includes the transition from the Old Stone

Age through Middle and New Stone Ages and the Metal Ages, to the present Industrial Age.

If we study the Pleistocene mammals of Europe, as Björn Kurtén of Finland has done so ably in his recent talented book (1968), we can find figures for the number of land mammals that became extinct in our European fauna at the different stages of the Ice Ages that started with the Günzian glacial phase about half a million years ago. There were four main periods of glacial advance (with some shortish glacial withdrawals within them which we call interstadials): Günz, Mindel, Riss and Würm, and periods of glacial retreat between (last, after) them which we call the interglacials Cromerian, Holsteinian, Eemian and Flandrian. These correspond exactly with the glacial advances and warm interglacials in Britain and Ireland, for which we use other

Years before present (approx.)	Number of land-mammal species that disappeared from Europe in each period†	Human key fossils	Culture (most typical sites are in France)
0–Flandrian interglacial	13(5)		–Industrial Age –Metal Age –Mesolithic and Neolithic
–	–		
Würm glacial advances	25(7)		–Upper Palaeolithic Aurignacian — Levalloisian — Mousterian
–	–		
0,000–Eemian interglacial	4(22)		
–	–		
Riss glacial advances	2(17)		Tayacian
–	–	● Swanscombe ● Steinheim	Acheulian
0,000–Holsteinian interglacial	14(32)		Clactonian
–	–		
0,000–Mindel glacial advances	19(11)	● Vértesszöllös	
–	–		
Cromerian interglacial	21(16)	● Mauer	
–	–		
0,000–Günz glacial advances	25(61)		Abbevillian
–	–		
0,000–Tiglian pre-glacial time	10(2)		

† Brackets denote new species detected in Europe for the first time in the period.

names – and with those in North America which have still other names.

We can date the episodes by radiocarbon if they are younger than 40,000 years (or 70,000 years at most) and by potassium-argon and other radio-dating methods if they are older than about 400,000 years. Between the two limits we can only date, so far, from the astronomical calculations of Milankovich and Emiliani of the variations in the amount of solar radiation received. These variations are calculable and can be correlated with the physical evidences of warmer and colder times discovered through digs in river-gravels and excavations in caves, as witnessed by plant and animal remains and the remains of once-frozen ground or wind-blown ground or ancient rivers and lakeshore ground.

All this sounds – and is – very complicated; but the sophistication of our quaternary (Pleistocene and Recent) geologists and their response to challenge is such that the detailed picture of the events of the last 3 million years and the icy episodes of the last half million when man first seems to have arrived in Europe, is developing rapidly.

Comparatively speaking, a lot of mammals became extinct during the first two (Günzian and Mindelian) glacial advances and the Cromerian interstadial between them. During the long Holsteinian interglacial and the Rissian glaciation and Eemian interglacial that followed the extinction-rate went down. It rose again in the Würmian glaciation and in the following Flandrian interglacial, which is the interglacial we are currently living in.

The Günz glaciation was preceded by a succession of climate changes from warm and dry to cool and wet that lasted for over 2 million years. In some parts of the world nearer the poles the cool-wet periods had produced glacial advances. During Günz there was a glaciation of Europe – perhaps the first in over 200 million years, for Ice Ages do not visit our planet very often, in the geological sense.

Man in Günzian times was a rare, presumably newly immigrant hunting animal in Europe, so rare that we have found but a few of his tools and none (yet) of his bones in Günzian European deposits. The animal extinction, therefore, can scarcely be ascribed to human overkill – most probably it was caused by the lack of preadaptation to glacial and subglacial conditions on the part of a high percentage of the fauna, and to their replacement by better-adapted evolutionary successors.

In the Günzian period more species appeared for the first time than became extinct, with a proliferation of ruminants and a great increase of rodents; and a similar thing happened in Holsteinian, Rissian and Eemian times. But in Würmian and Flandrian times four times as many mammals became extinct in Europe or left it, as evolved in Europe or colonized it – supposing that the figures closely approximate to true lasts and firsts which from my own study of the sophistication of the records of European fossil mammals I am convinced they do.

What emerges from this is that within the last 100,000 years there has been a Stone Age overkill in Europe, not quite as marked as that in North America (p. 196) which is connected with human invasion of the Continent. Humans invaded Europe about 500,000

Woolly mammoth.

142

Aurochs, as depicted in the Lascaux frieze in the earliest known sophisticated rock-paintings.

years ago. Not until Würmian times, and particularly Late Würmian times of 45,000 years ago or less (which, fortunately, are recent enough for radiocarbon dating to be of help) did man become populous or well armed enough to destroy his own prey stocks by overhunting.

The following list gives the terminal dates, as far as I can rummage them out of a voluminous but scattered literature, of as many as I can find of the European continental bird and mammal fauna since Late Würmian times. In the period covered the hunting cultures of Europe evolved from the later Aurignacian Palaeolithic through the improved Perigordian cultures of Châtelperron and La Gravette to the classic Upper Palaeolithic of Solutré (Solutrean) and Grotte de la Madeleine (Magdalenian). Species marked * are still living outside Europe.

Late Würmian (45,000 B.P. or less).

Dhole *or* red dog,* *Cuon alpinus*, Grotte de l'Observatoire, Monaco.

Leopard,* *Panthera pardus*.

Aurignacian, c. 26,000 B.P. Forest elephant, *Elephas antiquus*, picture Pindal Spain.

Magdalenian, C^{14}† 13,500 ± 450 B.P. Steppe bison, *Bison priscus*, Pont-du-Château, France.

Magdalenian, C^{14} 11,550 ± 450 B.P. Woolly mammoth, *Elephas primigenius*, Vailly-sur-Aisne, France. A C^{14} of 9500 ± 500 of this species, on bone, from Herttoniemi, Finland, may be too young.

Magdalenian, now dated between *c.* 17,000 and 10,000 B.P.

Cave chough, *Pyrrhocorax primigenia*, Massat, France.

European race of Sarus crane,* *Grus antigone primigenia*, Grottes des Eyzies, Grotte de Gourdan and Grotte de la Madeleine, France.

Spotted hyena,* *Crocuta crocuta*, Grotte de la Madeleine, France.

Woolly rhinoceros, *Coelodonta antiquitatis*, Grotte des Trois-Frères, France.

Saiga,* *Saiga tatarica*, Laugerie-Basse, France.

European tahr, *Hemitragus (jemlahicus?) bonali*, picture Cougnac, France.

Mesolithic?, C^{14} 9500 ± 500 B.P. Cave bear, *Ursus spelaeus*, on bone, Ranggiloch, Switzerland, may be too young; there are plenty of Late Magdalenian records. (A C^{14} of 7950 ± 530 on bone from Sainte Reine, France, may also be too young.)

Neolithic, between 6000 and 4000 B.P.

European wild ass, *Equus hydruntinus*, Dobrogea, Roumania.

Cave goat, *Myotragus balearicus*, Mallorca and Minorca, Spain.

Iron Age, between 2650 and 2450 B.P. Giant deer, *Megaloceros giganteus*, Styria, Austria.

Graeco-Roman, around 0 B.C./A.D. Lion,* *Panthera leo*, in S. Europe.

Modern (1600–present).

Seventeenth century A.D. Hermit ibis,* *Geronticus eremita*, Austria.

1627 Aurochs, *Bos primigenius* (ancestor of domestic cattle, *Bos taurus*), Jaktorowka, Poland.

c. 1774 Sardinian pika, *Prolagus sardus*, Tavolara, Sardinia.

1844 June 4, Greak auk, *Pinguinus impennis*, Eldey, Iceland.

At the famous cave at Lascaux in France which boasts the finest Palaeolithic animal paintings in the world, the late F. E. Zeuner identified the rhinoceros picture as the forest rhinoceros, *Dicero-*

† C^{14} means a radiocarbon date on carbon-14.

Ibex in the Swiss National Park, a large nature conservation reserve which concentrates on fostering populations of relict alpine animals and plants in the Engadine.

rhinus mercki, now known as *D. kirchbergensis*. Carbon from hearths in Lascaux has been C^{14} dated between $17,190 \pm 140$ and $15,516 \pm 900$ B.P.; but this may date from fires that people, probably of the Solutrean culture, lit to see the pictures by. I know of no European fossil of this rhino that is younger than Early Würmian. A C^{14} date of $> 29,900$ B.P. for this rhino from Mörschwil in Switzerland is minimal and the deposit could even be Eemian and thus at least 90,000 B.P., which would make it older than Early Würmian. Doubtless some at least of the Lascaux pictures are Early Aurignacian and more than 45,000 years old.

The forest rhino could have been driven out of Europe, or even exterminated, by Early Aurignacians, but we need more evidence to prove it. What is certain is that through the four main glacial advances and retreats of the Ice Ages, Europe had a real big-game fauna until the final, Flandrian, retreat of the ice. Now Europe knows no elephants, rhinos, wild horses or asses, giant deer, lions, leopards and hyenas. The sabretooths made their last stand in England (p. 121, where the terminal dates for the big game of Britain and Ireland may be compared). It is true that Europe still has a bison, which is a post-glacial, Flandrian colonist from Asia and may have come from Alaska and have a joint ancestry with the American bison. The European bison is now a conserved relic; no more than that. Bear, wolf and lynx all have relict distribution in Europe and are under grave pressure. Moose, reindeer and red deer survive largely by virtue of game laws. The bigger birds of prey have scarcely ever had it so bad.

Through the 10,000 Flandrian years European man has evolved farming, forest clearance, grazing, overgrazing, ploughing, over-ploughing, new kinds of hunting from falconry to the shotgun; heavy industry, heavy roads, heavy railroads, heavy ships and heavy aircraft, and a pollution system without any parallel in history. His only passports to a future oneness with nature and an international heald are education and democracy, the liberty to learn, the tradition of teaching, the right to research, the duty to dispute, the obligation of orderliness, the privilege of planning, and a love of land in the same league as his love of liberty.

In Europe we can be slow and slovenly, ignorant and idle, and have often proved it; but the conservation cadre of conscientious citizens in every country and clime is being fairly clever, on the whole cool, and scientifically canny and careful. European Conservation Year 1970 is not a vague united front, distinguished by its volume of paper. If a ton of paper could win a battle, most of our conservation battles would have been won by now. They haven't. But what can be won, and may now be being won, is the battle for the acceptance of conservation values in society.

This battle is, in essence, a planning battle – or a battle for planning. The best conservation ecology in Europe flourishes in countries which have deployed a network of conservation units, a mosaic defence of nature, with the least dissent of the captains of the industry and labour on which their economies depend. All countries fight pollution; those who fight best have the broadest view of what pollution is and include sight and sound offences in their blacklist of pollutions. Their virtue can be measured by the broadness of the terms of reference of the pollution commissions and committees they set up. Are these "front organizations?" the international and national critics ask. Can they really influence environmental policy as a whole – of which the pollution problem is but one important facet? Can they move from the vital correction of mistakes to the creation of environmental paradise? Many have.

The Scandinavian environment, still under less human population pressure than most of Europe, has enjoyed a mosaic defence for as long as any part of the Continent. Sweden designated half a dozen national parks as long ago as 1909 – the first in Europe – and now has ten more at least, and a mosaic of more than a thousand national nature reserves, habitat reserves and natural monuments under management and control. Norway's national nature reserve system dates back to 1923 and she now has two national parks. Iceland's reserve system started in 1905 and its first national park at the world's oldest parliament meeting-place at Thingvellir dates from 1928. Denmark's national nature reserves date from 1930, Finland's national parks and national nature reserves from 1938, much helped by the forest administration on which Europe's foremost timber economy depends.

In Western Europe West Germany's conservation mosaic is vast and now amounts to nearly 20 per cent of the total area of the republic, if we include all the nature parks, nature reserves and natural monuments. The relatively small natural monuments bring the designated land units up to more than 40,000 which is without parallel in the world.

The Netherlands network consists of well over 100 planned units which are administered by the departments of agriculture and

Seabird populations are protected on a now large chain of islands off the European coast. This puffin breeds on one of the Lofoten Islands of Norway.

The alpine marmot is another typical mammal of the Swiss National Park.

education; of these four are national parks, the rest national nature reserves. In 1952 Belgium started a system of what is now nine national nature reserves under an *ad hoc* national council with the support of two voluntary national associations. Luxemburg enjoys a large international trans-border nature park with West Germany.

France will shortly have 2,000 nature units all over the country and in Corsica, ranging from three national parks (the first opened in 1963) to national nature reserves (first, 1912) of three main categories. Some of these, like the vital zoological and botanical reserves of the Camargue (1928) at the mouth of the Rhône, and many of the new wetland reserves enjoy World Wildlife Fund support and are places of pilgrimage from all over the world.

Spain started national parks in 1918 and now has three in the Iberian Peninsula and two in the Canaries; since 1963 it has set up, with WWF help, one of the greatest international nature reserves in the world, the Marismas. At the delta of the Guadalquivir, this embraces the classic Coto Doñana, Las Nuevas and Hinojos areas. Here, in a mosaic of wetlands and desert, lives a fantastic community of flora and fauna which can be described as the best surviving sample of preindustrial Europe that it is possible to see. The herds of red deer and fallow deer, and the sounders of wild boar, remind history-lovers of England in Robin Hood's day; and the birds are so profuse that any energetic and fairly knowledgeable ornithologist can rely on seeing over a hundred species on any fine day at spring migration time. Portugal so far has no national park or national nature reserve arrangements in its "metropolitan" Iberian area.

Italy's national park system goes back to 1922, when by law the Gran Paridiso became one; it had been a hunting park since 1836 and a royal one since 1856. Now Italy has four substantial national parks and five national nature reserves, and further national nature reserves are projected in Calabria and Sardinia.

Switzerland's fine national park in the Engadine dates from 1914, is administered by a federal commission and is, in effect, a very big natural reserve with an ibex-chamois-eagle fauna. Besides this the Federation supports two national forest reserves, and there are at least eleven cantonal nature reserves and four more belonging to the Swiss League for Nature Protection. Austria's five nature reserves date from 1933 (the first) and its Tauern nature park from 1913.

Poland's national parks, which include the European bison reserve of Bialowieza (p. 150), date from 1947, although Bialowieza itself has been protected since 1919, and number twelve; besides these there are thirty-eight national nature reserves and no less than 462, mostly but not all small, special reserves. Of the national nature reserves Borki is also a bison sanctuary.

Czechoslovakia has three fine national parks (the first of them founded in 1948), fourteen national nature reserves (first, 1933) and five large "protected zones" (the first of which was set up still earlier) which correspond closely with the English-Welsh Areas of Outstanding Natural Beauty.

Hungary's Tihany National Park dates from 1952 and its six main national nature reserves from 1951; it also manages eighteen

minor reserves. Yugoslavia's list comprises seventeen national parks (the first dates from 1948) and twenty-five nature reserves (first, 1951) of which at least nine still harbour bears, five chamoix and two lynx. Albania's four national parks date from 1956. Greece's national park on Mount Parnès dates from 1953 and the national parks on Mount Olympus and Parnassus (set up in 1938) are being rehabilitated; another national park is projected at Pinde and another on Mount Ainos. Eight national nature reserves (first, 1937) and eight deer-hunting reserves are also on the national list. Bulgaria has a formidable list of twenty-five national nature reserves (first, 1931), five "Popular Parks" (first, 1954), twenty-six smaller reserves and 366 natural monuments. Roumania's single national park, Retezat, was created in 1935 and the first of its fifteen national nature reserves in 1932; it also has seven other minor reserves and is projecting another national park.

In Ireland the Irish Republic has had, since 1932, a national park in Killarney, the Bourn Vincent Memorial Park. Phoenix Park in Dublin (1925) is a recreational park, and six places are national bird reserves, including the Skellig Islands, of which the Little Skellig houses one of the largest gannet colonies in the world. In Northern Ireland a considerable system of private society nature reserves is already deployed and a national park network is being designed by the new Ulster Countryside Committee. Ireland as a whole, because it is under less population pressure currently than much of Western Europe, has a great chance of establishing a fine conservation mosaic, profiting by the experience of other countries that have been under greater pressure.

The protective mosaic of national parks and nature reserves now developing in nearly every country in Europe shows that, despite strong differences in historical background and political systems, Europeans talk one language and operate one system when they conserve together. The senior author of this book represented the U.K. at the inaugural meeting of the Council for Europe to steer European Conservation Year 1970. I have recently been on the U.K. delegation to a European conference on rural planning convened by the Food and Agriculture Organization of the United Nations. Both of us feel that the sharing of conservation problems and schemes is very peace-provoking.

The basic goal of rural conservation is the rehabilitation of wildlife, and the restoration to the ideas of all of us of "wilderness values," as the North Americans, who have still some wilderness to value, put it. All Europeans know that they have but one space to plan, and that without plan nature will fall into total disarray and life will become intolerable. International problem sharing is an essential for conservation progress – and it works.

The old Roman, Tacitus, no fool as a farmer and a lover of rural values said, nearly 1,900 years ago, "Ubi solitudinem faciunt, pacem apellant" – "When they make a wilderness, they call it peace." We can all take the message and enlarge upon it; for conservation cannot flourish without mutual international aid; and good country planning through nature conservation is not only a peaceful pursuit but a peace-promoting pursuit.

The only native bear of South America, the spectacled bear is now rare and relict in the northern part of the continent.

Russian Paradise

The skilful naturalists of the Soviet Union can offer us an historical picture of the progress of nature in their vast Eurasian country that is very similar to that in Western Europe. Their busy palaeontologists are unearthing (literally) a picture of Late Pleistocene big-game disappearance of Western European style; no woolly rhinoceros date younger than in Western Europe is yet available, though Russia could well have been the last refuge of this originally northern Asian species.

A steppe rhinoceros *Dicerorhinus hemitoechus* from the Jana River may have died out in Late Würmian times. The youngest woolly mammoth radiocarbon date I can find, in a country where at least the tusks (and often some of the other bones) of over 100,000 mammoths have been dug (mostly for the ivory trade) is 11,450 $\pm$ 250 B.P. from Taimyr. A mammoth from Kunda has a date of 9780 $\pm$ 260 B.P. on tusk which may be too young. Just as in Austria, the giant deer survived in the Black Sea area until Iron Age times of 700–500 B.C.

Soviet zoologists are enthusiastic members or correspondents of IUCN's Survival Service Commission and are jealous guardians of Russia's surviving big-game and other relict animals. The present network of conservation land in the country consists of a chain of fifty-one nature reserves some of which are of national park quality and size. One of the earliest of these is Lagodethi in Georgia, which dates from 1912. In some reserves experiments are conducted with the domestication of animals, among them the eland of Africa.

Reserves with endangered – i.e. currently listed in the IUCN's Red Data Book – animals in their fauna include:

In the RSFSR. Sikhote-Alin with tiger, goral and leopard; Caucasus with European bison and leopard; Oka with bison; Kiedrowaia Pad' with leopard; Soupoutinsk with tiger; and Priosko-Terrasny with bison.
In Kazakhstan. Aksov-Djebogly with snow leopard.
In Bielorussia. Bielovieja on the Polish border marching with Poland's Bialowieza Forest, with bison.
In Turkmenia. Badkhyz with onager and leopard.
In the Ukraine. Askania Nova with introduced and managed onager, Przewalski horse and bison.
In Uzbekhistan. Zaamin with snow leopard.

Part of the headquarters herd of the European bison now conserved and managed in some forests of Poland near the Russian border.

Asian Paradise

The earliest fossil man in Asia is *Homo erectus*, Java man, originally described from Trinil in Java as *Pithecanthropus erectus* by Dubois in 1894. He also has been found in deposits at Modjokerto and Sangiran in Java, which are of Günzian or Cromerian times (p. 141). These deposits are earlier, therefore, than the Mindelian deposits at Choukoutien near Peking where Black identified Peking man, *Sinanthropus pekinensis*, in 1927. Most modern anthropologists put Peking man in the same species as Java man, *Homo erectus*. It seems likely that by Mindelian times this ancestral species of ours extended in range from China to Western Europe and North Africa.

Another Chinese fossil was described by von Koenigswald in 1933 as *Gigantopithecus blacki* on the evidence of a molar tooth which came from a Hong Kong drugstore. A very recent paper by Pilbeam suggests with good evidence from new material that *Gigantopithecus* was not a man, and not a member of the family Hominidae, but a member of a group the Dryopithecinae, which is an extinct subfamily of the Pongidae, the family of the living great apes.

Homo erectus appears to have been the only true man in Asia in Early Pleistocene times, and an evolution to Sapient man in Asia appears to parallel that in Europe, though Lantian man of Konwanling in Shensi is not identical with what may be his evolutionary counterpart, Neanderthal man.

It is not yet certain when man first colonized Japan. The earliest radiocarbon dating I can find is Late Würmian 16,150±550 B.P. from a Palaeolithic culture horizon at Lake Nojiri. It is probable that when man arrived a Pleistocene big-game fauna, including elephant, giant deer and perhaps even the extinct Japanese race of tiger still flourished, as well as wild horse.

These are now extinct in Japan, but we cannot on the evidence be sure that their extinction was due to overkill. As the Japanese evolved in the Flandrian period through Neolithic and Metal Age cultures they seem to have developed an attitude to nature not unlike that of a counterpart archipelago in the eastern Atlantic – Britain and Ireland – with the same idea of analysis for analysis' sake and conservation for conservation's sake. This was fostered largely by the aristocracy and landowning classes, but based on firm popular support, particularly during the Tokugawa Shogunate from 1615 to 1865. After the Meiji restoration in 1867 animal protection virtually collapsed; but the first national parks were created in 1934 and the whole conservation system was strengthened by a new law of 1957.

Today Japan has twenty-three national parks of IUCN standard, twenty-four quasi-national parks, 240 prefectural (county) parks and no fewer than 1,148 nature reserves which are at least equivalent to the Sites of Special Scientific Interest of the British Nature Conservancy.

Several of the Japanese national parks house Red Data Book animals, such as Bandai-Asahi, Jo-Shin-Etsu Kogen, Chubu Gangaku, Nikko, Chichibu-Tama, Towada-Hachimantai, Yoshino-Kumano, Hakusan, Minami Alps and Rikuchu Kaigan, all with the

Orang utan, figured by Josette Gourley, the greatest of the Asian anthropoid apes, under serious human pressure in its last strongholds in Sumatra and Borneo.

The Asiatic race of the lion, surviving only in India, mainly in the Gir Forest of Kathiawar, this relict subspecies could be rehabilitated by a WWF-aided programme.

Wildlife Crisis

Japanese serow; and Fuji-Hakone-Izu with the Japanese race of the ancient murrelet, and Shiretoko where the Japanese race of the California sea lion lately survived.

Though it is aware that recent wild animal protection laws have been passed in mainland China, IUCN has been unable to obtain from the Chinese People's Republic any data about continental national parks and nature reserves. The Government of Taiwan (Formosa), however, reports three reserves inherited from the conservation-minded prewar administration by Japan. These are the Mount Yangming National Park (1936) and the reserve of the Taroko Gorge (1937, which shelters the Red Data Book Swinhoe's pheasant) and Mount Ali and Mount Morrison (1936).

Information from South Vietnam indicates projects to designate a national park, a forest park, four nature reserves and seven hunting reserves. Laos likewise has only projects at this stage, for four national parks. Since 1963 Cambodia has designated and administered the Angkor Wat area as a national park, and has set up six nature reserves, and some 200 forest reserves under the Water and Forest Service. Since 1962 Thailand has established nine national parks administered by the Royal Forest Department. Those with Red Data Book animals are Khao Yai (tiger), Khao Salob (tiger, Sumatran rhinoceros) and Khao Luanga (Sumatran rhinoceros).

In Malaysia there are two national parks in Malaya, Taman Negara and Templer. In Borneo Sabah has the famous naturalists' mountain, Kinabalu, as a national park and Sarawak has Bako. Taman Negara has rhinoceros and tiger; Templer has tiger; Kinabalu has orang utan, and sometimes the Sumatran rhinoceros. Malaya also has one game reserve; and Sarawak is planning no less than ten national parks.

The wild form of the Asiatic buffalo, here figured by Helmut Diller, has a population of 2,000 or less in a fractionated range in India and Nepal.

Indonesia has a big reserve system, with twenty national nature reserves in Java, including the Panjitan Nature Reserve at Udjung Kulon (the last stronghold of the Javan rhinoceros); twelve in Sumatra, including Indrapura (Sumatran rhinoceros, Sumatran race of serow) and Rafflesia Serbödjadi (orang utan); two in Kalimantan in Borneo, including Mandor (proboscis monkey); six in Celebes, including Tangkoko (maleo – a mound-building game bird – and anoa – a dwarf ox), Panna (maleo), and Tanggala and Bantimurung (anoa); and one in the Moluccas. Indonesia has also designated fifty-three other reserves and twenty-two more nature parks.

The Philippines, with a very special fauna and flora, have long been a problem area for conservation. Indigenous specialities such as the monkey-eating eagle and the tamaraw are in grave danger. Forest clearance has led to the extinction or relict status of several bird species, especially on Cebú. Of the thirty-six national parks on the Government's list in 1967 twenty-three were found acceptable to IUCN* under its rules. On Mindanao Mount Apo is, or was, an headquarters of the rare monkey-eating eagle.

Burma has one important nature reserve, which it calls a "game sanctuary" at Pidaung in the north, which has a tiger population. IUCN does not log "above the line" eleven rather small hunting-reserves.

India's oldest national park is Corbett (formerly Hailey) National Park in Uttar Pradesh founded in 1935; she now has four others in Bihar, Maharashtra and Madhya Pradesh. Wildlife sanctuaries go back to 1908 when Kaziranga in Assam was so designated. This large national nature reserve may soon become a national park; among other Red Data Book animals it houses the great Indian rhinoceros, the barasingh and about a third of the world population of the wild Asiatic buffalo.

In all, the Indian Board for wildlife has eighty wildlife sanctu-

* IUCN has its own rules of categorization of areas designated by countries as national parks, nature reserves, etc. An area that IUCN accepts will often be referred to in the following pages as "mainstream."

aries of which Kaziranga and eight others rate full recognition by
IUCN as mainstream nature reserves. Red Data Book mammals
guarded by the others and some of the national parks include
great Indian rhinoceros at Manas in Assam and Jaldapara in
West Bengal, Asiatic buffalo at Manas, the Asiatic race of lion
(virtually the entire world population) at Gir in Gujarat and the
barasingh at Kanha National Park in Madhya Pradesh. The rare
hangul race of the red deer is guarded by a wildlife sanctuary at
Dachigam in Kashmir which may soon be elevated to national
park status. Many of India's wildlife sanctuaries and national
parks have elephant, tiger and leopard populations and a rich bird
fauna, and they are an effective insurance of the perpetuation of
India's big game.

Up to 1967 only two national parks in Pakistan reached the
mainstream list of IUCN. Now, largely as a result of Guy Mountfort's missions and expeditions in 1966 and 1967, it looks as if, with
WWF support, a positive conservation programme is now advancing in a vital sector of the subcontinent that is overgrazed,
ecologically degraded and three-quarters eroded.

With European and North American help, the Government of
Pakistan is designing a new system of national parks and nature
reserves in both West and East Pakistan and before long we can
expect, under active conservation *management*, at least four NPs
and five reserves to be set up in West Pakistan and at least three
NPs and four reserves in East Pakistan.

The danger to wildlife in Pakistan through over-hunting for food,
fur, skins and the aviculture and zoo trade has been such that many
animal species, notably ungulates and spotted cats, were being
lately considered for the Red Data Book. Pakistan has now
prohibited the export of the skins of *all* wild animals, showing an
initiative that should be copied by all countries with endangered
wildlife – which means, today, most countries of the world.
Pakistan is now pro-rhino, pro-tiger, pro-crocodile and pro-life in
general, and developing the idea that enlightened tourist-orientated
improvements to its national park system are good for the national
economy as well as for wildlife. There will be cooperation with
India, for instance, over the stocking of the improved Sunderbans
Reserve in East Pakistan with great Indian rhinos from India's
Kaziranga National Park not far away up the Brahmaputra.

Nepal has, for more than a decade, taken a positive conservationist attitude to its national natural treasures and looks after
two fine sanctuaries through its Forest Department. These are
Sukla Phanta in the Kanchanpur district of the Terai region of the
Ganges Plain, which still has a fine community of big game, and
the Chitawan in the Rapti Valley. The Chitawan Sanctuary
contains the second largest great Indian rhinoceros population in
the world. The status of the rhino here was seriously threatened
by farming developments between 1959 and 1964; but now no less
than 4,000 people have been rehoused and refarmed in other parts
of Nepal, and the rhinos have free range over about 76,000
hectares, guarded by nearly 200 trained wardens and officers.

Afghanistan has no national parks or national nature reserves.
Iran and Iraq had nothing that qualified for the IUCN mainstream list in 1967. But the Persians are refining their protection

laws and foresee the deployment of protected conservation areas, of which a model has been already set up in the northeast and named after H.I.M. the Shah. The Iraqi laws also foresee a reserve system; but they have not got one as yet.

Middle and Near East Paradise

Iran and Iraq bring us to the Fertile Crescent, where, as the last Ice Age came to an end, man first invented civilization as we know it. Remains at Jericho, from Jordan's Mesolithic past, have now been radiocarbon dated back to $11,166 \pm 107$ B.P.; Jericho must rank as the oldest known city in the world.

The archaeologists and palaeontologists have worked together for years, now, on the vast array of fossil man and his cultures and the animals he lived with, preyed on and domesticated. The oldest human remains yet discovered in the Middle East are a few small fragments from Tell Ubeidiya in the Central Jordan Valley just south of the Sea of Galilee, associated with an archaic pebble industry and the bones of some thirty-seven species of mammals, at least thirty of which are extinct. These included Lower Pleistocene spectaculars like an ancient species of sabretooth, the European zebra, the primitive horse *Hipparion*, the Etruscan rhinoceros, the hippopotamus, a camel, a giraffe, the ancient ox *Leptobos* and antelope. The date of this famous deposit remains to be worked out, but it is very old indeed.

Hippopotamus photographed in the Queen Elizabeth Park, Uganda, by Donald Paterson.

155

Wildlife Crisis

We can measure man's transition from hunter to farmer by logging his domestications. The first domestic animal we can now date from this vital area in the evolution of civilized man is, not surprisingly, man's hunting ally, the dog, which turns up in a stratum radiodated at around 11,480 B.P. in Belt Cave in Iran. The farmer's breakthrough shows with the earliest domestic sheep in a later horizon at Belt Cave with 8845 ± 500 B.P.; but domestic sheep have been dated earlier at Zawi Chemi Shanidar in Iraq, where a radiodate of $10,800 \pm 300$ is the earliest I've ever read of. The domestic goat was first domesticated at the same time, judging by a date of around 10,790 for a level containing it at Jericho. So it was in Mesolithic times that farm animals first came in.

At Khirotikia in Cyprus a Neolithic horizon dated 7635 ± 100 B.P. discloses domestic pig and domestic cat, and the pig is found in an equally early Neolithic dig, also of the eighth millennium B.P., at Arpachiyah in Iraq. Arpachiyah, and Banahilk in Iraq which is of the same period, have what may be the first certain domestic cattle. Horse remains at Tepé Sialk in Iran of the seventh millennium B.P. may have been of domesticated animals, as may camel remains of *c.* 4500 B.C. at Yarmuq in Israel. The earliest donkey I can find is of the fifth millennium B.P. from Gerza in Egypt. The ancient Egyptians, since Old Kingdom times (2900 B.C. onwards) were fanatical experimenters with domestication. They kept zoos, and tried out several species of antelopes and even hyenas, monkeys, mongoose and hares, as well as birds of all sorts, including ostriches and cranes and geese.

The closeness of our link with the past in the Fertile Crescent and round it are the tentacles real history thrusts into periods which elsewhere are the pure province of the archaeologists. Woolley at Ur in Iraq dug up the museum of a fellow archaeologist, the Princess Bel-Shalti-Nannar daughter of Nabonidus, the last of the Babylonian kings. This museum was built in *c.* 550 B.C. as part of the royal priestess's girls' school; it contained objects dating as far back as *c.* 2280 B.C. and even the earliest museum label made by a previous curator of the collection in the seventh century B.C.

The earliest level at Troy in Turkey is Early Bronze Age, and Abraham was a man of the Bronze Age.

Since the classic times of the first true flowering of European civilization in the Fertile Crescent and Near East there has been an ecological deterioration there. This has climatic reasons, but it is primarily due to pressure of human population, erosive farming and overgrazing. With international help, all the nations concerned are trying to correct this trend, with varying success. Many of us in Western Europe think that a final solution can come only when a peace by negotiation can bring about that pooling of scientific talent and conservation experience which is necessary for the thorough rehabilitation of an ecological unit that stretches from the Black Sea and the eastern Mediterranean to the Persian Gulf, the Red Sea and the Nile.

If national parks of an effective kind be a test of fitness, Turkey has good prospects, for seven mainstream national parks have been created there since 1958, and seven more are under development or planned. These guard Red Data Book animals such as the

156

Anatolian race of leopard in Kusadasi (Mount Samson) National Park which is totally protected and under research programmes run by Istanbul University.

Syria has, as yet, no conservation deployments which IUCN can report, and Lebanon has only the beginnings of an FAO-aided network of forest reserves and plans for four national parks. Cyprus is developing a national park and nature reserve system with British and other advice.

In 1965, with British scientific advice, Jordan created the Azraq Desert National Park and put it under the administration of the new Division of National Parks and Historic Monuments of its Tourism Authority. This lovely, big oasis of 400,000 hectares could be a model for all the desert countries; and three other national parks are planned by Jordan, as well as two national historic monuments and a network of forest reserves.

Israel has the deepest development, so far, of a conservation mosaic in the desert. The Mount Carmel National Park, accepted by IUCN as mainstream, which has within it four national nature reserves under complete protection designation and management, is another fine desert model for a park. Israel has established twelve other national nature reserves, too. These are run by the Nature Reserves Authority which works closely with the voluntary Society for Nature Protection of Israel and with the Institute of Nature Protection and Ecology, set up in 1965 at Tel Aviv University.

The scientific line of Israel's conservation authority is ecological and holistic, and careful attention is paid to the botanical communities – which comes naturally to a nation of plant-lovers and devoted biologists. Under development are two more national parks and about 120 more smallish nature reserves, whose designation gives Israel, alone in the Near East, a pattern resembling that in the most forward-looking conservation countries of Europe, and conservation-minded states and provinces of North America. Israel shares planning conferences and dialogue more deeply with Europe than with the rest of the Near East and Fertile Crescent for political reasons that are only too obvious. When peace finally comes, this newly established nation can lend marvellous intelligence and experience to the rural rehabilitation of the cradle of civilization.

Meanwhile, Saudi Arabia makes no response to IUCN's invitation to disclose its conservation plans. Neither does Yemen. Aden confirms that it has no national parks or nature reserves. WWF's relations with Arabia are progressing and special schemes, e.g. for the conservation of the highly endangered Arabian oryx have made measurable advances. Egypt, which harbours quite a number of Red Data Book animals, does not answer IUCN questionnaires and has but one detectable hunting reserve at Wadi Rishrash.

The world population of the exclusively North American trumpeter swan is now well over 2,000, largely as a consequence of active conservation management in Montana, Wyoming and Idaho; the species is officially regarded by the IUCN as now out of extinction danger.

The Arabic-speaking peoples have a long tradition of natural history interest. Aboru ben Masoweih (d. 857) wrote a fine natural history of animals; Avicenna (980–1037) improved on the work of Aristotle, and the Spanish-Arabian Ibn-Rushd (Averroës, 1126–98) was doubtless the most scholarly and knowledgeable naturalist of his time in the world. Abdallatif (1162–1231) published a natural history of the Nile that was packed with original scientific

161

observations on crocodiles and hippopotamuses. Sakanja ben
Muhammed El Kasvini (thirteenth century) from Persia wrote a
philosophical *Wonders of Nature* with many original observations.
Albulbeka el-Damiri of Cairo (d. 1405) wrote a monumental *Life
of Animals*.

Arab intellectuals led the world in scientific biology at significant points in medieval times. Since then their output of works has
continued, but their bias of interest in nature has tended rather to
shift to an interest in animals in the service of man, and their
medicinal properties.

Lately, however, we can detect in the universities of some Arab
countries, a renaissance of an interest in general analytical
natural history, and the rise of a cadre of conservationists of
whom a benign leader is H.M. the Hashemite King of Jordan.

North African Paradise

In North Africa, which is ecologically distinct from the rest of
Africa and has much habitat affinity to the Near East, conservation
is in a similar state. The evolution of systems is slow, but starts
can be recognized. In Libya IUCN cannot yet recognize mainstream units, but seven reserves in Cyrenaica, several forest
reserves in Tripolitania and a hunting-reserve in the Fezzan
provide a basis for development.

Tunisia's Bou-Hedma State Park has full IUCN recognition and
is a good faunal reserve. A national park is projected at Ghardi-
maou on the Algerian border, and two forest reserves have been
designated. Conservation is administered by the Forest Service
under the Ministry of Agriculture and has been deployed at
Bou-Hedma since 1936.

Algeria's Chréa and Ouarsenis National Parks in the north of

Barbary race of leopard, now
confined to Morocco with a
relict population not thought to be
over 100, photographed by
Charles A. Vaucher.

Zebra photographed in the Northern Frontier District, Kenya by Donald Paterson.

the country date from 1925 and 1924 respectively and are good nature parks with public access, administered by the Water and Forest Service of the Ministry of Agriculture. Eleven other designated national parks are developing and some will doubtless reach the IUCN mainstream list soon.

In Morocco the Tazzeka National Park dates from 1934; it is under the Water and Forest Administration. The Park is a beautiful cedar forest with a good fauna. In winter it has lately been visited by the Barbary race of leopard which is nearly extinct. The Toubkal National Park is still under pressure from nomadic herdsmen and is overgrazed and somewhat eroded; the Barbary leopard has disappeared from it, and it cannot figure on IUCN's mainstream list yet. Nearly 500 faunal and floral reserves are also reported by Morocco, a country in which good conservation could rapidly evolve, with a strong hand on the helm.

There are no designated conservation areas in Tangier.

African Paradise

Africa south of the Sahara is the theatre of the evolution of man. It is the home of the Australopithecines, the extinct subfamily of our own Hominidae family that, in the course of evolution, gave rise to the Hominines. An early Australopithecine, *Proconsul*, lived in Kenya in Miocene times and has been radiodated at 15.9 ± 1.5 million years. On, or near the hominine line, and younger are Leakey's famous *Australopithecus boisei* from Bed I at Olduvai in Tanzania which has an Early Pleistocene radiodate of *c.* 1.75 million years. At *c.* 1.5 million years lie *Australopithecus africanus* of Dart from Makapansgat and Taung in South Africa and *A. transvaalensis* of Broom from Sterkfontein in South Africa.

Later, in times (equivalent to Europe's Günzian) of 500,000 years ago or a little less, come more South African ape-men of Broom, *Australopithecus* (or *Paranthropus*) *robustus* from Kromdraii, and *A.(P.) crassidens* from Swartkrans.

Wildlife Crisis

From Koobi Fora on the east side of Lake Rudolf in Kenya the Leakey family and their colleagues have very lately reported* the results of their new digs in 1968–69 in an area never previously explored by palaeontologists. They found flint artifacts and hominid bones in a stratum which could be radiodated by the potassium-argon technique as 2.61 ± 0.62 million years old. The choppers and flakes they found are a million years older than any other ancient stone tools that have been dated. Among the five hominid specimens a cranium closely resembles *Australopithecus boisei* and the others, yet to be fully described, belong either to *Australopithecus gracilis* or to "a very early representative of *Homo*." As no tools have yet been found associated with *Australopithecus boisei* the ancient artifacts may prove to belong to the other species, perhaps the earliest known true man, on which Professor J. Murgai's report from University College at Nairobi is eagerly awaited.

Full Hominines from Africa are – the earliest presently certain – Leakey's *Homo habilis* from Bed I at Olduvai *c.* 1.75 million years, and two fossils which are now referred to *Homo erectus* of a date of *c.* 340,000 years old or less from Bed II at Olduvai (equivalent to European Early Holsteinian); and (north of the Sahara) from Ternifine in Algeria equivalent to the European Mindelian. *Homo rhodesiensis* of Smith Woodward is from the equivalent of an Early Würmian horizon at Broken Hill in Zambia and is here about 80,000 or 90,000 years old. It is regarded as a Neanderthaloid. This form has also been discovered at Saldanha near Cape Town in South Africa.

Was there a Pleistocene overkill of big game in Africa in Stone Age times? In his stimulating recent book, *The Evolution of Man*

* (1970 April 18), *Nature* 226 (5242): 223–30.

African lion with a dead zebra, photographed in Serengeti National Park, Tanzania, by Donald Paterson.

The western race of the giant eland, drawn by Cécile Curtis in 1966, has a relict distribution in West Africa and a red sheet in IUCN's Red Data Book.

and Society (1969), Professor C. D. Darlington states that "In Africa 100,000 years ago men with Acheulian flint weapons exterminated many genera of great mammals which they killed for food." P. S. Martin in the *Pleistocene extinctions* symposium volume (1967), points out that roughly fifty mammal genera disappeared from Africa in the Pleistocene and that "The living genera of African big game represent only 70 per cent of the middle-Pleistocene complement;" he concludes that "despite its extraordinary diversity, the living African fauna must be regarded as depauperate, albeit much less so than that of America or Australia." Some, but little extinction of big game occurred in the last 20,000 years; there was thus less overkill in Late Würmian and Flandrian times than went on in Europe.

It is abundantly clear that of all countries in the world Africa possesses the most varied megafauna (which is only scientific not-so-shorthand for big game) at present. It has, in fact, a Pleistocene fauna, which has remained essentially unchanged during the last 20,000 years.

A full analysis of the first and last dates of the mammal members of the African Pleistocene fauna remains to be made; and very interesting it would be. The educated guess of most of the palaeontologists with whom I have discussed the subject is that there *was* an overkill period in Africa when Stone Age man *did* raise the extinction-rate over that imposed by climate and natural evolution, and this period, they guess, was probably around 175,000 to 40,000 years ago. Perhaps it went on a little later.

It was an earlier overkill, however, than can be detected anywhere else in the world, and it ran down before the end of Ice Age times. The Pleistocene big game of Africa evolved on that continent – and nowhere else – in the long, full sense, along with evolving man. Though this big game surrendered to man's stone spears and killing tools for a period, its survivors, still recognizable as a Pleistocene-type fauna, reached a state of not-exactly-peaceful but stable coexistence with man some time before the last glaciation was over. In Africa the glaciations in Europe were paralleled by "pluvials," when the precipitation was significantly higher than in the dry "interpluvials," which were the equivalent of the interglacials. During the last pluvial, if not before, the African mammals may have evolved new fear of man, and new avoidance behaviour-patterns, which cut his crop of them to a tax that could be paid by their reproductive potential, rather than an extinction.

Only now, in the new epoch of shotgun man, zooman, tree-cutting man, dust-raising man, industrial man, does overkill rear its head again in Africa. By a paradox, one of the solutions now under discussion for the conservation of Africa's wildlife is a gradual cessation in vital areas of domestic animal, overgrazing husbandry, and a return to a *planned* cropping of some (but not all) of the wild species. The paradox is that, under proper management, a planned system of wild protein cropping can actually *conserve* the wild species that provide protein and stabilize their numbers to the carrying capacity of the land. This, in the past and in the present, is what the *natural* predators did, and can still do.

Lions do not overkill antelopes; they take a sparable crop

A token of survival of the great Pleistocene big game in Africa is this African elephant herd at Nyeri in Kenya, photographed by Arthur Rothstein.

which does not hinder the main antelope population from keeping within the limitations of its feed. Lions are skilful killers, and kill only when hungry; but they are not skilful enough to be over-killers. Humans *are* skilful enough; so, like all good Western sportsmen, they have to ration and plan their take. They have to make rules against overkill and observe and refine those rules. This is real conservation, and it is being gradually, carefully and often tentatively deployed in Africa.

It is often said, and has been so said for years, that the only place to understand what a Pleistocene fauna looks like is in Africa, and that the only place to see one now is in an African national park. The origin of the deployment of African national parks was in African colonial times, and it was a sign that the era of the gun demanded the designation, dedication and management of conservation land as part of the self-denying ordinance that was essential for the gunners. National parks in Africa often started their evolution as game parks. As they proliferated, they got results; but they cannot be said to have cured overkill in the ordinary, undesignated rural game country. Here overkill is in some areas still the order of the day.

We can measure, all the same, the success of conservation, and the conservation skills of each African country, by their national parks and reserve systems. The emergent nations have mostly seized on conservation as a tool of the national economy, and have come to recognize the areas where their fauna still thrives in

Pleistocene style as part of the scenery that tourist pilgrims love, and happily pay to visit.

Let us sweep, then, through Africa with a glance at the conservation treasures, starting in Mauritania. Here the only reserve in the IUCN mainstream list is the Mauritanian Isles off the coast, where a fine seabird and waterbird fauna is looked after by the Water and Forest Service. Another coastal reserve is being developed at Lévrier Bay and an inland elephant reserve at El Agher.

In Sénégal the Niokolo Koba National Park (1962) protects a rich Pleistocene fauna, including the endangered western race of the giant eland; and the Djovol Nature Reserve (also set up in 1962) protects a community of wetland birds. Both are under the management of the Water and Forest Department, which is also developing bird reserves at Djeuss and Boundoum.

Little Gambia has no national parks or game reserves yet, but has designated eighty-eight forest parks. Portuguese Guinea has no mainstream IUCN areas but under hunting law has created three reserves.

Guinea has had, since 1944, the Nimba Mountains Nature Reserve, an international reserve which reaches over the Ivory Coast border, and remains, as in colonial days, under Water and Forest Department inspection. This is good chimpanzee country. Sierra Leone so far is still at the planning stage but may soon develop Konsilica National Park and three nature reserves. Liberia likewise is at the planning stage, has mapped three putative national parks, and may consider entering its own sector of the

Another Pleistocene animal of Africa, the black rhinoceros which has the highest population of the living rhinos. Photographed by Donald Paterson at Amboseli, Kenya.

Nimba Mountains into the international nature reserve that
Guinea and the Ivory Coast have maintained since 1944. Besides
its share of the Nimba Mountains, Ivory Coast has a fine fauna
and flora of full Pleistocene character totally protected in the
Bouna Reserve; and is developing two other national parks and
three other reserves.

Mali's Boucle du Baoulé National Park is of true Pleistocene
standards (p. 166) faunally (henceforth I shall refer to this as
"P-type") and protects some Red Data Book western giant elands
which are under severe hunting pressure in the rest of Mali.
Besides this key area, Mali is developing five other nature reserves
for total protection, and a largish forest reserve. Upper Volta, in
its eastern corner, shares the W. National Park with Dahomey
and Niger with a P-type fauna. This international park is truly
internationally run and managed with a single permit system.
Upper Volta is also developing six nature reserves.

In Ghana's Mole Game Reserve protection is complete under the
Forest Division, with a P-type fauna; and another game reserve
and five game sanctuaries are being developed. Togo has three
IUCN mainstream areas at the Koué Forest Reserve (a P-type
fauna with lowland gorillas and chimpanzees), the Kamassi Game
Reserve (another gorilla sanctuary) and the Kéuan Game Reserve;
Togo is also developing two more game reserves. Besides the
W. National Park, Dahomey has the Boucle de la Pendjari
National Park (also P-type) and is developing twenty-eight forest
and twenty-two faunal lesser reserves. Niger's only National Park
is W., where she is developing a northwest game reserve extension
with total protection.

Nigeria's only IUCN mainstream area is the Yankari Game
Reserve (P-type); but another game reserve and six lesser reserves
are under development. Chad has two fine P-type national parks at
Zakouma (with elephant and black rhino) and Manda (elephant);
and is developing four nature reserves.

Cameroun has three P-type national parks at Boubandjidah
(black rhino), Benoué (black rhino) and Waza (fine birds) and is
developing a dozen nature reserves. Sudan has three national
parks, six mainstream game reserves and nine more game reserves
under development. Most of the national parks and main game
reserves have a P-type fauna, with the endangered white rhino at
Southern and Nimule National Parks and Shambe and Juba Game
Reserves, and black rhino at Mongalla and Badigeru Nature
Reserves.

In Ethiopia the National Park of Menagasha was formed in 1958
by proclamation of H.I.M. The Emperor of Ethiopia. So far, it is
the only conservation area in Ethiopia that has reached mainstream status in IUCN's books. This is not for want of trying, for
the Imperial Ethiopian Government since 1963 has received a
number of missions from UNESCO – starting with that lively
conservationist Sir Julian Huxley – and from WWF. Ethiopia's
main difficulty is in the deployment of conservation measures in a
country where farming erosion, overgrazing and hunting overkill
are rife. Yet several Red Data Book animals are indigenous to this
country and no other, and are in real danger, notably the Tora and
Swayne's races of hartebeest, the Walia ibex and Prince Ruspoli's

Facing:
The Galápagos flightless cormorant
breeds on but two of the
Galápagos Islands in the equatorial
Pacific 600 miles west of Ecuador,
and has a population of under
1,000.

turaco. The senior author of this book was among those on a recent visit which could be classed as a WWF mission.

It is hoped that the relict P-type faunas will be protected by a strengthening of the Wild Life Conservation Department and the development of a great new system of national parks and game reserves to IUCN standards, notably the Semien Mountains National Park (Walia ibex's sole habitat), the Metahara or Awash National Park, the Maji or Omo National Park, a new national park in the Bale and Arussi Mountains (mountain nyala), and game reserves in the Danakil area (Somali wild ass), the Lake Ruspoli region (Swayne's hartebeest), the Rift Valley Lakes (waterfowl) and at least five other areas.

The personal interest of H.I.M. The Emperor in conservation makes us confident that Ethiopia, home of so much of the classic African P-type fauna, will become a model conservation country to the world in general, and forward-looking Africa in particular.

In French Somaliland two national parks were designated before the war and two reserves have been also designated, but in the absence of information about their management, IUCN has not put them on its mainstream list. In Somalia one complete reserve at Bubasci *is* mainstream (with black rhinoceros, Hunter's hartebeest and beira); a national park and six more reserves are under plan.

Kenya has a fine conservation record with five mainstream national parks and seven mainstream reserves; and three more national parks and two more reserves under development. Red Data Book animals protected include the black rhino (at Tsavo, Aberdare, Mount Kenya, and Nairobi National Parks, and at Masai Mara, Meru, Isiolo Buffalo Spring, and the Samburu Uaso Nyiro Reserves), and all the mainstream areas are P-type. The wardening service is big, well trained and skilful; four of the mainstream game reserves are managed by county councils, the rest by the Trustees of the National Parks of Kenya and by the Forest Department.

All Uganda's conservation areas are P-type; in IUCN's mainstream list are three national parks and four game reserves; also developing are two white rhino sanctuaries and a mountain gorilla sanctuary which adjoins that in Rwanda (another gorilla reserve is developing), and forty other reserves. The parks are managed by the Trustees of the National Parks of Uganda and the game reserves by the Ministry of Animal Industry. Like Kenya, Uganda is inspired by a forward-looking and scientific view of conservation. The white rhinoceros is an endangered animal which has been introduced at the Murchison Falls National Park and is also conserved at the Lumunga Game Reserve and the two special white rhino sanctuaries of Mount Kei and Mount Otze. The black rhino is present at Murchison Falls.

Tanzania can be safely assigned, with Kenya and Uganda, to the Big Three conservation countries of East Africa. All its five mainstream national parks and three reserves are P-type, as are most of its eight other developing reserves in Tanganyika; in Zanzibar there are three developing forest reserves on the main island and two on Pemba. A Red Data Book animal, the black rhino, is preserved in Serengeti, Ruaha, Lake Manyara, Ngurdoto Crater/

The red uakari is confined to the forests of the Brazil-Peru border and under severe over-hunting pressure.

171

Not discovered until early in the present century, the okapi of the Congo forests is the only other living member of the giraffe family besides the giraffe. It is not thought to be in present survival danger but its status is being carefully watched.

Momella Lakes National Parks, and in the Ngorongoro and Tarangire Reserves. The Serengeti-Ngorongoro complex provides one of the largest P-type spectacles in the whole of Africa. Appropriately, it lies not far from Olduvai Gorge, where Louis Leakey and his family have made their classic discoveries of ancient African men and ape-men.

Rwanda has two fine national parks, with a P-type fauna. At Kagera black rhinos, introduced from Tanzania, first bred in 1961. At Albert, despite ecological damage in the revolution of 1959, a mountain gorilla population survives. Burundi has no mainstream area, but is developing a game reserve on Lake Rwihinda and, with FAO and IUCN advice, is planning a fully protected reserve on the Ruzizi Plain near Kihanga. Congo (Kinshasa) has three great national parks – Upemba, Albert and Garamba – and is developing a nature reserve at Mount Kahuzi. All have a P-type fauna. At the volcanic Albert Park, which extends over the Rwanda border with the same name, the fauna includes mountain gorilla and okapi and is a classic African rain-forest community. Garamba has a white rhinoceros population. Congo (Brazza) has the P-type Odzala National Park (with lowland gorilla) and three developing reserves.

Gabon has a national park at Okanda and a nature reserve at Ofoué, with a typical forest fauna. Another reserve has been projected. In Angola mainstream areas with P-type fauna are the national parks of Quiçama and Iôna and the nature reserves of Cangandala and Luando. Under development are another national park and a reserve system in four areas. Black rhinos are present in Iôna and the Red Data Book giant sable antelope in Luando and Cangandala.

All Zambia's mainstream areas, the Kafue National Park and seven game reserves, are of P-type fauna; and three more game reserves are under development. Black rhinos are found at Kafue and at the game reserve of Mweru. In Malawi the Malawi National Park is a mainstream conservation P-type fauna area; but five developing game reserves were under too much human pressure from poaching, and, in one case, cultivation, to reach the IUCN main list. In Mozambique the Gorongoza National Park, likewise, is a mainstream conservation P-type fauna area with black rhinos; under development are reserve systems in four areas.

Conservation has reached a sophisticated level throughout southern Africa. In Rhodesia three national parks are not on IUCN's list because of their small size, and numerous nature reserves are "controlled hunting areas" or private, and do not yet rate inclusion; nor do four official reserves. But the mainstream list embraces no less than ten national parks and six game reserves. These all have P-type faunas. Protected Red Data Book animals are the black rhino in Wankie and Rhodes Matopos National Parks, and in Cheware, Matusadona, Chizarira and Mana Pools Game Reserves; and the white rhino in Rhodes Matopos and Kyle Dam Game Reserves; it has been safely translocated to the latter from South Africa.

In Botswana the area adjoining South Africa's Kalahari Gemsbok National Park became an official game reserve in 1965 having been one in effect since 1944. This has mainstream status as a valuable extension of Gemsbok, with similar P-type fauna. Five other sanctuaries or reserves are under development. In Southwest Africa the P-type fauna Etosha Game Park is mainstream, with its mountain zebras and black rhinos; and six other game reserves are still developing.

In the Republic of South Africa is the greatest deployment of conservation areas in the continent. Six national parks are administered by the National Parks Board of Trustees under an Act of 1962. The greatest of all of them, Krüger, was created Sable Game Reserve by President Krüger as early as 1898 and became the Krüger National Park in 1926. All the South African national parks have P-type fauna; the white rhinoceros lives at Krüger, and the black at Addo Elephant.

The protected mainstream land in Cape Province comprises three nature reserves and the de Hoop Wildlife Farm. The bontebok, which is also present in Bontebok National Park, lives also in the Cape of Good Hope Nature Reserve.

In Natal one of the fourteen mainstream reserves is the Royal Natal National Park, and another the St Lucia Park; the rest are designated nature reserves. All have been most efficiently managed by the Natal Parks, Game and Fish Preservation Board since it was set up in 1950. All have P-type faunas. The black rhinoceros lives in Umfolozi, Mkuzi and Hluhluwe, and the white rhinoceros has done so well at Umfolozi and Hluhluwe that many have been translocated to other reserves, parks and park zoos.

In the Orange Free State the mainstream Willem Pretorius Game Reserve houses a typical P-type local fauna.

The five mainstream reserves of the Transvaal house both African rhino species at Loskop Dam, whence the white rhinoceros has been translocated. All have a P-type fauna, including Barberspan Nature Reserve whose Pleistocene-type animals are birds, notably the two species of African flamingos and other lovely wetland birds like spoonbills and herons.

Two new South African national parks are on their way; and under development also are a dozen more nature reserves in Natal and seven in the Transvaal. Municipal reserves are now deployed in Cape Province (ten), Orange Free State (two) and the Transvaal (nine). There are also five reserves in Cape Province under divisional councils; many private reserves; sixty-seven forest nature reserves under the Department of Forestry, and on the coast five rock lobster reserves and thirty-three state guano islands where the seals and seabirds are totally protected. In Lesotho there is no reserve; in Swaziland there is the Milwane Game Sanctuary, a P-type mainstream conservation area with white rhinos.

The South African conservation network is an exemplary model of the deployment of nature care thoughtfully, and not cheaply, on the continent that has the best surviving Pleistocene fauna. South African brains, hard-won knowledge, and hard work have done wonders of which they are proud, and of which the world is proud. They are the real experts on the African heald.

The Indian Ocean islands, which support the Madagascan subfauna, are crowded with conservation problems. Madagascar,

The aye-aye, drawn by Josette Gourley. This relict of an unique family of the lemurs is in serious danger and under careful conservation management supported by WWF.

now known as the Malagasy Republic, was first invaded by man, of Indonesian rather than African culture, in about 1800 B.P. or the second century A.D. It is not easy, on present evidence, to list precisely those members of the now-fossil fauna that survived until after this date, but an overkill by man is beyond doubt.

Of the rocs or elephant birds, the heaviest birds ever known, possibly all seven known species died out after the coming of man. The largest of all, the great elephant bird *Aepyornis maximus*, survived in south Malagasy to *c.* 1649, quite some time after the island had been colonized by Europeans.

Other fossil birds which may have survived until after the first human invasion are the dwarf snake bird, *Anhinga nana*, the Sirabé sheldgoose, *Alopochen sirabensis*, Forsyth Major's duck, *Centrornis majori*, Robert's water hen, *Hovacrex roberti*, and the primeval coucal, *Coua primaeva*.

Fossil mammals which may also have survived up to this time are some sixteen species of lemurs, nearly all of which were bigger than the surviving lemurs; all of them were diurnal and probably fitted into niches occupied in Africa by cercopitheque monkeys, baboons and apes. At least three of these species have been found in fossil strata containing human pottery, one of them with a skull dented by an axe. One of these was not much bigger than a present lemur, another the size of a baboon and another the size of a small chimpanzee. There were also two small species of hippopotamus and a water hog. We know the approximate dates of the following extinctions since 1600:

Great elephant bird, *Aepyornis maximus*	1649
Delalande's coucal, *Coua delalandei*	1930
Giant aye-aye, *Daubentonia robusta*	1930

So there seems to have been an overkill in Malagasy, and we cannot say that it has abated until we get better evidence on the dating of the fossils. Presently ten full species of the lemur infra-order (p. 232, and some races of five others) are in Red Data Book danger, and four species of birds, the Alaotra dabchick, the Madagascar teal, the long-tailed ground roller and the small-billed false sunbird.

The emergent Malagasy Republic is beginning to take conservation very seriously and has had much help from France and from the WWF. The two national parks and thirty-one nature and special reserves in Malagasy all have mainstream status on IUCN's books except for one nature and one special reserve. Most are designed to support those biological treasures of the island, the lemurs. Reserves and national parks that are known to harbour Red Data Book animals are:

Tsingy du Bémaraha: Cocquerel's mouse lemur, fat-tailed lemur, red-tailed race of weasel lemur, red-fronted race of black lemur, fork-marked mouse lemur, grey gentle lemur and Verreaux's sifaka.
Ankarafatsika: fat-tailed lemur, red-tailed race of weasel lemur, mongoose lemur, western race of woolly avahi, Verreaux's sifaka.
Andohahelo: weasel lemur, Verreaux's sifaka.
Zahamena: weasel lemur, grey gentle lemur, indris.

174

Tsaratanana: fossa.

Tsingy de Namoroka: fat-tailed lemur, red-fronted race of black lemur, mongoose lemur, western race of woolly avahi, Verreaux's sifaka.

Tsimanampetsotsa: fat-tailed lemur, red-tailed race of weasel lemur, Verreaux's sifaka.

Betampona: weasel lemur.

Lokobé: Nosy-bé race of weasel lemur, typical race of black lemur, ruffed lemur.

Montagne d'Ambre National Park: grey gentle lemur, Sanford's race of black lemur, crowned race of mongoose lemur, fork-marked mouse lemur.

Nosy-Mangabé: aye-aye, ruffed lemur.

The special efforts being made to conserve key lemur species like the unique aye-aye are described on p. 232.

East of Malagasy in the Indian Ocean are three 'Mascarene' islands of volcanic origin, which have only a tiny native mammal fauna but a strong bird one. Réunion was not discovered by any human beings until 1507 or 1513 and was colonized stably by Europeans in 1662. Thereafter the fauna quickly began to disappear: approximate extinction dates are:

Bourbon pink pigeon, *Columba duboisi*	1669
Bourbon parakeet, *Necropsittacus borbonicus*	1669
Solitaire (Réunion's representative of the dodo), *Raphus solitarius*	1746
Réunion fody, *Foudia bruante*	1776
Mascarene parrot, *Mascarinus mascarinus* (died in Munich)	1834
Bourbon crested starling, *Fregilupus varius*	1862

Birds presently in danger are the Réunion petrel and the Réunion cuckoo shrike. The island is a French colony and no conservation designation has yet been made of any part of it.

Mauritius, discovered in 1505, was a Dutch colony from 1598 to 1710, a French colony from 1715, and was captured by the British in 1810; it is now self-governing. As on Réunion, its extraordinary bird fauna suffered instant overkill from the European colonists and their African slaves. Approximate extinction dates are:

Broad-billed Mauritian parrot, *Lophopsittacus mauritanus*	1638
van den Broecke's red rail, *Aphanapteryx bonasia*	1675
Dodo, *Raphus cucullatus*	1681
Mauritius blue pigeon, *Alectroenas nitidissima*	1830
Commerson's scops owl, *Otus commersoni*	1837

Presently in danger are the Mauritius kestrel, the Mauritius pink pigeon, the Mauritius cuckoo shrike and the Mauritius race of the olivaceous bulbul.

Two mainstream reserves established in 1951, are administered by the Ministry of Education and Cultural Affairs at Bel-Ombre and Macabe-Mare Longue; these harbour introduced and feral wild boar, deer and monkeys. Seven smaller reserves are being developed.

Rodriguez, discovered in 1645, was first colonized in 1691 by the French and seized by the British in 1809–10. It is a dependency of

Mauritius and has no present conservation reserves. Its bird fauna, too, suffered instant overkill; approximate extinction dates are:

Rodriguez blue pigeon, *Alectroenas rodericana*	1693
Flightless night heron, *Nycticorax megacephalus*	1730
Flightless blue rail, *Aphanapteryx leguati*	1730
Rodriguez parakeet, *Necropsittacus rodricanus*	1730
Rodriguez little owl, *Athene murivora*	1730
Rodriguez solitaire (the representative of the dodo), *Pezophaps solitaria*	1791
Leguat's starling, *Fregilupus rodericanus*	1832
Rodriguez ring-necked parakeet, *Psittacula exsul*	1875

Presently in danger is the Rodriguez warbler.

Also in the Indian Ocean the British Indian Ocean Territory embraces the islands of Aldabra, the Chagos archipelago and some other coral islands. No government reserve dedications have yet been made, but Aldabra (which has been discussed for development as a staging airfield) is a large atoll with a remarkable indigenous fauna which is presently under intensive research (supported by the WWF) by the Royal Society and visiting naturalists from many parts of the world. The fauna is too vulnerable to stand an airfield invasion and it is hoped that the island will soon be given at least nature reserve status.

In the Seychelles Territory, this beautiful archipelago has presently no official government conservation deployments; but with WWF help the nature reserve of Cousin Island has been purchased, and it is hoped that this will be but the first of a network of reserves among those lovely and vulnerable islands where no less than six indigenous full species of birds are in Red Data Book danger of extinction. These are the Seychelles kestrel, the Seychelles owl, the Seychelles magpie robin, the Seychelles warbler, the Seychelles black paradise flycatcher and the Seychelles fody.

Australian Paradise

The Australasian fauna of the world is to be found east of Wallace's Line between Bali and Lombok in the East Indies and occupies Australia and New Guinea and the chain of East Indian Islands from Lombok to beyond Timor. Celebes and the islands between it and New Guinea are in a blend-zone where the Oriental and Australasian faunas mix. New Zealand and Oceania (the Pacific archipelagos) have a mainly Australasian-type fauna. Hawaii, however, falls in a blend-zone where American elements mix with Australasian; and some people would classify the interesting and rather special New Zealand fauna as a subfauna of the Australasian fauna, which has colonized that archipelago entirely across the sea because New Zealand has never had a land bridge linking it with anywhere else. Antarctica, too, can be said to support its own small subfauna.

When man first colonized Australia its fauna, as now, had a few placental mammals – rodents and bats that had drifted there or flown from Southeast Asia – but its major land mammals were all marsupial. They had evolved into an assembly of big-game and smaller elements whose members had ecological counterparts in other faunas all over the world but which had reached their place in nature by entirely independent, convergent evolution. Of the monotremes, the aquatic duck-billed platypus has no ecological counterpart anywhere; but the echidnas are paralleled by armoured anteaters, which have independently evolved in other parts of the world. The thylacines are the counterpart of dogs; the phalangers of arboreal carnivores and rodents, the numbat of unarmoured anteaters, the koala of tree sloths, the wombats of fairly heavy, slow, ground rodents, the kangaroos and wallabies of deer and antelopes and gazelles, the bandicoots of insectivores, and the marsupial moles of moles.

Carbon-dating of charcoal at an early human stratum on the Keilor terrace of the Maribyrnong River in Victoria, Australia, gives a date of $31,600 + 1100$ or -1300 B.P. This, published in 1968, is the earliest date for man in Australia. If we collect the fauna of Upper Pleistocene and Flandrian Australia from deposits known to be no older than this we find that a Pleistocene megafauna, a real big-game array of evolved marsupials, was present in the Australian continent when man arrived. All the larger elements of it have disappeared.

Unfortunately for the record, we cannot make much of the birds. No less than forty-one extinct Upper Pleistocene birds are known from Australia, all but a few of them described by the palaeontologist C. W. De Vis between 1884 and 1906; but all but one come from deposits that we cannot (so far) confidently date at less than 32,000 years old. Most of them come from the Darling Downs deposits of Queensland, or from South Australia. The noble emu, *Dromaeus patricius*, however, is an extinct species which has been found in the Wellington Caves of New South Wales, where a fossil dingo and an alleged fossil human tooth were also found. The presence of the dingo in any Australian deposit is, of course, a human marker because early man brought it to Australia: there are certainly several dingo deposits that are earlier than the only one so far dated by radiocarbon, at Fromm's Landing in South Australia, which gave $3170 + 94$ B.P.

The human invasion of Australia produced what we must now recognize as an overkill pattern comparable with that in the Americas (p. 196). The truth will doubtless be much refined as digging and dating proceed in Australia, where two Universities now have their own radiocarbon teams. From man-associated deposits in New South Wales and Victoria we can now recognize the following species as extinct: an echidna, a devil (smallish carnivore) in the same genus as the Tasmanian devil, two thylacines (marsupial "dogs"), a bandicoot, a phalanger, a ring-tailed phalanger, five wombats and a musky rat kangaroo. These were fairly small game; but unquestionably in the megafaunal or big-game league were: the "marsupial lion," *Thylacoleo carnifex*,

Leadbeater's possum, by Josette Gourley, has a relict population in not more than eight places in Victoria.

177

which was described by the great palaeontologist Sir Richard
Owen in 1859. Placed in a family of its own between the phalangers
and the wombats, this biggish animal is still a mystery. Most of its
early excavators thought that it was, in fact, the biggest carnivore
that the Australian marsupials could be found to have produced;
but while its skull (more than ten inches long) has enormous,
pointed, canine-like first incisors and big crushing premolar
teeth, the true canines were tiny and it may have been adapted to
tearing apart termite hills and trees and living on insects and
vegetation or a combination of both. Its limb bones suggest that it
was a fairly nimble animal; and it may well have occupied a niche
similar to that of the small or medium extinct ground sloths of
the Americas.

Also probably in this niche, but corresponding rather to the
giant ground sloths, were the members of another marsupial
family, the Diprotodonts. Two that are known from human
horizons are *Nototherium mitchelli* and the even larger *Diprotodon
australis*. Both these, like *Thylacoleo*, had enormous first incisors,
adapted for cutting rather than piercing, and molars adapted for
hard, sharp chewing. *Diprotodon* had a skull more than three feet
long and was itself ten and a half feet long, about the same size as
a rhinoceros. It walked flat-footed and was doubtless a browser
like the ground sloths.

In the kangaroo family there were three species of the extinct
genus *Sthenurus*, *Procoptodon rapha*, which was a giant kangaroo,
and *Palorchestes azael*, which was the biggest kangaroo known,
had an eighteen-inch skull and may have stood eleven and a half
feet high. Besides these, there were at least seven extinct species
of the modern genus of the large kangaroos, *Macropus*. Most of
these were big, and one, *M. ferragus*, was a giant version of the
living great grey kangaroo; we might call it the giant grey
kangaroo, if we only knew that it was grey. So far I have been able
to identify twenty-eight mammal species that survived in Australia
to the time of man but are now extinct.

Since 1600, our date for the beginning of modern extinction, one
bird and seven mammals are generally agreed to have become
extinct in Australia. In order of date these are Gilbert's rat
kangaroo, 1840, the eastern barred bandicoot, 1867, the brown hare
wallaby, 1890, the broad-faced rat kangaroo, 1906, the speckled
marsupial mouse, 1910, the Lord Howe (Island) whiteye, 1918, and
the Toolache wallaby, 1938.

In survival danger are the cereopsis goose, the Lord Howe
woodrail, seven members of the parrot family, the two scrub birds,
a whipbird, a grass wren, a honeyeater and the Norfolk Island
starling; and among the marsupials two planigales, a phascogale,
a sminthopsis, a jerboa marsupial, a dasyure, the thylacine, a
bandicoot, three possums, four wallabies and five kangaroos.
The Stone Age Australian colonists may have had an overkill with
the big game; Western colonists have made and are possibly still
making a fairly quick overkill of the little and middle game that
survives in the continent.

If present overkill points up the need for conservation in
Australia and the trends towards habitat degeneration, erosive
farming and some overhunting that are the main causes of it, there

Thylacine, the "Tasmanian
Wolf", drawn by Peter Scott.
This interesting marsupial
carnivore is now confined to,
and very rarely encountered in the
dense bush of western Tasmania.

is another side to the coin. Nature reserves or national parks have not yet been deployed in Australian New Guinea; but on the continent itself no less than seventy-two protected territories were on IUCN's mainstream list of 1967, spread over every state and the Northern Territory, and administered by the state and commonwealth governments. Besides these at least 100 other areas are under development. More than sixty of the mainstream areas are national parks; the rest are wildlife reserves; in which a number of endangered species are fully protected, and – just as important – a number of native animals that *could* become endangered by habitat destruction are protected in good populations.

IUCN gets very good intelligence from the zoologists and botanists of the government agencies and universities of Australia; and it is clear that a sound conservation policy is evolving in a country that now has a tradition, well over a century old, of energetic natural history research and scientific scholarship.

New Zealand Paradise

e North Island Kiwi,
ew Zealand.

Man first set foot on the New Zealand archipelago in about A.D. 950 (as we can calculate from genealogy), when a small fleet of boats – small ships of the Polynesians – landed on the main islands and the Chatham archipelago and established the pre-Maori moa-hunting culture there. They encountered a major country that had always been geologically and physically separate from the rest of the world, whose only land mammals were two bats (and possibly a rodent), and whose birds had evolved into the occupiers of the "mammal niches" in the environment.

The main order of grazing and browsing birds consisted, as the fossil record now tells us, of twenty-seven moas and four kiwis; of these it is likely that twenty-two of the moas and three (possibly all four) of the kiwis were still living when the Polynesians arrived. Three kiwis still survive; but all the moas have now gone. Many other species of birds have gone, too; and it is possible (with the aid of the records of sophisticated New Zealand archaeology and some carbon-datings) to make a tentative chronological list of New Zealand full species extinctions from the first colonization times to the present.

Dates are terminal, A.D.; those marked * are based on radiocarbon analysis:
Graceful kiwi, *Pseudapteryx gracilis*, island unknown, possibly survived after *c.* 950.
New Zealand owlet frogmouth, *Megaegotheles novaezealandiae*, North and South Islands, *50, possibly after *c.* 950.

Probably (*provedly) after *c.* 950.

Pygmy lesser moa, *Pachyornis pygmaeus*, North Island.
Mappin's lesser moa, *Pachyornis mappini*, North Island.
Owen's lesser moa, *Pachyornis oweni*, North Island.
*Oliver's lesser moa, *Pachyornis septentrionalis*, North Island.
Short lesser moa, *Euryapteryx curtus*, North Island.
Slender lesser moa, *Zelornis exilis*, North Island.

Huia, by J. Kühn, one of the three known members of the specially New Zealand bird family Callaeidae, which became extinct (last on North Island) in 1907.

Wildlife Crisis

*Von Haast's lesser moa, *Zelornis haasti*, South Island.
Ostrich-like great moa, *Dinornis struthoides*, North Island.
*Owen's great moa, *Dinornis novaezealandiae*, North Island.
Gigantic great moa, *Dinornis giganteus*, North Island.
Hercules great moa, *Dinornis hercules*, North Island.
*Finsch's shelduck, *Euryanas finschi*, South Island.
North Island tarepo (goose), *Cnemiornis gracilis*, North Island.
Chatham Island duck, *Anas chathamica*, Chatham Islands.
Chatham Island sea eagle, *Haliaeetus* species, Chatham Islands.
Cave rail, *Capellirallus karamu*, North Island.
*Little weka (a rail), *Gallirallus minor*, Chatham, North and South Islands.
Giant rail, *Diaphorapteryx hawkinsi*, Chatham Islands.
*Hodgen's gallinule, *Pryamida hodgeni*, South Island.
Chatham Island snipe, *Coenocorypha chathamica*, Chatham Islands.

Hokioi (eagle), *Harpagornis moorei*, North and South Islands, *1150.
Turkey-like lesser moa, *Anomalopteryx didiformis*, North and South Islands, *1185.
Hutton's lesser moa, *Emeus huttoni*, South Island, *1185.
Crane-like lesser moa, *Euryapteryx geranoides*, North and South Islands, *1185.
Robust great moa, *Dinornis robustus*, South Island, *1185.
Greatest moa, *Dinornis maximus*, South Island, *1320, perhaps later.
Elephant-footed lesser moa, *Pachyornis elephantopus*, South Island, fourteenth–sixteenth centuries.
Heavy lesser moa, *Emeus crassus*, North and South Islands, fourteenth–sixteenth centuries.
South Island tarepo (goose), *Cnemiornis calcitrans*, South Island, fourteenth–sixteenth centuries.
Large New Zealand harrier, *Circus teauteensis*, North and South Islands, fourteenth–sixteenth centuries.
New Zealand coot, *Nesophalaris chathamensis*, Chatham and South Islands, fourteenth–sixteenth centuries.
Giant flightless wood hen, *Aptornis otidiformis*, North and South Islands, fourteenth–sixteenth centuries.
New Zealand *or* Moriori crow, *Corvus moriorum*, North and South Islands, fourteenth–sixteenth centuries.
Burly lesser moa, *Euryapteryx gravis*, North and South Islands, *1640, possibly after 1773.
Brawny great moa, *Dinornis torosus*, South Island, *1670.
Poua (swan), *Cygnus sumnerensis*, Chatham Islands, c. 1690.
Tokoweka (moa), *Megalapteryx didinus*, North and South Islands, *1785.
Kermadec megapode, *Megapodius* species, Sunday Island, Kermadec Islands, 1876.
Stephen Island wren, *Xenicus lyalli*, Stephen Island, South Island, 1894.
Chatham Island rail, *Rallus modestus*, Chatham Islands, c. 1900.
Auckland Island merganser, *Mergus australis*, Auckland Islands, 1905.
Huia (Callaeid), *Heteralocha acutirostris*, North Island, 1907.
Chatham Island banded rail, *Rallus dieffenbachi*, Chatham Islands, 1940.

Thus forty-five birds – full species – have become extinct, and globally extinct, on New Zealand in the space of a thousand years.
Of the following New Zealand full species listed in the Red Data Book (the sole land mammal is an introduction from Australia), several are in the gravest danger of present extinction.
Brown teal, *Anas aucklandica*.
Takahé (rail), *Notornis mantelli*.
New Zealand shore plover, *Thinornis novaeseelandiae*.
New Zealand snipe, *Coenocorypha aucklandica*.
Black stilt, *Himantopus novaezelandiae*.

Kakapo (parrot), *Strigops habroptilus.*
Antipodes Island kakariki (parakeet), *Cyanoramphus unicolor.*
Yellow-crowned kakariki, *Cyanoramphus auriceps.*
Orange-fronted kakariki, *Cyanoramphus malherbi.*
New Zealand laughing owl, *Sceloglaux albifacies.*
Bush wren, *Xenicus longipes.*

Saddleback (Callaeid), *Creadion carunculatus.*
Kokako (Callaeid), *Callaeas cinerea.*
Chatham Island robin, *Petroica traversi.*
Piopio (whistler), *Turnagra capensis.*
Stitchbird, *Notiomystis cincta.*
White-throated wallaby, *Macropus parma* (extinct in Australia).

Takahé, a photograph from the New Zealand Department of Internal Affairs of the flightless rail which, when rediscovered in 1948, had been thought to have been extinct for years. Its population (200–300 birds) is now protected in a nature reserve of over 200 square miles round Takahé Valley in South Island.

When the Polynesians discovered New Zealand, the number of indigenous bird species breeding in the archipelago was of the order of 150. Nearly a third of the original fauna has died out in a thousand years of human ecological domination. The European colonists have brought the bird list nearly back to the old Pleistocene number with the aid of 35 successful introductions; and some wild birds have colonized from Australia. But New Zealand once had a Pleistocene-type fauna and now no longer enjoys one – though introduced deer and other mammals (like chamois, tahr (a goat) and wild boar) occupy the old moa food niches.

In proportion to its size, New Zealand has a conservation territory network that is fully up to Australian, South African, European or North American standards. IUCN recognizes the ten New Zealand national parks (three in the North Island, seven in the South Island) as mainstream; and under the National Parks Authority are nearly a thousand developing special, historic or other reserves. The takahé, the classic flightless rail which is the badge bird of the New Zealand Ornithological Society, is protected by the vast Fiordland National Park which embraces all the takahé habitat, and a kakapo population in its more than 1 million hectares. The orange-fronted kakariki is protected in Arthur's Pass and Mount Cook National Parks.

The whole network of New Zealand conservation is planned by integrated government authorities: the National Parks Authority and its Board, the Department of Scientific and Industrial Research and the Department of Tourism and Publicity, working in a sensible and democratic dialogue with groups of intellectuals and enthusiasts, private conservation and natural history societies and the great universities, schools and regional museums of the archipelago.

New Zealand is blessed with vast wilderness areas in its national parks, and significant parts of them, containing rare and relict populations of the fascinating indigenous fauna, are by no means fully explored and are a challenge to nature-minded New Zealand youth.

The greatest moa is now only a twelve-foot ghost striding through the pages of books or animating museum skeletons. Public opinion in New Zealand does not want any more ghosts, and through its elected government is pushing a very decent and effective slice of taxpayers' money into the maintenance of the national parks system. This is a real investment: a nature defence budget.

Kakapo, a virtually flightless parrot, photographed by P. Morrison, which has been extinct on New Zealand's North Island for nearly forty years, and survives in South Island's Southland with a population of probably under 100 birds.

Oceanian Paradise

The still wild archipelagos of the Pacific Islands were first colonized by man from east Asia. Indonesian voyagers, in rafts or canoes, spread through Melanesia before 2000 B.C., thence into Micronesia, and later still into the scattered Polynesian islands. By c. A.D. 300 the colonization was widespread. Some islands of the archipelagos have quite early carbon-dates for human sites, like c. 420 B.C. in the New Hebrides. But for the open sea islands the dates are generally later. C. A.D. 1010 is the earliest radiodate for the Society Islands (Moorea) though it seems very likely that Tahiti was colonized c. A.D. 700 or before. It was from Tahiti that both New Zealand and Hawaii were colonized, and radiodates at camp sites on Hawaii range from c. A.D. 1004 on; much earlier dates of A.D. 128 and even 300 B.C. probably need rechecking. The remotest of all Pacific Islands, Chile's Easter Island has a very early radiodate of c. A.D. 380 which may well represent a South American colonization rather than a Polynesian one. Fiji appears to have been occupied by man since c. 46 B.C., the Marquesas since the amazingly early radiodate of c. 130 B.C., New Caledonia since c. 800 B.C. All the main islands of the Pacific were colonized by A.D. 1500.

Faunas on small islands have been specially sensitive to the ecological interference of man, and the extinction-rate of island species and forms has been, and still is, the highest of all. In Oceania, the Solomons lost a peculiar and interesting pigeon on Choiseul in 1904; in the Carolines, Kusaie lost a starling in 1827 and a rail in 1828; in the New Hebrides, Tana lost a ground dove in 1774; New Caledonia, a lorikeet in 1860, an owlet frogmouth in 1880 and a wood rail in 1904; Fiji, a bar-winged rail and the long-legged warbler in 1890; Samoa, a wood rail in 1873. In the Society Islands, the Raiatea kakariki, mysterious starling and thrush were seen by the Cook Expedition of 1774 and have never been seen since, and in Tahiti the Tahiti sandpiper was last recorded in 1777, the kakariki in 1884 and the red-billed rail in 1925.

Birds in Oceania that are listed by IUCN as endangered species are:

Marquesas:	Marquesan ground dove.
Samoa:	tooth-billed pigeon.
Tonga:	Pritchard's megapode.
Fiji:	MacGillivray's petrel, masked parakeet.
New Caledonia:	kagu (a bird of a unique monotypic family), cloven-feathered dove, giant imperial pigeon, horned parakeet.
Carolines, Ponapé:	mountain starling, giant whiteye.
Carolines, Truk:	monarch, great whiteye.
Marianas:	La Pérouse's megapode, Tinian monarch.
Palaus:	ground dove, owl, fantail.

In these archipelagos government conservation is deployed only in New Caledonia and Fiji. In the former, five reserves are under development but none has reached the IUCN mainstream list, but the colonial government, backed by the Ornithological Society of

Tuatara, *Sphenodon punctatus*, by Josette Gourley, is the last living survivor of a very ancient order of reptiles, the Rhynchocephalia, over 200 million years old. It is now confined to about twenty islands off the New Zealand coast, on some of which it survives in good populations and most of which are under strict protection.

Oceanian Paradise

New Caledonia, protects the kagu by law and is developing a reserve for it at Rivière Bleue.

In Fiji mainstream nature reserves are administered by the Forestry Service on Vanua Levu at Ravilevu and on Viti Levu at Nadarivatu, and three other reserves are under development.

By far the deepest conservation system in the Pacific is deployed in the Hawaiian archipelago. It is part of the great U.S. network. The Hawaii Volcanoes National Park was created in 1916, and part of it made into the separate Haleakala National Park in 1961. The State of Hawaii is busy encouraging the development of a reserve network elsewhere in the islands and in protecting the endangered fauna.

When the Polynesians colonized Hawaii there is no evidence that they overkilled the remarkable indigenous fauna; as far as can be detected, the sixteen extinctions all date from the Western takeover of the islands and from the days of habitat destruction, farming erosion, a certain amount of hunting and collecting and the introduction of exotic birds and the bird diseases they carry.

Half the sixteen Hawaiian native birds extinct between 1837 and 1945 were members of the peculiarly Hawaiian honeycreeper family, the Drepanididae, of which only fourteen species survive, many in danger. The rest are three rails, a warbler and four honeyeaters of the Australasian family. Nineteen native birds are listed as presently in danger, several with red sheets in the Red Data Book (p. 217). The néné or Hawaiian goose has been the subject of an effective WWF-aided rehabilitation programme. So has the Laysan teal. The unique Hawaiian monk seal is holding its own under careful watching.

Antarctic Paradise

The only area of the world where man appears to be deployed in a totally benign system of complete international scientific co-operation is the Antarctic continent, which has now become virtually an international park. The Antarctic scientists at their well-run and well-financed stations are not there to claim or exploit, to extract and erode. They have but one motto: Find Out; and having found out, another motto: Do What's Right. And they find out and do.

There is presently but one endangered animal in the Antarctic – Ross's seal whose population and breeding-life is still a mystery. Someone will soon find it out.

In peace, the analysis of Antarctica proceeds, with work-sharing and station-sharing and ship-and-transport-sharing that trans-cends the differences in political systems and philosophy of the exploring nations. If the world's nature problems as a whole (or, come to that, space problems) could be tackled in the style of the Antarctic problems our species could become less terrible.

The world is full of young people unhappy about their environment and their style of life in it. If there is a big enough challenge, as in the exploration and analysis of the Antarctic or space, the response can transcend politico-philosophical, historico-national, racial, faith and age differences.

Conservation is as big a challenge as landing on the Moon or Mars. Its leaders are of very different nations with very different systems; and yet it has an amazing pool of common thought and experience. Conservation has borrowed a slogan from hard international politics: Peaceful Coexistence – with nature.

If the world can reach this we members of the club of *Homo sapiens* will not have to look for another world. We can make our own planet a garden of nature, a living theatre of all the interdependent organisms that have risen therein, and continue to rise and change, prosper and wax and wane, by evolution through natural selection. We want to relieve nature's network of the human pressures which have hashed up the habitat, scarred the soil, extinguished the endemic organisms, polluted the ponds, negated nature. We try; by the ordinary methods of analysis, seeking and finding, or – as the Scandinavians say – ransacking. This is the kind of ransacking we want; *research ransacking*, not the other kind. The new ransackers of conservation are the antithesis of the old ransackers who chopped nature, left it barren and dead, and moved on to chop elsewhere.

The world is a very interesting place, with a net of fauna and flora that has taken 3 billion years to evolve, yet could be destroyed in a few decades. Growing in the world at present is a new movement, the Conservation International, which could become a force for peace, progress and prosperity that the world has not experienced, badly needs and is beginning, we believe, to demand.

West Indies Paradise

When Columbus discovered the West Indies in 1492 they had a population now estimated to have been at least 2 million Amerindians. The dominant culture was Arawakan, which may have colonized from the direction of South America about a thousand years earlier. But men probably entered the Caribbean Islands much earlier than that, in about the eleventh millennium B.P. It seems certain that they perpetrated a classic overkill on the vulnerable, specialized island fauna. A list follows of the birds and mammals in approximate chronological order which became extinct after the first human colonization of the West Indies; though that all of them were extinguished by man cannot be proved. I have included races because in archipelagos these are rather more significant than usual. Man arrived at or before the beginning of Flandrian times, so that any postglacial fossil is a bone of the time of man.

Flandrian not further dated
Asphalt stork, *Ciconia maltha*, Cuba.
Secret caracara, *Caracara latebrosa*, Puerto Rico.

Anthony's snipe, *Gallinago anthonyi*, Puerto Rico.
Lesser Puerto Rican ground sloth, *Acratocnus odontrigonus*, Puerto Rico.

Hispaniolan solenodon, drawn by Peter Scott. An insectivore of a peculiarly West Indian family now rare in the wilder areas of the Dominican Republic.

* This was a monster, as large as today's American white-tailed deer.

West Indies Paradise

Lesser Hispaniolan ground sloth, *Acratocnus comes*, Hispaniola.
Greater Puerto Rican ground sloth, *Acratocnus major*, Puerto Rico.
Greater Hispaniolan ground sloth, *Parocnus serus*, Hispaniola.
Anguilla giant rodent, *Amblyrhiza inundata*, Anguilla.*
Cuban short-tailed hutia, *Geocapromys columbianus*, Cuba.
Least Hispaniolan hutia, *Plagiodonta spelaeum*, Hispaniola.
Montane Hispaniolan hutia, *Aphaetreus montanus*, Hispaniola.
Agouti-like spiny rat, *Heteropsomys insulans*, Puerto Rico.
Agouti-like rodent, *Homopsomys antillensis*, Puerto Rico.
Narrow-mouthed Hispaniolan spiny rat, *Brotomys contractus*, Hispaniola.

Estimated c. 3000–1500 B.P.
Square eagle, *Calohierax quadratus*, Great Exuma in Bahamas.
Glover Allen's eagle, *Titanohierax gloveralleni*, Great Exuma in Bahamas.
Haitian barn owl, *Tyto ostologa*, Haiti.
Mighty barn owl, *Tyto pollens*, Great Exuma in Bahamas.
Giant Cuban barn owl, *Tyto* species, Cuba.

Estimated as probably later, but still Pre-Columbian
Camao (rail), *Nesotrochis debooyi*, Puerto Rico; last known St Croix and St Thomas.
Ghost quail dove, *Oreopeleia larva*, Puerto Rico.
Concordia macaw, *Ara autochthones*, St Croix.
Cave barn owl, *Tyto cavatica*, Puerto Rico.
Otero's owl, *Ornimegalonyx oteroi*, Cuba.

Post-Columbian and pre-1600
Guadelupe violet macaw, *Anodorhynchus purpurascens*, Guadelupe.
Puerto Rican giant heptaxodon (rodent), *Heptaxodon bidens*, Puerto Rico.
Puerto Rican giant elasmodontomys (rodent), *Elasmodontomys obliquus*, Puerto Rico.

Quemi (giant rodent), *Quemisia gravis*, Hispaniola.
Hispaniola hutia (rodent), *Hexolobodon phenax*, Hispaniola.
Puerto Rican hutia, *Isolobodon portoricensis*, Puerto Rico.
Haitian isolobodon (rodent), *Isolobodon levir*, Hispaniola.
Broad-mouthed Hispaniolan spiny rat, *Brotomys voratus*, Hispaniola.

Post-Columbian, probably post-1600
Eastern Cuban nesophontes (insectivore), *Nesophontes longirostris*, Cuba.
Western Cuban nesophontes, *Nesophontes micrus*, Cuba.
Hispaniolan nesophontes, *Nesophontes zamicrus*, Hispaniola.
Puerto Rican nesophontes, *Nesophontes edithae*, Puerto Rico.
Puerto Rican long-nosed bat, *Monophyllus frater*, Puerto Rico.
Cuban fig-eating bat, *Phyllops vetus*, Cuba.
Puerto Rican flower bat, *Phyllonycteris major*, Puerto Rico.
Greater Cuban spiny rat, *Boromys offella*, Cuba.
Lesser Cuban spiny rat, *Boromys orrei*, Cuba.

Extinct since 1600
Haitian flower bat, *Phyllonycteris obtusa*, Hispaniola, after 1600.
Cuban race of large funnel-eared bat, *Natalus major primus*, Cuba, after 1600.
Martinique macaw, *Ara martinica*, Martinique, 1658.
Guadeloupe parrot, *Amazona violacea*, Guadeloupe, 1722.
Martinique parrot, *Amazona martinica*, Martinique, 1722.
Guadeloupe conure, *Aratinga labati*, Guadeloupe, 1722.
Guadeloupe red macaw, *Ara guadeloupensis*, Guadeloupe, 1722.
Jamaican red macaw, *Ara gossei*, Jamaica, 1765.
Dominican green-and-yellow macaw, *Ara atwoodi*, Dominica, 1791.
Jamaican green-and-yellow macaw, *Ara erythrocephala*, Jamaica, 1810.
St Michel nesophontes, *Neso-*

phontes paramicrus, Hispaniola, late nineteenth century.

Atalaye nesophontes, *Nesophontes hypomicrus*, Hispaniola, late nineteenth century.

Jamaican race of least pauraque, *Siphonorhis americanus americanus*, Jamaica, 1859.

Jamaican rice rat, *Oryzomys antillarum*, Jamaica, 1877.

Jamaican race of diablotin, *Pterodroma hasitata caribbaea*, Jamaica, 1880.

St Lucia rice rat, *Oryzomys luciae*, St Lucia, 1881.

Cuban red macaw, *Ara tricolor*, Cuba, 1885.

Martinique race of house wren, *Troglodytes aedon guadeloupensis*, Martinique, 1886.

Jamaican race of uniform crake, *Amaurolimnas concolor concolor*, Jamaica, 1890.

Antigua race of burrowing owl, *Speotyto cunicularia amaura*, Antigua, 1890.

Guadeloupe race of burrowing owl, *Speotyto cunicularia guadeloupensis*, Guadeloupe, 1889.

Bayamo race of Cuban solenodon, *Atopogale cubana cubana*, Cuba, 1890.

St Vincent rice rat, *Oryzomys victus*, St Vincent, 1897.

Jamaican flower bat, *Phyllonycteris aphylla*, Jamaica, 1898.

Martinique rice rat, *Oryzomys desmaresti*, Martinique, 1902.

Barbuda rice rat, *Oryzomys audreyae*, Barbuda, 1902.

Hispaniolan fig-eating bat, *Phyllops haitiensis*, Hispaniola, 1917.

Grand Cayman thrush, *Turdus ravidus*, Grand Cayman, 1938.

Grenada race of hook-billed kite, *Chondrohierax uncinatus mirus*, Grenada, 1955.

In present survival danger: in IUCN's Red Data Book

Caribbean generally
Caribbean monk seal, *Monachus tropicalis*.
Caribbean race of West Indian manatee, *Trichechus manatus manatus*.

Black-billed whistling duck, *Dendrocygna arborea*.

Lesser Antilles
Grenada dove, *Leptotila wellsi*, Grenada.
St Vincent parrot, *Amazona guildingi*, St Vincent.
St Lucia parrot, *Amazona versicolor*, St Lucia.
Imperial parrot, *Amazona imperialis*, Dominica.
Virgin Islands race of Puerto Rican screech owl, *Otus nudipes newtoni*, St Thomas.
Grenada race of Euler's flycatcher, *Empidonax euleri johnstonei*, Grenada.
St Vincent race of house wren, *Troglodytes aedon musicus*, St Vincent.
St Lucia race of house wren, *Troglodytes aedon mesoleucus*, St Lucia.
Guadeloupe race of house wren, *Troglodytes aedon guadeloupensis*, Guadeloupe.
Martinique race of brown trembler, *Cinclocerthia ruficauda gitturalis*, Martinique.
White-breasted thrasher, *Ramphocinclus brachyurus*, Martinique and St Lucia.
Barbados race of yellow warbler, *Dendroica petechia petechia*, Barbados.
Semper's warbler, *Leucopeza semperi*, St Lucia.

Puerto Rico
Red fig-eating bat, *Stenoderma rufum* (lately in Virgin Islands).
Puerto Rico race of plain pigeon, *Columba inornata wetmorei*.
Puerto Rican parrot, *Amazona vittata*.
Puerto Rico race of short-eared owl, *Asio flammeus portoricensis*.
Puerto Rican whip-poor-will, *Caprimulgus noctitherus*.

Hispaniola
Hispaniolan solenodon, *Solenodon paradoxus*.
Cuvier's hutia, *Plagiodonta aedium*.
Dominican hutia, *Plagiodonta hylaeum*.
Hispaniolan race of least pauraque, *Siphonorhis americanus brewsteri*.

Facing:
The western race of the ring-tailed rock wallaby now has only one relict population, in the Flinders Range of South Australia.

HELMUT DILLER

West Indies Paradise

Jamaica
Jamaican short-tailed hutia,
  Geocapromys browni.

Cuba
Eastern race of Cuban solenodon,
  Atopogale cubana poeyana.
Bushy-tailed hutia, *Capromys
  melanurus.*
Dwarf hutia, *Capromys nana.*
Cuban hook-billed kite, *Chondro-
  hierax wilsoni.*
Gundlach's hawk, *Accipiter
  gundlachi.*
Cuban race of sandhill crane, *Grus
  canadensis nesiotes.*
Zapata rail, *Cyanolimnas cerverai.*
Fernandina's flicker, *Nesoceleus
  fernandinae.*

Cuban race of ivory-billed woodpecker, *Campephilus principalis
  bairdi.*
Zapata wren, *Ferminia cerverai.*
Zapata sparrow, *Torreornis
  inexpectata.*

Bahamas
Bahaman hutia, *Geocapromys
  ingrahami.*
Bahaman race of Cuban parrot,
  *Amazona leucocephala
  bahamensis.*
Bahaman races (three) of West
  Indian red-bellied woodpecker,
  Melanerpes superciliaris.

Bermuda
Cahow, *Pterodroma cahow.*

A brief glance at the preceding list may convince the reader that the West Indies have had an overkill situation ever since man set foot in them, and that it may still be chronic. In the West Indies no present conservation land unit to mainstream standards is recognized by IUCN except in Cuba (four), the Dominican Republic (one) and Puerto Rico (one). Nowhere does any British Commonwealth Island in the archipelago have a national park or nature reserve of IUCN standards – not even the largest islands, Jamaica and Trinidad. There are no reserves in the French Antilles at all.

Conservation planning needs a pattern of total Caribbean problem-exchange to arrive at a great plan for the Caribbean life-community, which is a real, ecologically separate subunit of the neotropical fauna and which also has its separate botanical personality. The pressures of human population, habitat destruction, overhunting, and in places erosive agriculture are great. Of the recognized reserves only three, as far as I know, guard endangered species: in Cuba Cupeyal and Jaguani Reserves which have reported populations of ivory-billed woodpeckers (one of the rarest birds in the world); in Puerto Rico, the fine Luqillo Experimental Forest, which is virtually the only climax forest left on the island, guards the Puerto Rican parrot.

The task for most of the West Indies is to identify their own good conservation trends and develop them cooperatively. Good starts have been made here and there; for instance in 1961 the Bermuda Government designated as bird sanctuaries more than twenty-five acres of islands, including most of the key islands that can offer breeding grounds to their unique cahow – another of the rarest birds in the world.

The Bahamas, now developing a high cost but also a high standard of living could afford reserve designation for their tender fauna and flora, especially on places like the flamingo paradise of Great Inagua. They have made a start with a designation of East Plana Cay as a sanctuary for the typical race of the Bahaman hutia, an animal listed as in danger of extinction in IUCN's Red Data Book. Besides its recognized Nature Reserve of

Confined to New Caledonia, where it is now very rare in the forests, the kagu represents an unique suborder of the crane-rail order.

Puerto Rican parrot, painted by
Paul Barruel.

Haina-Duey the Dominican Republic could develop its three
designated national parks and four other nature reserves, and
Haiti, which has neither, could follow and help build a reserve
mosaic in Hispaniola that could give a real defence to the
threatened fauna of that beautiful island. Cuba has four national
parks in the making, one of them in the vital Zapata Swamp area
where several endangered animals live; this is integrated with a
nature reserve where special efforts are already being made to
preserve the last, relict population of the unique Cuban crocodile.

Jamaica has four good botanic gardens, two beauty-spots, one
hill sanctuary and a tender fauna, and must soon progress into
new realms of conservation from this smallish start. Trinidad's
forest reserves (thirty-six) cover nearly a third of the island but are
mainly dedicated to pure commercial forestry; it also has four
largish game sanctuaries and five small or smallish nature
reserves; but nothing is yet mainstream to IUCN.

In the Lesser Antilles the Windwards have three forest reserves,
St Vincent four forest reserves and four bird sanctuaries, Mont-
serrat a forest reserve and Antigua two public parks which are
mainly recreational. These are all developments to build up on.

The West Indies are very accessible to naturalists both from the
Americas and from Europe and are well worked by them in
consequence. The files of knowledge of the wildlife situation are
good, and will continue to be good while we have men of the
calibre of James Bond (the real, not the fictional one) to "do" the
birds. WWF missions and projects in the West Indies so far have
scarcely got farther than Trinidad. Is it too much to think that by
the half millennium of Columbus's "discovery" of America in the
West Indies the whole glorious archipelago will have a mosaic of
conservation land, a recovered fauna and flora, and an international plan for its happy integration with prosperous farming,
forestry, industry, tourism and recreation? What a target for 1992!

Middle American Paradise

The earliest radiodate for a human in South America comes from Venezuela and is $14,300 \pm 500$ B.P. This means that man must have colonized Middle America before then, though the earliest radio-dating I can find from this area is $11,003 \pm 500$ B.P. from peat containing imperial mammoth remains associated with stone implements at Santa Isabel Iztapan in México.

The early Mexicans had megafaunal encounters on a scale comparable with that in North America (p. 196) though the digs do not give us so long a list of species. The Santa Isabel Iztapan date is the oldest for man associated with extinct fauna; two other digs in which he is so associated, but not radiodated, both in México, are at Tequixquiac and Hueyatlaco. At San Bartolo Atepehuacan, also in México, charcoal associated with human implements and an unspecified mammoth radiodates at 9670 ± 400 B.P.

The association list for man of extinct animals in México includes the La Brea condor, *Breagyps clarki*, Grinnell's eagle, *Spizaetus grinnelli*, a race of the La Brea caracara, *Caracara prelutosa grinnelli*; and the big-game mammals, *Brachyostracon*, a glyptodont or carapaced edentate; a short-faced bear, *Arctodus*, about a foot taller than and twice the weight of a big grizzly; the American mastodon, *Mammut americanum*; the imperial mammoth, *Elephas imperator*, fifteen foot at the shoulder; horses, *Equus*; a flat-headed peccary, *Platygonus*; the camel, *Camelops*, a fifth up in linear dimensions on the surviving dromedary; the giraffe camel, *Titanotylopus* which stood eleven and a half feet tall with its long neck and has not been found as a fossil north of México at any Upper Pleistocene horizon; the little American antelope, *Capromeryx*; the four-horned antelope, *Tetrameryx conklingi*; a bison or bisons, *Bison*; and a shrubox, *Euceratherium*.

Middle America had its time of overkill, then; but since 1600 there have been no detectable extinctions on its mainland. The only two higher vertebrates are birds which died out on isolated Guadalupe Island, 150 miles off the Pacific shore of México's Baja California: the Guadalupe caracara in 1900 and the Guadalupe storm petrel in 1912. Birds and mammals currently in danger include the volcano rabbit, the Central American tapir, the giant pied-billed grebe, the horned guan, the thick-billed parrot, the imperial woodpecker, the tufted jay, and the slender-billed and Nicaraguan grackles.

The present active deployment of national conservation in Middle America is mainly in the north. Only in México and Guatemala has dedicated land reached mainstream level in IUCN's files – thirteen of the forty-eight national parks of México (one of which goes back to 1898) and four of Guatemala's eleven. In Guatemala the world population of the Atitlan grebe is embraced by the Atitlan National Park, and the Rio Dulce National Park protects a population of the Central American tapir. In both countries government administration is in the hands of the Forestry Department.

In the rest of the isthmus British Honduras operates an unlisted nature reserve and sixteen unlisted forest reserves, Nicaragua

Central American tapir, now very rare and relict in the forests from México south, photographed by the New York Zoological Society in the Bronx Zoo.

operates an unlisted national park, Costa Rica three unlisted nature reserves, Panama is developing a (unlisted) national park system to seven units and has some good forest reserves, and in the Canal Zone of Panama the U.S. Smithsonian Institution operates a mainstream nature reserve and research station on Barro Colorado Island. Honduras and Salvador have no units. The chief enemies of progress in Middle America are those of habitat degradation, especially lumbering, and the hunting pressure (much from lumber camps and estates) that goes with it.

South American Paradise

Of the 154 living families of birds, no fewer than 23 are exclusively neotropical, that is, confined to South and Middle America and the West Indies, and of the 122 living families of mammals, 18 are exclusively neotropical. Colombia, Brazil, Ecuador and Venezuela, in that order, have bigger bird lists than any other countries in the world. South America is the heartland of vertebrate variety on our planet.

The earliest radiocarbon-datings of man in South America are $14,400\pm435$ in Venezuela, $10,720\pm300$ in the very south of Chile, $10,430\pm160$ in Peru, $9,720\pm128$ in Brazil, $9,030\pm144$ in Ecuador and $8,060\pm100$ in Argentina. This means that Stone Age hunters may have explored their way through the whole length of South America to the Strait of Magellan in less than 4,000 years. The invading men met a fauna new to them, and there is evidence of an overkill, though its extent cannot be fully judged until more digs have been dug and dated and more material is available. In the cave faunas of Lagoa Santa in Brazil and in several caves in southern South America is evidence of a vast pampas Pleistocene-type assemblage of big game that could have competed as a show of specialized monsters on even terms with any other fauna of the time, including that of Africa. Some of the extinct genera encountered and, I think, exterminated by early man in South America belong to families now extinct. Among those present in the fauna of 11,000 years ago or less in South America, and now extinct, are:

Lydekker's stork, *Prociconia lydekkeri.*
Fighting shelduck, *Neochen pugil.*
Opossum-type American marsupials.
Giant marmoset, *Callithrix primaevus*, which was twice as big as any modern species of the genus.
Ground sloths – probably members of all three extinct families of this extinct superfamily of the edentate mammals survived until the time of man in South America, including the giant *Eremotherium* which was so big that it could stand on its hind legs and browse seventeen feet from the ground, as can a tall giraffe, and the *Megatherium* which was nearly as big. Certainly found at human levels in the deposits were the sloths *Megalonyx cuvieri, Glossotherium* and *Mylodon.*
Greatest anteater, *Myrmecophaga gigantea*, which was of the same genus as the living great anteater but the size of an ox.
Great giant armadillo *Chlamytherium*, as big as a tapir.
Two species of *Hoplophorus*, glyptodonts – giant armoured edentates related to armadillos.
Various extinct carnivores.
Proboscideans (elephant order) represented by the two extinct families of the mastodons; the Gomphotheriids, represented by the grazing mastodon *Stegomastodon* and by *Cuvieronius*; the Mammutids, represented by the browsing mastodon *Mammut.*
Horses, represented by the primitive extinct genus *Onohippidium* and extinct South American species of the modern genus *Equus.*
Tapirs (perhaps living species).
Peccaries, including extinct species.
At least two species of the big, extinct genus of llamas, *Palaeolama.*
An extinct species of American antelope.

Since 1600 IUCN can find no bird or mammal extinction *proved* on the South American continent; though this does not mean there has not been any. The colossal area of South America and the variety of its wildlife has meant that systematic scholarship and depth of biogeographical record for the continent has lagged behind that of more temperate continents where universities, scientific societies and institutions are more numerous and older. In the Galápagos Islands the only extinct forms that I know are a race of Darwin's finch and four species of rice rats. But those who go through the South American list will find (among others) no less than six monkeys, three armadillos, four carnivores, the Amazonian manatee, two tapirs, the vicuña, three deer and at least ten species of birds which are considered to be in survival danger.

What is happening to nature's richest continent, as many call it, is an over-extractive deployment of human energy. In parts of South America classic type-specimens of forest overslash, over-grazing, cultivation erosion, soil denudation and overhunting can be encountered as living, real, awful warnings. All South American governments face these problems and most are organizing what conservation measures they can, as far as their budgets allow.

Colombia's system, just coming into action, is designed for wide

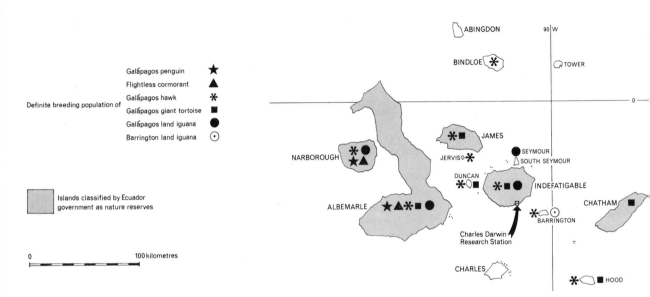

Galápagos penguin ★
Flightless cormorant ▲
Galápagos hawk ✳
Galápagos giant tortoise ■
Galápagos land iguana ●
Barrington land iguana ⊙

Definite breeding population of

Islands classified by Ecuador
government as nature reserves

0   100 kilometres

ABINGDON   90 W
BINDLOE ✳   ◯ TOWER
                                        0
                        ✳■ JAMES
NARBOROUGH ✳●   JERVIS◦✳   ● SEYMOUR
         ★▲   ◻ SOUTH SEYMOUR
                DUNCAN
                ✳◯■   ✳■ ● INDEFATIGABLE
ALBEMARLE ★▲✳■ ●   CHATHAM ■
                        ✳◯⊙ BARRINGTON
              Charles Darwin
              Research Station
CHARLES   ✳◯ ■ HOOD

The special situation of wildlife in the Galápagos Islands.

coverage of this amazingly varied land of mountain, forest, wetland and coast with a record fauna. Of six national parks designated (but not all confirmed) three may soon reach mainstream IUCN status. All of these harbour Red Data Book animals: the mountain tapir lives in Las Farallones de Cali and Purace, the spectacled bear is found here too and also in the Sierra de la Macarena, and the pudu deer is preserved in Purace.

Venezuela has a sophisticated conservation structure and in many ways serves as an headquarters of the conservation movement in South America. Seven national parks are mainstream; and under development are another three rural national parks, two nature reserves and six forest reserves. The rare spectacled bear has a population in the (Andean) Sierra Nevada de Merida National Park.

Guyana's sole national park is at Kaieteur, the escarpment and gorge of what may well be the world's most spectacular waterfall, in a zone of primeval and near-primeval tropical forest; its fauna is P-type, in so far as South America offers such faunas today, for jaguar, ocelot, tapir and some of the deer could be said to be Pleistocene-style animals.

Surinam, with much Dutch conservation experience to call on, has deployed a good, firm Nature Reserve Protection Law since 1954 and its Forestry Service looks after six mainstream nature reserves, many of which house rich wetland faunas of birds and reptiles.

French Guiana has no detectable conservation structure; but it will be consulted when the WWF plan to construct a Tucumanque National (international) Park on the border (also on the Surinam border) gets under way.

Presently Brazil has eleven mainstream national parks and nine others under development or designation. None of the mainstream parks is in Amazonian or Matto Grosso Brazil; all are in the eastern part of the country where human pressure tends to be at its greatest and control of exploitation, hunting and recreation most important. The reorganized Brazilian National Parks

194

Commission is energetically pursuing this type of development.

Also re-examining its national park and nature reserve plans with care is the Republic of Ecuador which, 600 miles offshore, has one of the greatest nature treasures in the world, the Galápagos Islands, where Darwin was so deeply inspired to evolutionary thoughts in 1835. In the Galápagos, Santa Cruz Island is itself largely a huge nature reserve and the headquarters of the international Charles Darwin Foundation for the Galápagos. The whole archipelago may earn special status; if it does not all become one national park at least national park and nature conservation enforcement systems could, and should be applied to all the islands. These face grave problems of habitat destruction by cultivation erosion, overgrazing (especially by feral goats) and some kinds of human disturbance. WWF is a Galápagos project backer, and very heavily involved.

On the mainland of Ecuador no territory is a mainstream reserve like the present Galápagos National Park; but about ten areas are under designation or plan as national parks or nature reserves from the coast to the High Andes.

Peru has three national parks under development as well as sixteen forest and at least two nature reserves. One of the nature reserves looks after a population of the threatened vicuña in the High Andes. Peru is wrestling manfully with the problem of correcting habitat degradation and may soon raise some of its units to the IUCN mainstream list. Bolivia is in the same boat; her six national parks are not yet mainstream, but could soon be. Paraguay has no conservation territory as yet but is planning national parks legislation.

Uruguay has four mainstream national parks and at least eight others under development. As is appropriate in a developed country much trouble is taken to provide facilities for public access to the national parks and camping and boating within them, in the style of the U.S. and U.K.

Chile, too, has four mainstream national parks, of which the southernmost is at Cape Horn itself. Under development is an array of at least eighteen more units which could become recognized national parks or nature reserves. Park laws began as early as 1931, and conservation administration is the responsibility of the Forest Department.

All the twelve conservation units of the Argentine Republic have been put on the IUCN mainstream list. All are national parks save the Petrified Forest Natural Monument, and they embellish a huge area of the country from the Rio Pilcomayo to Tierra del Fuego. Many of the parks lie in the thrilling territory of the southern Andes' east side. Argentina has a National Parks Council, and a forward-looking national parks policy, and is skilfully developing tourist visits to its treasure areas in a style which does not put undue pressure on the scenery or wilderness values.

In the Falkland Islands two nature reserves were created in the archipelago in 1964 (when the government set up legal conservation control) and these now have full IUCN recognition. Other island reserves are planned to look after a subantarctic fauna in which seabirds and seals and sea lions are tremendously important.

Galápagos tortoise, by Josette Gourley. Represented by race, or races, on nearly every island in the Galápagos archipelago 500 miles west of Ecuador, this giant tortoise has relict populations of many races, and four races are probably extinct. With WWF aid a conservation programme for the survivors is now deployed under the administration of the Charles Darwin Foundation Station on Santa Cruz (Indefatigible).

195

North American Paradise

The fauna and flora of the Americas evolved, with native monkeys but no apes or men, a community of life which is still the most varied array in the world.

Man arrived in the Americas by crossing the Bering Strait during the last glacial period of the Ice Ages, in what is called the Wisconsinian epoch of the Pleistocene. Sea-level was lower than it is now, because so much more of the planet's surface water was locked up in polar and alpine ice than is at present.

The date of man's arrival has yet to be determined, but the radiocarbon-dating of Stone Age hearths, peat, wood and bone, developed in the last two decades, has now established that he had reached the United States by 15,000 years before the present, and southernmost South America near the Strait of Magellan 10,000 years ago. "Hearths" associated with animal bones but not for certain with human implements, in the deposits at the sites investigated have been radiodated as at least 40,000 years B.P. in Texas and at least 37,000 B.P. in California. But it is not proved that these are human hearths.

Whenever man *did*, in fact, arrive in North America, his coming can be linked with a swift extinction of big game, birds and mammals, such as has no parallel in America at any previous time in the Pleistocene Ice Ages of the last million years with a comparable climate. The economical hypothesis is that most, though not all, of the species were killed off by him. He is known from straightforward palaeontological evidence to have preyed on the megafauna, and to have been able to kill, and subsequently butcher, the largest animals – elephants and mastodons (with Clovis stone "points") and bison (with points of the Folsom culture).

So deep has been the palaeontological work of the naturalists of the great universities and museums of the United States that it is possible to arrange a demise list in chronological order from carbon-dating of the youngest specimen of each species presently known.

Here, then, is a "Pleistocene overkill" list for North America.* I go back to 32,000 B.P., in case the suspicion that Stone Age man was around at that time proves correct.

Facing:
Camels of several species formerly ranged widely over the Americas (the evolutionary home of their family), Asia and North Africa. In the New World they were probably extinguished by Stone Age man; and in the Old World the only surviving wild populations are two groups in the Chinese and Mongolian parts of the Gobi Desert, of the wild race of the Bactrian camel.

Overleaf: Freshwater Lake Saimaa in Finland has been cut off from the sea for about 8,000 years, during which the resident population of common seal, estimated at *c.* 200–50 in it and its adjoining lakes in 1966, has evolved into a race or subspecies separate from the Baltic form.

* Helped importantly by the recent compendious cooperative treatise *Pleistocene Extinctions the Search for a Cause* (1967), published by Yale University and edited by P. S. Martin and H. E. Wright, Jr.

Terminal dates (youngest presently known) of mammals and birds (full species) extinct in North America since the thirty-second millennium before the present. Radio-carbon-dates (and correlation dates*) are B.P. (before the present), the "present," as usual, being taken to be A.D. 1950.

Years B.P.

Years B.P.	
32,000+	Giant bison, *Bison latifrons*, American Falls, Idaho. (Another dating for the deposit of 29,700±1000 may be at a different horizon.)
31,000±6,000	Allen's bison, *Bison alleni*, Wilson Ford, Kansas.
23,000	A glyptodont, *Boreostracon* species, Sims Bayou, Texas.

Years B.P.

Years B.P.	
22,540	Snow muskox, *Bootherium nivicolens*, Fairbanks, Alaska.
20,000	Sinclair's horned owl, *Bubo sinclairi*, Potter Creek Cave, California.
20,000	Fossil Aplodontia, *Aplodontia fossilis*, Potter Creek Cave, California.
20,000	Sinclair's pocket gopher, *Thomomys microdon*, Potter Creek Cave, California.
19,500±500	Cope's flamingo, *Phoenicopterus copei*, Manix Lake, California.
19,500±500	Dwarf flamingo, *Phoenicopterus minutus*, Manix Lake, California.

196

HELMUT
DILLER.

9,098 ± 1074 Extinct rabbit, *Sylvilagus* species, Groesbeck, Texas.

9,098 ± 1074 Extinct ground squirrel, *Citellus* species, Groesbeck, Texas.

17,800 + Extinct freetail bat, *Tadarida* species, New Cave, New Mexico.

Between 16,325 ± 2000 and 4450 ± 200 Rancho La Brea, California; radiodatings of this big tarpit deposit, containing the richest fossil Pleistocene fauna in the world, range from 40,000 + to 4450 ± 200 B.P. The following species are unlikely to have terminal dates before 16,325 ± 2000 B.P. but the exact horizon of their youngest bone between the 16,325 and 4450 horizons is not certain.
Dice's deer mouse, *Peromyscus imperfectus.*
Anderson's coyote, *Canis andersoni.*
Petrol coyote, *Canis petrolei.*
Wetmore's wood ibis, *Mycteria wetmorei* (unlikely to be younger than 10,300).
Graceful teratorn, *Cathartornis gracilis.*
La Brea towhee, *Pipilo angelensis.*
La Brea cowbird, *Pandanaris convexa.*

The following species are more precisely dated:

13,890 ± 280 Shultz's American bear, *Ursus optimus*, Rancho La Brea, California.

13,890 ± 280 Daggett's puma, *Felis daggetti*, Rancho La Brea, California.

13,890 ± 280 Le Conte's peccary, *Platygonus compressus*, Rancho La Brea, California. (This species is, on bone, 4290 ± 150 from Warren Beach, Ohio, whence it is doubtless dated too young, though it is likely to be younger than this Rancho La Brea record and could be younger than the 10,000 year unspecified *Platygonus* from Texas, see below.)

13,890 ± 280 Miller's dire wolf, *Canis milleri*, Rancho La Brea, California.

13,890 ± 280 Asphalt stork, *Ciconia maltha*, Rancho La Brea, California. (Possibly survived until 9800 ± 550 or even 4450 ± 200 at Rancho La Brea but the correlations of the material are not certain.)

13,890 ± 280 La Brea condor, *Breagyps clarki*, Rancho La Brea, California.

13,890 ± 280 La Brea owl, *Strix brea*, Rancho La Brea, California.

13,000 California sabretooth, *Smilodon californicus*, Maricopa, California.

12,460 ± 320 Early western bison, *Bison preoccidentalis*, Upper Cleary Creek, Alaska. (A skull has provisionally been referred to this species and a horizon of date 6320 ± 140 at Russell in Manitoba.)

12,300 ± 35 Scott's moose, *Cervalces scotti*, Berrien Springs, Michigan.

11,800 ± 800 Santa Rosa owl, *Asio priscus*, Santa Rosa Island, California.

11,500* Short-faced bear, *Arctodus simus*, Burnet Cave, New Mexico.

11,500* Plains horse, *Equus excelsus*, Burnet Cave, New Mexico.

11,500* Sangamon deer, *Sangamona* species, Burnet Cave, New Mexico.

11,500* Frick's caribou, *Rangifer fricki*, Burnet Cave, New Mexico.

11,500* Stock's pronghorn, *Tetramerix onusrosagris*, Burnet Cave, New Mexico.

11,500* Sinclair's shrubox, *Euceratherium sinclairi*, Burnet Cave, New Mexico.

11,480 ± 160 Ohio giant beaver, *Castoroides ohioensis*, Northern Lights, Ohio. (Wood dated 10,890 ± 350 at Fitchburg Park, Michigan, may have been chewed by this species.)

11,400 ± 400 Jefferson's mammoth, *Elephas jeffersoni*, Genessee County, Michigan.

11,370 ± 170 Mexican wild ass, *Equus conversidens*, Cochrane, Alberta.

11,300 ± 160 Santa Rosa dwarf mammoth, *Elephas exilis*, Santa Rosa Island, California. (Some dates on bone are younger.)

11,300 ± 1000 Pennsylvania peccary, *Mylohyus pennsylvanicus*, Lloyd's Rock Hole, Pennsylvania.

11,300 ± 1200 Western horse, *Equus occidentalis*, Ventana Cave, Arizona.

11,220 ± 500 Imperial mammoth, *Elephas imperator*, Domebo, Oklahoma. (Last date México 11,000 ± 300, from Santa Isabel Iztapan, based on surrounding peat; from its own bone it has been carbon-dated at no more than 2640 ± 200 years old, but this record is not fully accepted; other carbon-dates from the site are all over 9000. Another from Berrien Springs, Michigan, has been dated on tusk at 8260 ± 300; though this may be too young it could be younger than the Domebo specimen.)

11,170 ± 360 Tarpit pronghorn, *Breameryx minor*, Blackwater, New Mexico.

10,600 ± 250 Harlan's ground sloth, *Paramylodon harlani*, Big Bone Lick, Kentucky. (Possibly survived until 4450 ± 200 at Rancho La Brea, California, but correlation uncertain.)

10,600 ± 250 Eastern horse, *Equus complicatus*, Big Bone Lick, Kentucky.

10,600 ± 250 Extinct muskox, *Bootherium bombifrons*, Big Bone Lick, Kentucky.

10,365 ± 110 Fierce jaguar, *Panthera atrox*, Kincaid, Texas. (Possibly survived until 4450 ± 200 at Rancho La Brea, California, but correlation uncertain.)

10,365 ± 110 Lambe's horse, *Equus lambei*, Kincaid, Texas.

10,365 ± 110 Extinct pronghorn, *Capromeryx* species, Kincaid, Texas.

10,000 ± 175 Extinct peccary, *Platygonus* species, Levi, Texas.

The great Indian bustard's population has now been reduced to relict status in India and West Pakistan, where it is now officially protected by law but not out of danger.

New Mexico deposits on the Wisconsian (or late glacial)/ Flandrian (or postglacial) threshold, which is around 10,300*

	Conkling road runner, *Geococcyx conklingi*, Conkling Cavern and Shelter Cave.
10,000±175	Thick-billed cowbird, *Pyelorhamphus molothroides*, Shelter Cave.
	Willett's eagle, *Spizaetus willetti*, Howell's Ridge Cave.
	Conkling pronghorn, *Tetrameryx conklingi*, Shelter Cave.

Rancho La Brea, California, deposits in the Early Flandrian (or postglacial) time between 10,300* and 4450±200 B.P.

	Graceful goose, *Anabernicula gracilenta*.
	Western black vulture, *Coragyps occidentalis*.
	Merriam's teratorn, *Teratornis merriami*.
	Grinnell's eagle, *Spizaetus grinnelli*.
	Loye Miller's hawk, *Buteogallus fragilis*.
	Woodward's eagle, *Morphnus woodwardi*.
	American neophron, *Neophrontops americanus*.
	Loye Miller's vulture, *Neogyps errans*.
	La Brea caracara, *Caracara prelutosa*.
	La Brea turkey, *Parapavo californicus*.
	La Brea blackbird, *Euphagus magnirostris*.
Early Flandrian	Woodland muskox, *Symbos cavifrons*, Fulton County, Illinois.
9800±500	Taylor's bison, *Bison taylori*, Plainview, Texas.
9550±375	Extinct armadillo, *Holmesina septentrionalis*, Ben Franklin, Texas.
9540±120	Ancestral California condor, *Gymnogyps amplus*, Rocky Arroyo, New Mexico. (Possibly survived until later at Rancho La Brea, California; but its distinction from *G. californianus*, the living California condor, is at this date uncertain.)
9540±120	Collin's shrubox, *Euceratherium collinum*, Falcon Hill, Nevada.
9400±250	Extinct tapir, *Tapirus* species, Evansville, Indiana.
9400±250	Jefferson's ground sloth, *Megalonyx jeffersoni*, Evansville, Indiana.
8910±150	American mastodon, *Mammut americanum* Ferguson Farm, Ontario. (The date 5950±300 from Russell Farm, Michigan, is widely quoted but doubted by some; 8550±100 La Mirada, California may be from a younger stratum.)
8527±250	Shasta ground sloth, *Nothrotherium shastense*, Gypsum Cave, Nevada.
8527±250	Dire wolf, *Canis dirus*, Gypsum Cave, Nevada. (Possibly survived until 4450±200 at Rancho La Brea, California, but correlation uncertain.)
8527±250	Stevens's long-legged llama, *Tanupolama stevensi*, Gypsum Cave, Nevada.

8274±500	Ancient bison, *Bison antiquus*, Allen, Nebraska. (Possibly survived until 4450±200 at Rancho La Brea, California, but correlation uncertain.)
8240±960	Columbian mammoth, *Elephas columbi*, Whitewater Draw, Arizona.
8240±960	Western camel, *Camelops hesternus*, Whitewater Draw, Arizona. (Possibly this species 7100±350 Wasden, Idaho; possibly survived until 4450±200 at Rancho La Brea, California, but correlation uncertain.)
7670±170	An American mammoth, *Elephas* species, Peace River, British Columbia.†
7350±100	Western bison, *Bison occidentalis*, North Saskatchewan River, Saskatchewan.
7290±260	Beautiful armadillo, *Dasypus bellus*, Miller's Cave, Texas.
6370±260	Alaska horse, *Equus alaskae*, Sullivan Creek, Alaska.
6730±260	Woolly mammoth, *Elephas primigenius*, Sullivan Creek, Alaska.
5070±250 or younger, Law's flightless scoter, *Chendytes lawi*, San Nicolas Islands, California.	
4283±250	Extinct bison, *Bison* species, Lubbock, Texas.
1850±480 (A.D. 100) Richardson's bison, *Bison crassicornis*, Plum Creek, Indiana.	
815±110 (A.D. 1135) Extinct horse, *Equus* species, Hemlock Park, Ontario.	

The following full species of mammals and birds of North America became extinct in historical times. Years (A.D.) are of last known live sightings.

Steller's sea cow, *Hydrodamalis stelleri*, last in North America at Monterey Bay, California, by radiocarbon 18,940±1100 B.P.; last seen 1768, Bering Island, Bering Sea, Siberia.

Cooper's sandpiper, *Calidris cooperi*, only known specimen collected 1833, Long Island, New York.

Townsend's bunting, *Spiza townsendi*, only known specimen collected 1833 May 11, New Garden, Pennsylvania.

Great auk, *Pinguinus impennis*, last recorded New World, harvest taken for food 1785 July 5, Funk Island, Newfoundland; last 1844 June 4, Eldey, Iceland.

Sea mink, *Mustela macrodon*, last c. 1860 (or c. 1894), Maine.

Labrador duck, *Camptorhynchus labradorium*, last 1875, Long Island, New York.

Passenger pigeon, *Ectopistes migratorius*.

Carolina parakeet, *Conuropsis carolinensis*.
Last individuals known died 1914 in the Cincinnati Zoo, Ohio, the pigeon on September 1.

† A mammoth, *Elephas* species, in a peat bed dated 5560±245 at Alliance, Ohio, is doubtless older than the peat.

If we date the coming of man at 32,000+ years ago, then at least sixty full species of mammals and thirty-three of birds have become extinct in North America since then. If we take the more conservative and well-established date of *c.* 15,000 B.P., the extinct mammals number fifty-two, birds thirty.

Some of the animals were certainly big game; among the edentates one of the ground sloths was a giant; the terrible wolf was a superwolf, the short-faced bear a superbear, the fierce jaguar a superjaguar much bigger than a lion, the sabretooth a big carnivore that preyed on young elephants, the mastodon and the four big mammoths huge animals, especially the imperial mammoth. The woolly mammoth survived longer in Alaska than in its original Eurasian home. The eight extinct bison were mostly bigger than the surviving American bison. The camel and llama were tall giants compared with their surviving counterparts in the Old World and South America. None of the six horses, incidentally, was domesticated by the early Indians who inherited the horses of Wild West days from Spanish introduction of our Eurasian *Equus caballus*.

The birds of prey included several giants and Merriam's teratorn was the largest ever known to have lived, save for the incredible teratorn, *Teratornis incredibilis* of Nevada, which had a sixteen to seventeen foot wingspan.

Study of the list shows that the main period of overkill was between 14,000 and 8,000 years ago, after which it tailed off. The early hunters of North America did not cease to be hunters when the bigger game died out. Instead, in the so-called Archaic period of culture that they entered, they adapted their weapons for smaller game, and contrived to establish more stable hunting villages. At many of these successions of Stone Age culture can be traced for thousands of years.

More than 9,000 years ago basketry developed in Nevada; but the transition to the equivalent of the Old World Neolithic culture with farming and pottery was slow in coming. It arrived, finally, in about 2000 B.C. Metal did not really enter the aboriginal Amerindians' world until Hopewellian times of *c.* 500 B.C. when artistic copper ornaments became quite widespread. However, these cannot be said to have constituted any kind of Bronze Age equivalent or counterpart in North America. When the whites came the Americans were still growing their vegetables and corn with stone tools of cultivation.

But hunting went on; the one surviving bison, the American bison, had a vast population in the Great Plains and was a staple of the Amerindian aboriginal population until a century ago. In 1869, the railroad link to the Pacific coast at San Francisco was at last completed, and within thirty years only a few hundred bison remained of herds once estimated to total 60 million.

All the evidence is that the Plains Indians were in a balanced predator-prey relationship with the one surviving bison species before the railroad-based bison-business men made the type of "industrial overkill" of a wild animal. Only public conscience, and the leadership of the educated classes of the new masters of the West, saved the last American bison from extinction.

As everybody knows, the first Europeans (as opposed to Asians) to discover America were not the men of Columbus's expeditions but Vikings. In the ninth century Norwegians colonized Iceland and, skilful seamen that they were, sighted Greenland when voyaging west in 877. In 982 Eirik Raudhes – Eirik the Red – sailed to southwest Greenland where he founded Norse colonies. These spread quite a little and survived for 400 years until bad climate and Eskimo competition brought them to an end. One of the early Greenland Norsemen, Bjarni Herjulfsson, blown off course on a visit there, sighted the Canadian coast in 986 or 987.

In about 1000 Leif Eiríksson, son of the Greenland colony's founder, voyaged from Greenland to explore this new country; on the grounds of recent archaeological evidence we believe that he landed in northern Newfoundland, and may even have reached New England.

In the eleventh century Norse Greenlanders voyaged to Hudson's Bay and until the fourteenth century they visited Canada, probably for timber, and occasionally penetrated to what is now the United States as far as Minnesota. They encountered Amerindians on these journeys and may have even contributed to the gene-stock of the northeastern American aboriginals. But there is no evidence that they contributed their skill with iron to the hunting culture of Pre-Columbian North America.

Columbus discovered the West Indies in 1492, and much of the early colonization of the North American continent was from the southeast by Iberian Europeans. Ponce de Léon, the first European – apart from Norsemen – to set foot on the continental United States, did so in eastern Florida in 1515. But the present pattern of American life can be said to derive its historical and cultural nucleus from the English who founded Jamestown in Virginia in 1607. By 1800 the population of the United States was more than 5 million; it had doubled by 1830, again before 1860, again by 1880, again by 1920; and again, reaching more than 200 million, by 1970.

This book is not a history of man; but never has a continent undergone such ecological change so quickly as North America with its burgeoning human population of the last century and two-thirds. If the founders of the United States and Canada had not been blessed with a deep cultural and educational tradition, and a vast and varied continent to explore and colonize, there might have been another story to tell. Ecological crises have been, and still are, rife; but their impact has been somewhat buffered by the dedication the North American democracies apply to the solving of environmental problems by dint of rating – as they try to do – spiritual, intellectual, historical and scientific values on a par with economic and industrial exploitation.

The philosophical dialogue in the United States began long before the shades of the greatest European philosophers helped write the Declaration of Independence in 1776 and the Constitution in 1787. The American Philosophical Society began publication in 1744, the American Academy of Arts and Sciences in 1780.

Going back to John Josselyn, who published the first botanical description of New England, in 1672, there was always a tradition of the *analysis* of nature and natural history in America by colonists and visitors like Catesby, Bartram and Forster.

Benjamin Franklin was a scientific polymath of the topmost

California condor, photographed by E. D. Sibley in southwest California, has a world population of little over forty birds, breeding in only two Californian counties.

calibre; Thomas Jefferson, the third President of the United States, was as good a naturalist as the twenty-sixth President, Theodore Roosevelt, who did so much for conservation, national and international, and the conservation laws of the Americas.

In Canada, equally free, the early explorers and rural developers did not call the analysis that so many of them made "ecological;" but that is what a lot of it was.

The first of my own many visits to North America was in the spring and summer of 1953 when Roger Tory Peterson planned a combined bird-watching national parks tour and (for me) people-watching trip which took us, in a hundred lively and profitable days, from Newfoundland to Alaska by way of México. A pay-off line that I contributed to our book of the trip, *Wild America*, was "never have I seen such wonders or met landlords so worthy of their land. They have had, and still have, the power to ravage it; and instead have made it a garden."

A recent visit to the United States included an official call at the National Parks Service to talk mutual business, as representing the U.K. Countryside Commission (formerly the National Parks Commission) and to hatch plans for the mutual celebration of 1972 March 1 – the hundredth anniversary of Yellowstone National Park, the first national park in the world.

Nothing has happened between this late visit and my first to upset my firmly held view of North American leadership in nature and environmental conservation. The United States, like all other great industrial countries, has terrible and escalating pollution and planning problems. Conservation has to compete for national budget with other strong causes – health, education, social welfare, housing, defence, space exploration. What is now emerging, however, is the recognition that the environment is a resource – and to those who work for it, *the* resource – without which life is intolerable. There is only one environment, and the profits of its conservation cannot be costed in the old style of income-and-expenditure, profit-and-loss account.

What is the income of America's national parks, national monuments and wilderness areas? The very existence of these treasures is the income, for scores of millions yearly. What is the profit of conservation? What are the California condor, the ivory-billed woodpecker, the woodland bison, the redwood trees, *worth*? If you've seen one redwood, you've seen them all, said one prominent American nonconservationist at a recent election time. The situation *could* arise that if you can see one redwood, you may be seeing them all.

I have already tried to describe some facets of the American intellectual background that led to the introduction of a practical conservation programme as early as 1872. Conservation is done by people; and among those people are the analysts – the scientific naturalists – and the designers. Sometimes people are both. Often they become heroes of what is now a great international conservation movement. The planning of the West is very different now from a century ago; but that fact does not erase the heroic contribution of some Western pioneers to the West's conservability.

I have already erected Thoreau and Audubon as heroes of American conservation. So was Audubon's great friend John

Bachman. Let me add those pioneer explorers of the West, Meriwether Lewis and William Clark, both excellent naturalists; the pioneer vertebrate zoologists Alexander Wilson and George Ord, who began publishing in 1808; early field men and systematic naturalists like Prince Charles Lucien Jules Laurent Bonaparte, Richard Harlan, and John Davidson Godman (who died young); the formidable ornithologist Thomas Nuttall; the Western explorer and landscape-expert Samuel Parker; the polymathic English naturalist P. H. Gosse; New York's zoogeographer James Ellsworth De Kay; California's ornithologist William Gambel; the government naturalist-explorer Titian Ramsay Peale; vertebrate zoologist Spencer Fullerton Baird; ornithologist John Cassin; James Graham Cooper and George Suckley who together reported on the natural history of the northwest U.S. as they followed the traverse of the Pacific Railroad; ornithologist and zoologist Thomas Mayo Brewer; ornithologist and scholar Elliott Coues; Henry Wood Elliott, clerk in the U.S. Treasury who was a more than competent naturalist and artist whose work on the Pribilof seals inspired, among others, Rudyard Kipling; the palaeontologist Edward Drinker Cope; William Healey Dall and Henry M. Bannister, pioneer Alaska naturalists; and Titus Fey Cronise of California who had an ecological attitude.

All these men were at work and publishing their work before the date of the now-famous camp-fire in the Yellowstone, and their words were not idle. History has rewarded some of them in the vernacular names of animals like Audubon's warbler, Bachman's warbler, Kirtland's warbler, Lewis's woodpecker, Clark's nut-cracker, Wilson's snipe, Bonaparte's gull, Harlan's ground sloth, Nuttall's woodpecker, Gambel's quail, Peale's peregrine, Baird's sandpiper, Cassin's auklet, Cooper's sandpiper, Brewer's blackbird, Coues's rock sandpiper and Dall's sheep.

Before the Yellowstone confirmation there was an interesting portent from California, where by Act of Congress the incredible Yosemite Valley in the Sierras was withdrawn from homesteading as early as 1864 and became a state park. It was made into a national park in 1890, along with neighbouring Sequoia National Park; it had probably never been seen by other than Indian eyes until 1851.

Yosemite Valley has been carved through solid granite by the Pleistocene ice of the last million years. It is a vertical-sided trough about 4,000 feet deep and a mile and a half wide, with about a third of all the over-300-foot-high hanging waterfalls in the world ribboning its vertical (or overhanging) grey granite sides. Ribbon Fall has a free drop of 1,612 feet, the second or third highest in the world.

Yosemite has many animal treasures and its own classic grove of the world's largest tree, the "big tree" *Sequoia gigantea*. The Grizzly Giant is probably 4,000 years old and weighs nearly as many tons, and is the third largest of its kind known. The Wawona Tree, through which a coach tunnel was cut in 1881, has lately fallen.

In near-by Sequoia National Park grow the densest and most uniform groves of big trees in the world. Public pressure on these two classic Sierra parks is now very great in the season and the

National Park Service is facing difficult problems with great skill.

The fourth U.S. National Park was confirmed in 1899 – the colossal extinct volcano of Mount Rainier in Washington State. This is a high alpine unit that dominates the northwestern landscape with its snows and glaciers and self-made weather. The heart of the fifth, Crater Lake in Oregon confirmed in 1902, had never been seen by a white man until 1853. In that year John Wesley Hillman first reached the lip of this huge extinct crater at nearly 9,000 feet and peered over into the deep blue lake that fills it, six miles wide, embellished with a cone-island and a jagged lava-islet. Crater Lake is one of the most perfect collapsed volcanoes in the world; the last eruption was less than 5,000 years ago.

The U.S. rule that evolved for national park dedication was wilderness and wildness. The whole network of thirty-two national parks is federally owned and controlled. It is lived in only by staff and – in carefully designed concessionary accommodation – visitors.

I can only list a few of the parks in detail. Mesa Verde in Colorado (dedicated in 1906) is a fascinating archaeological area based on the towns and houses of a classic site of the old Pueblo desert culture. Glacier National Park in Montana (1910), marches with the Canadian border and forms an international park with Alberta's Waterton Lakes National Park (1895). In 1916 the Hawaii Volcanoes National Park was brought in, in what is now the fiftieth state, and in the following year Mount McKinley National Park was confirmed in Alaska, preserving North America's highest mountain, and a huge area of glaciated range.

In 1919 Grand Canyon in Arizona was promoted from National Monument to the status of national park. This phenomenal gorge of the Colorado River, eroded during the last 2 million years or so, is 217 miles long, on average over 8 miles across, and 1 mile deep from the south rim – deeper from the north. It contains several fantastic towers standing to the height of the surrounding tilted plateau, and its walls and precipices are gloriously colourful. Already 1,000 cubic miles of rock have been eroded away; the present erosion rate of the whole Colorado River system from source to canyon bottom is over 500,000 tons of silt a day.

It is the greatest and most perfect canyon in the world and attracts – and provides tidy accommodation for – nearly 1 million visitors a year. Its surroundings are full of interesting animals and plants and its north rim houses one of America's rarest and most beautiful animals – the Kaibab squirrel. As in all U.S. national parks, the fauna and flora are carefully wardened by the National Park Service and the park naturalists.

In 1930 the Great Smoky Mountains in North Carolina and Tennessee became a national park. These are the climax of the Appalachian Mountain chain of the eastern U.S. and are forested to its top. There are 131 native species of trees in the Park alone, more species than in the whole of Europe; it is a paradise for the botanist and the bird watcher.

Shenandoah in the Virginian Appalachians was established in 1935. Here an old lumbered forest is regenerating under careful forestry to a new and benign climax, and with beautifully designed motor access well over 2 million people now enjoy it every year.

Two great, and comparatively late, parks in the southeast U.S. are particular favourites of mine. These are Big Bend in Texas (1944) and the Everglades in Florida (1947). Big Bend marches with the Méxican border on the Rio Grande, and is a desert paradise with agave and cactus stands. At the Santa Elena Canyon the south cliff overhangs a thousand feet and one can stand in Texas with México's Chihuahua overhead, while around in the cactus bush the deer and the antelope play.

The Everglades National Park in south Florida is the third biggest in the U.S. and the biggest wetland park in the world. On average not much more than eight feet above sea-level, it is a vast area of water slowly flowing through sawgrass vegetation, past a complex of low limestone islets clad with palms, pine, gumbo-limbo and other trees; mangrove swamps adorn the salt-water rim at the coast.

The wetlands have a big fauna with birds galore, many rare insects, and mammals like the aquatic manatee, for which they are the last refuge in the United States, and a good population of the declining American alligator.

The whole system has recently been endangered by Florida development plans which have threatened to lower the water-table and inflict a noisy new jetport close by; the dangers have so far been staved off, but conservationists remain anxiously on the alert.

The U.S.A. also has forty-two national monuments – reserves of natural history, landscape, geological and often archaeological and historical importance. Katmai in Alaska is the largest of these. There are also two national memorials and many national capital parks. The American conservation effort also takes in six national seashores, including Cape Cod in Massachusetts; four national recreation areas; twenty national wildlife refuges, of which the Arctic National Wildlife Refuge is by far the largest; and eighty-nine state parks. National forests can be broken down into fourteen wilderness areas, twenty-nine wild areas, and forty primitive areas.

The Boundary Waters Canoe Area in Minnesota adjoins, and forms a sort of international park with Quetico, an Ontario Provincial Park which was confirmed in 1913.

North of the border Canada has eighteen national (federal) parks, of which Glacier National Park in British Columbia (1886) is the earliest and Wood Buffalo National Park in Alberta by far the largest. There are also at least 172 provincial parks, of which Algonquin Park in Ontario (1895) is the earliest and Parc de la Vérendrye in Québec the largest.

Endangered animals in Canadian parks are the wood buffalo and the whooping crane, both of which are protected in Wood Buffalo National Park, Alberta.

Paradise in Peril:
An American Epilogue

Stewart L. Udall
U.S. Secretary of the Interior 1961–69

The American people have consistently shown a remarkable
ambivalence towards the wildlife of our continent. Some of the
most savage episodes of wildlife slaughter in the world's history
have occurred in the United States. Every conservationist would
like to forget the extermination of the passenger pigeon, the
decimation of the buffalo and the hunting down of other irreplaceable species that were trapped to near extinction in the nineteenth
century.

But there have also been notable achievements – moments in
our history when the instinct to preserve prevailed. We invented
the national park concept (and the inviolate status it gives to
resident wildlife populations). And in this century the people of
this country, acting through their government, have set aside
more acres as permanent refuges for wildlife – and done more to
nurture the sensitive science of wildlife management – than
perhaps any other nation in the world.

Yet, once again, the integrity of our ecosystem is being impaired
– this time by the reckless use of poisons and pesticides and the
overpowering pollution of a throwaway industrial system. The list
of endangered wildlife is longer today than ever before. It is
shockingly symbolic that our national bird, the bald eagle, may be
half-way down the road to extinction (along with the osprey, the
condor, and other magnificent birds) as a result of the DDT and
other pesticides that we have already broadcast indiscriminately
on to our land and into our waters – and cannot now eradicate.

Despite our increasing efforts to understand the intricate web
of life that sustains wild things, science still falls short when
confronted with the massive environmental intrusions of modern
agriculture and industry. The destroyers of our time are not
greedy trappers or "market hunters;" they are "good farmers"
attempting to enlarge the yields of their farmlands, and captains
of industry who are ecological ignoramuses, intent only on
achieving new goals of gross production.

The battle to save the land and its creatures is never-ending –
and never really won. But to succeed in the 1970s will require
drastic changes in our industrial practices, a fresh definition of
social "progress," and a new, more sensitive life-style for individual citizens as well.

Even a decade ago most Americans were complacently convinced that the new science of wildlife management would show us
how to save and sustain thriving wildlife populations. We
belatedly recognize today that we grossly underestimated the
power of technological man to alter and destroy the natural
balances that support life. And we also consistently misjudged the
damage being done by the ever-widening wave of pollution and

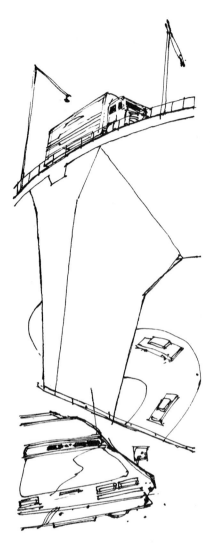

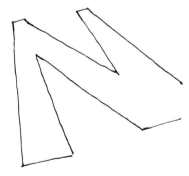

contamination that was the foreseeable result of an affluent, high-energy, goods-oriented civilization.

Today, even the most remote refuges for wildlife are no longer safe sanctuaries. It was, for example, the discovery that DDT was present in the bodies of the penguins of Antarctica, a thousand miles from any point of application, which spelled out the peril of long-lived pesticides. We now realize that oil spills, air pollution – and even the SST and its sonic boom – can diminish and slowly destroy the life-nurturing qualities of these reserves that early generations supposedly "saved" for all time. Nearer to our population centres, the paving over of the American land (at a rate of 1 million acres per year) and the filling and pollution of those barrens and marshes and estuaries that are the essential nurseries of our fish and wildlife populations pose a more immediate threat to the "urban" wildlife we desperately need to enhance the livability of blighted cities.

Today, our need for wildlife resources goes far deeper than the ready provision of food or of profit – we need wild things now as ever-present emblems of the beauty and hope of life itself. In an increasingly ugly, dehumanized world, wildlife in all its myriad forms is part of the geography of hope: its health and presence re-creates our spirits, and gives us daily assurance that nature's life machine is still functioning.

In a curious way, the wildlife policies of the United States evolved out of an antipathy towards English royalty. (My friend Prince Philip will, I am sure, delight in the irony of this historical circumstance!) When the colonists first came to this country, they brought with them English common-law concepts about game and fish resources which had their genesis in the Magna Carta of 1215. Before that time, ownership of wildlife had been vested in the King of England as a person for "his own benefit and pleasure." After the Magna Carta modified the kingly privileges, however, the king owned the wildlife only in his sovereign capacity as trustee for the people.

So the colonists, in turn, wrote into their charters the idea that the ownership of wildlife was a trust held by the sovereign (i.e. the state) for the people at large. This concept was transplanted into the state constitutions of the original Thirteen Colonies – and became the pattern that governs wildlife ownership and management in the United States today.

This underscores one of the important differences between contemporary U.S. and most European wildlife management. In England and most European countries the landowner owns the resident game and controls its cropping. Here, the game belongs to the state, and the management and control of wildlife is a public trust responsibility of public agencies. Thus, ancient England has bequeathed us a system within which every citizen has a right to assert an interest in the laws and policies and regulations that determine the future of wild things in this country.

As one result of this policy, large and vigorous citizen conservation organizations like the National Wildlife Federation, The Audubon Society, The Izaak Walton League, etc., have become organized ombudsmen for wildlife. Another result has been that the public agencies which administer our national estate have

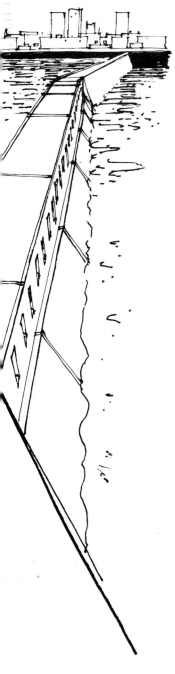

been required to assemble large staffs of biologists, habitat managers and enforcement personnel to carry out their assigned function of scientific management.

During the last decade the leaders of the International Union for the Conservation of Nature and Natural Resources and the World Wildlife Fund have not only made us face the world-wide problems of endangered species; they have helped us expand our outlook and made us think in terms of the planet as a fragile spaceship. They have told us we must care about the Arabian oryx, the blue whale, and the polar bear not simply because these are threatened species – but because their extinction will become yet another entry on a fateful scoreboard which tells us man's own prospects on this planet are uncertain.

As the World Wildlifers fight their battles on many continents, I am convinced the wildlife crisis in this country will increasingly centre on these areas of concern:

1. *We must recognize that the United States has a population problem.* We are the super-rich – and the super-polluters too. Each newborn American will pollute this planet more in his lifetime than will eighty citizens of India in theirs. The levelling off of population growth in this country is the most urgent conservation undertaking of the next generation. We cannot hope to control contamination and blight if we race headlong down the road to a doubled population – and a certain quadrupling of the national demand for water, raw materials, energy and open space.

Overpopulation will, *ipso facto*, drive much of our wildlife to extinction. Because most larger animals must have a separate habitat, they cannot thrive and reproduce in close proximity with man. If we double and redouble our population, these animals can no longer exist. The eagle and the elk will become memories, or rare phenomena of some remnant wilderness which must be permanently banned to man in order to ensure their survival. But weeds will remain with us, and with them weedy birds and animals such as the rat, the roach, and the starling, the species that thrive in man's polluted personal environment.

2. *The rollback of air and water pollution is vital.* Pollution is the paramount, immediate threat to wildlife. Unless tough, effective pollution control laws are passed and rigorously enforced in the next five years, we run the risk that millions of acres of land and water will become so befouled that in all parts of the United States wild things will slowly expire – the victims of our ruthless drive for material goods and goals.

3. *We need a national land use policy.* We must slow down the needless asphaltizing of the land and preserve the oxygen-producing open space that future generations will require. We also desperately need to purchase all the available beaches, parklands, marshes and open spaces near the urbanized areas of the country to preserve the environmental values they offer both man and wildlife.

4. *Dams, seacoast dredging and river "channeling" projects in all*

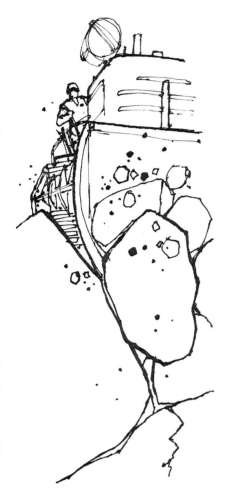

parts of the country must be halted and each one questioned on environmental grounds. I am convinced that this generation will be more honoured by posterity for the dams and canals we *don't* build than for those we do. Some of the nation's finest areas of unspoiled habitat are involved in these plans. Already over 10,000 miles of rivers and streams in the Appalachian Mountains have been choked by acid drainage from coal strip mines. This is typical of the tragic price we have been willing to pay for short-term national growth.

5. *We must develop scientific guidelines that will enable us to sharply restrict, or eliminate, existing "predator control" programmes.* These programmes are currently being pressed by stockmen in various parts of the country. More than the survival or destruction of the coyote, the mountain lion, the wolf and the golden eagle is involved, for potent poisons and other lethal devices have a chain reaction on other wildlife. It is urgent that sensitive, ecologically sound policies be developed to replace the outdated "kill-bounty" programmes of the past.

Above all, henceforth, we must think and act as stewards, not just of the American earth, but of this planet. There can be no higher task, nor one that concerns us more intimately. As we attempt it, this injunction of the Santa Barbara Declaration of Environmental Rights could serve as our personal creed:

> "We must find the courage to take upon ourselves
> as individuals responsibility for the welfare of the
> whole environment, treating our own back yards as if
> they were the world and the world as if it were our
> back yard."

Regaining Paradise

The object of this book is to tell some of the story of world conservation, to show that the problems are global and that they have to be internationally shared, and to demonstrate that, while conservation is a job – indeed, a duty – for governments and the taxpayers that support them, it is also viewed as a job by private citizens the world over, who have formed a new international movement.

The World Wildlife Fund was founded in 1961 and by its tenth birthday it will have raised and spent £2 million or nearly $5 million. As its target, WWF International has worked out the sum of £2.3 million or $5.6 million *annually*, to be raised and spent all over the globe on our planet's environment and all the plants and animals that dwell therein. This figure is a highly educated estimate of the order of annual expenditure that *could* enable the ecology of environment to emerge from its present crisis and turn the corner.

That thoughtful zoologist and conservationist Desmond Morris called a recent book of his *The Naked Ape*, and the thousands who read it were stirringly reminded of Animal Number One's place in nature. The whole point is that man is a very intelligent and powerful higher animal, who is, and always must be, part of nature, and that he can only tidy up the world by knowing himself, understanding his own instincts and drives, and evolving a situation in which, organized freely and internationally, he can create a campaign from which he emerges as the servant, and no longer the master, of the environment he shares with over a million other animal species.

From Desmond Morris's book title we can steal APE, a good acronym for the three main tasks of the Conservation International. This currently presents itself in the form of two great, cooperative, brother bodies: the International Union for Conservation of Nature and Natural Resources (IUCN), and the World Wildlife Fund (WWF). Until lately, IUCN and WWF have shared headquarters in Morges, Switzerland, in a country that is a great host to international causes. WWF is now moving down the road to Geneva to give IUCN more room at Morges; but the link remains as strong as ever.

APE = Analysis + Programmes + Education; and that is just what WWF spends its money on.

Without Analysis and the intelligence files and systems that go with it international conservation could not get off the ground. The principal international analyst is IUCN, supported by the research departments of great foundations and universities the world over, and by other closely related international organizations such as ICBP (the International Council for Bird Preservation), IBP (the International Biological Programme) and the official internationals UNO, UNESCO, FAO and WHO, not to mention the Council of Europe and the Organization of African Unity.

Under the Analysis heading then, WWF supports a world survey for conservation requirements, without which no programme can be designed. Based on this survey, action under the P for Programmes heading can be, and is being, deployed.

Programmes are of three main kinds:

1. Survival Programmes concentrated on the preservation and rehabilitation of endangered animals and plants, based on the Red Data Books kept by IUCN's Survival Service Commission. Special drives are now under way to conserve vulnerable mammal groups like lemurs, great apes, big cats, rhinos and some antelopes and deer, endangered bird groups like birds of prey, waterfowl and some parrots; overhunted reptile groups like marine turtles and the members of the crocodile family; relict fishes and amphibians; rare butterflies; and succulent plants.

2. Habitat Programmes, which concentrate on what the international conservationists now call "biotopes" – ecological communities whose very pattern and network is in danger of destruction or grave erosion by human development. High on the programme list are the conservation of endangered wetlands, which man has been claiming from nature for hundreds of years under the pious-sounding double-talk slogan that he is somehow "reclaiming" them.

Mountain ranges have marvellous "island"-type special faunas and floras each with its own unique ecological personality. Many of these, all over the world, are under development pressures. Oceanic islands, as biotopes, have been under terrible pressures, and have the highest extinction-rate of any habitats in the world.

And some biotopes of the sea are in grave danger from over-fishing and pollution, for it is to the sea that the rubbish and excretions of man's burgeoning, effluent society go. Wildlife can still be suffering from the aftermath of a disaster like the wreck of the *Torrey Canyon* years after the industries concerned have written off their financial losses.

3. Regional Programmes, which concentrate on countries that have special problems and need special help. Most of them lie in the continents that begin with A. In Africa special IUCN and other missions, and funds provided by the WWF, have been and are helping Ethiopia, Kenya, Malagasy, Tanzania and Uganda. In Asia such programmes are serving Indonesia, Pakistan and the Philippines, in particular. In the Americas Ecuador and Peru have special support, because conservation is a vital facet of their development.

The E of APE stands for Education; for the promotion of conservation teaching and training. As I write a whole system of specialized schools in wildlife management is evolving in Africa, especially in those areas where the language of teaching can be English or French.

Under the A for Analysis heading the WWF has given generously to surveys all over the world. By 1970 the WWF's annual grant to the IUCN for all its devoted work had reached $100,000 (£41,666); this embraced all the commissions of the IUCN whose staff are based on Morges and whose members (whose attendance visits are usually financed by their national academies, conservation societies and foundations, or are paid for out of their private pockets) are drawn from over fifty nations all round the world.

WWF's own international Board of Trustees has as its President H.R.H. The Prince of the Netherlands, with the distinguished conservationists Peter Scott of the U.K. and Dr Lukas Hoffman of Switzerland serving as Vice-Presidents. Its members come from Germany, India, Peru, the United States, France, Sweden and South Africa, thus representing ten of the countries with strong private and charitable funding of nature conservation.

Besides the international Board of Trustees, there are fourteen National Appeals of the WWF. With their Presidents, these are Great Britain (H.R.H. The Duke of Edinburgh), U.S.A. (past-President General Dwight D. Eisenhower, present President Dr Ira N. Gabrielson), Switzerland (Dr Karl Brunner), The Netherlands (H.R.H. The Prince of the Netherlands), Germany (Dr Eugen Gerstenmaier), Austria (Konsul Manfred Mautner Markhof), Belgium (S.A. le Prince Antoine de Ligne), India (Lt.-Col. H. H. Maharaja Fatesinghrao, Gaekwad of Baroda), Italy (Marchese Mario Incisa della Rochetta), France (Ministre Jean Sainteny), Canada (General Samuel Findlay Clark), Pakistan (General A. M. Yahya, F.P.K., H.J., President of Pakistan), Republic of South Africa (Dr Anton E. Rupert) and Spain (H.R.H. Prince Don Juan Carlos de Borbón). National Appeals may be organized soon in Sweden, Japan and Brazil. Of the money collected by the National Appeals, as much or more is spent abroad as in the country that originates the National Appeal.

WWF's great grant to IUCN keeps it going and has been until lately its chief source of funds. The analysis and intelligence role of IUCN has a vital Operations Intelligence Unit, which works through six commissions: the Commission on Ecology, the Survival Service Commission, the Commission on Landscape Planning, the Commission on Legislation, the Commission on Education and the International Commission on National Parks.

Besides IUCN there are other closely associated international conservation units whose work the WWF nourishes. The International Waterfowl Research Project works closely with Project MAR, whose job is the rehabilitation of the wetlands of the world, starting with those of Europe, North Africa and the Middle East. MAR has so far concentrated largely on the wetlands of France from which so much can be learned. Thousands of pounds have already been wisely spent by the two bodies, with a hundred wetland reserves in France alone to show for it.

Another strongly grant-aided body is the International Council for Bird Preservation. This works in permanent liaison with IUCN, especially with IUCN's Survival Service Commission, for which it undertakes the compilation of the bird volume of the Red Data Book.

The WWF has also financed, and continues to finance, special continental analytical missions which have surveyed and reported on the conservation situation in Australasia, the Indo-Pakistan subcontinent, Indonesia, the Philippines and other countries of Southeast Asia, Central America, México, Ecuador and other South American countries, Ethiopia and other African countries. The gamut of activity round the world shows the World Wildlife Fund to be an international grant body with extremely positive notions of balanced duty to the cause of conservation. The money is tidily and effectively spent, and there are results to show for it.

Conservation is in, and these days world leaders neglect it at their peril. Some world leaders fortunately have their heart in it. India's Prime Minister, Mrs Indira Ghandi, spoke most eloquently for them, and for us all, in her address to the tenth General Assembly of IUCN, which took place in New Delhi in 1969.

"Man has lived by the notion that he has unrestricted licence to exploit Nature and its resources. Through agriculture and animal husbandry he learnt early in history that the land takes care of him only if he took care of it. Even so, his respect for forest and pasture was always subjected to his own greed. With the advent of the industrial age, exploitation took new shape. The problems created by pollution of air and water, and by fear of the depletion of the mineral resources of the earth, have created a belated realization that we should be conservers, not destroyers, of this planet. For the first time we have also become aware of the problems created by the geometric progression of human population. Administrators and Governments are now conscious that it is only through the rational use of the earth's resources that they can ensure the future welfare of mankind. But the conservationists are still at the beginning of the battle. People must be re-educated to take a long-term view of the human environment."

Extinct and Endangered Birds and Mammals of the World

1969 December 31 as known to IUCN

ull endangered and extinct species are listed, with the exception of some species in the Red Data Book on which information is relatively small and which are omitted for reasons of space; and a selection of species is also made of which one or some, but not all races are extinct or in danger. The complete Red Data Books can be purchased from IUCN, 1110 Morges, Switzerland. The expression "relict" is used to describe a distribution that has declined and become fractioned into very small local populations.

HEAVY TYPE Species living in 1600 now globally extinct. Races, of species still living, globally extinct since 1600.

GREEN TYPE Formerly in danger but now out of it enough for its sheet in the official Red Data Book of the International Union for Conservation of Nature and Natural Resources to have been replaced by a green sheet, which means a formal withdrawal from the Red Data Book.

RED TYPE In such danger as to earn pink (red) sheet in the Red Data Book "a critically endangered form."

ORDINARY TYPE Other endangered forms.

Order SPHENISCIFORMES
Family SPHENISCIDAE, penguins.

Galápagos penguin, Spheniscus mendiculus. Confined to the Galápagos Islands, Ecuador. Population estimated c. 5,000 birds 1962 December but since 1965 perhaps no more than 2,000. A

Order AEPYORNITHIFORMES
Family AEPYORNITHIDAE, elephant birds.

Great elephant bird, Aepyornis maximus. Survived in south Madagascar to c. 1649.

Order APTERYGIFORMES
Family EMEIDAE, lesser moas.

Okoweka, Megalapteryx didinus. North and South Islands, New Zealand, latest date not earlier than A.D. 1785, South Island.

Burly lesser moa, Euryapteryx gravis. North and South Islands, New Zealand, latest dates South Island c. A.D. 1640 or possibly early European times (A.D. 1773 or after).

Family DINORNITHIDAE, great moas.

Brawny great moa, Dinornis torosus. South Island, New Zealand, latest date c. A.D. 1670.

Order PODICIPITIFORMES
Family PODICIPITIDAE, grebes.

Titicaca grebe, Podiceps micropterus. Small population confined to Lake Titicaca, Bolivia.

Junin grebe, Podiceps taczanowskii. Small population confined to Lake Junin, Peru; in pollution danger.

Alaotra dabchick, Podiceps rufolavatus. Small population confined to Lake Alaotra, Madagascar.

Giant pied-billed grebe, Podilymbus gigas. Confined to Lake Atitlan, Guatemala, where c. 100 pairs 1929 and 1936. In 1964 only 100 birds, in 1966 only 86 birds. Wardening began 1965.

Order PROCELLARIIFORMES
Family DIOMEDEIDAE, albatrosses.

Waved albatross, Diomedea irrorata. Breeds only on Hood Island in Galápagos, Ecuador, where c. 6,000–7,000 birds 1962.

Short-tailed albatross, Diomedea albatrus. Formerly nested on at least 8 islands in the North Pacific, where the population in the 19th century may have been a million. Since 1936 has bred only on Torishima off Japan. Here fowlers reduced the population to under 100 in 1953. Wardened since 1957, the island population recovered from 7 occupied nests in the late 1950s to 23 in 1966. Volcanic eruptions (last 1965) may endanger the colony.

Family PROCELLARIIDAE, petrels and shearwaters.

Majenta petrel or Chatham Island taiko, Pterodroma majentae. Known from but 1 specimen collected in 1867; but may be represented by bones collected on Chatham Island, New Zealand. This island is to be explored in search of this mysterious species.

Diablotin, Pterodroma hasitata.
P.h. caribbaea, the Jamaica race, probably became extinct in c. 1880.
P.h. hasitata formerly bred abundantly on Guadeloupe, Hispaniola (Haiti), Dominica and Martinique in the West Indies, but in the first half of the present century

all known colonies had disappeared, and the species was known only from records at sea until c. 4,000 breeding birds were found on Morne la Salle in Haiti.

Cahow, Pterodroma cahow. Confined to Bermuda, where discovered and heavily exploited for food in the early 17th century, this petrel was unknown for nearly 3 centuries until rediscovered in 1906 and 1935. A nesting colony was found in 1951 on small islets in the Castle Harbour Island group of the archipelago. The number of occupied breeding burrows in the 1960s was just over 20 (with an annual output of 6 to 8 young) and the sites are now protected and managed.

Family OCEANITIDAE, storm petrels.

Guadalupe storm petrel, Oceanodroma macrodactyla. Formerly bred on Guadalupe Island off Baja California, Pacific México; considered extinct since 1912.

Order PELECANIFORMES
Family SULIDAE, gannets and boobies.

Abbott's booby, Sula abbotti, nested on Assumption Island in Indian Ocean to c. 1936, but now confined to Christmas Island (same ocean), where latest count of 2,000 or more pairs in 1967 may represent a real increase in population during the previous quarter-century.

Family PHALACROCORACIDAE, cormorants.

Spectacled cormorant, Phalacrocorax perspicillatus. North Pacific; last alive on Bering Island, eastern Siberia c. 1852.

Galápagos flightless cormorant, Nannopterum harrisi. Breeds only on Albemarle and Narborough in the Galápagos Islands, Ecuador. A population estimated at 3,000–5,000 birds in 1962 had dropped to c. 1,000 in 1965 and perhaps fewer in 1969.

Family FREGATIDAE, frigate birds.

Ascension frigate bird, Fregata aquila. Confined to Boatswain Bird Island off Ascension Island, South Atlantic, where c. 8,000–10,000 breeding birds 1958.

Order CICONIIFORMES
Family ARDEIDAE, herons.

Flightless night heron, Nycticorax megacephalus. Rodriguez Island, Indian Ocean, where survived to c. 1730.

Wildlife Crisis

Family CICONIIDAE, storks.

White stork, *Ciconia ciconia*, 3 races. The Korean or Oriental race, *C.c. boyciana*, formerly bred in Russian Amurland, and may have bred in Manchuria and Korea. Now it is probably confined to Japan where it is presently restricted to one hill in west-central Honshu, and has a tiny population (in 1966 only 9 adults) in Hyogo prefecture, and an even smaller one in Fukui prefecture. Despite Government protection it remains one of the rarest birds of the world.

Family PLATALEIDAE, ibises and spoonbills.

Giant ibis, *Thaumatibis gigantea*. Confined to the Mekong basin in Cambodia, with a world population probably not more than a few hundred. **B**

Japanese crested ibis, *Nipponia nippon*. Formerly nested north to Russian Ussuriland, west to Shensi or possibly Szechwan in China, south to Chekiang in China, east to Japan. By 1930 reduced to c. 25–40 birds on the Noto Peninsula and Sado Island in west Honshu, Japan; by 1967 probably only 8 individuals on Sado. The bird, one of the rarest in the world, enjoys complete protection. **C**

Order ANSERIFORMES
Family ANATIDAE, swans, geese and ducks.

Poua, *Cygnus sumnerensis*. New Zealand; last Chatham Island c. 1690.

Trumpeter swan, *Cygnus buccinator*. This had a wide breeding range in North America before the shotgun days of the 19th century. By 1932 the whole population on nesting grounds in the U.S. outside Alaska was estimated at no more than 57 adults, mostly in and near Yellowstone National Park. Since then the Montana-Wyoming-Idaho population has been built up under government protection and colonies have been established in South Dakota, and a breeding population has been discovered in Alaska. In 1961 the Alaskan-Canadian (British Columbia, Alberta and now Manitoba) population was estimated at c. 1,300 birds, and by 1966 the total (world) North American population at c. 2,200.

Néné or Hawaiian goose, *Branta sandvicensis*. Formerly bred on Hawaii and Maui in the Hawaiian Islands; declined, after European colonization, in 18th century; probably extinct Maui by 1900. By 1947 only 50 birds – wild and captive – were estimated to be left on Hawaii, and none anywhere else. Captive breeding by the Wildfowl Trust in England started at Slimbridge, Gloucestershire, in 1952 and when the first imported gander died in 1963 he was the ancestor of over 230 birds. By 1966 the world population was over 500 and captive-bred stock from

A Galápagos penguin

B Giant ibis

C Japanese crested ibis

D Cereopsis *or* Cape Barren goose

Hawaii and (mostly) Slimbridge had been released in Hawaii and had restocked Maui. Slimbridge bred 283 nénés in 1952-69 and has sent 144 to Maui in 5 consignments 1962–69. In the State of Hawaii two sanctuaries totalling 18,000 acres were declared by 1964 and under intensive management the official bird of the fiftieth American state now thrives.

Cereopsis *or* Cape Barren goose, *Cereopsis novaehollandiae*. Australia; islands of west and south coasts and in Bass Strait; recovering from a low population. **D**

Crested shelduck, *Tadorna cristata*. Known only from southern Russian Ussuriland, Korea and Japan; was believed extinct by 1943; but sight records near Vladivostok in 1964 may be valid. **E**

White-winged wood duck, *Cairina scutulata*. Rare and decreasing throughout its wide range from northeastern Assam through Burma, Western Thailand and Malaysia to Sumatra and Java, under hunting pressure and habitat degradation.

Mallard, *Anas platyrhynchos*, 5 races. Hawaiian duck or koloa, *A.p. wyvilliana*. Formerly resident in most of the Hawaiian Islands is now restricted to Niihau, Kauai and eastern Oahu. In 1964, after some recovery, the population was estimated as c. 500, mostly on Kauai; of this total 60 or 70 were in captive collections.

Laysan teal, *Anas laysanensis*. Restricted to Laysan at the far western end of the Hawaiian archipelago, where reduced to 20 birds or less in the 1920s and 1930s. The island population rose (after rabbit clearance) to a maximum of c. 688 in 1961 and holds up despite occasional hurricanes. The population in world aviculture is over 150, most of which are captive bred.

Madagascar teal, *Anas bernieri*. Extremely rare, and perhaps found only in the Bekopaka-Maintirano area of west central Madagascar.

Brown teal or pateke, *Anas aucklandica*, 3 races. Auckland Island flightless teal, *A.a. aucklandica*, Auckland archipelago of New Zealand, where extremely rare or extinct on main island, but apparently holding its own on 6 off-lying islets. New Zealand brown teal, *A.a. chlorotis*, main islands of New Zealand, where now restricted to Auckland province in North Island, Southland in South Island, and the Stewart Island archipelago where it is rare.

Campbell Island flightless teal, *A.a. nesiotis*, is restricted to Campbell Island 500 miles south of New Zealand; race is based on single specimen collected in 1886 and on a pair collected in 1944; has only been otherwise recorded from sight records in 1943 and 1958. May be extinct and is certainly in danger.

Pink-headed duck, *Rhodonessa caryphyllacea*. **India; last recorded Bihar 1935; last captive in England 1944.**

Labrador duck, *Camptorhynchus labratorium*. **Eastern North America; last shot on Long Island, New York 1875.**

Auckland Island merganser, *Mergus australis*. **Auckland Island, New Zealand where extinct 1905.**

Order FALCONIFORMES
Family CATHARTIDAE, New World vultures.

California condor, *Gymnogyps californinus*. This, and a directly ancestral species, ranged in Pleistocene times over California, Nevada, Arizona, New Mexico, Florida, Texas and Nuevo Léon in México. By the 19th century it had withdrawn to the states west of the Rockies, and by the 20th century was probably breeding only in California. By 1946–47 the Audubon Society survey found only 30 non-nesting adults, 10 adults at 5 nests and 20 others, chiefly immature. From 1960 the population fell to c. 42 in 1963–64, with 20 non-nesting adults, 8 adults at active nests and 14 others of which at least 10 were immature. The breeding grounds, now in only 2 counties, are threatened by poisons, hunting, and a dam project, and defended by law and public opinion. The future of this classic bird depends on improved law enforcement.

Family ACCIPITRIDAE, vultures, hawks and eagles.

Cuban hook-billed kite, *Chondrohierax wilsoni*. Now reduced to a relict population near Guantánamo, in Oriente province of Cuba.

Snail kite, *Rostrhamus sociabilis*, 4 races. "Everglade kite," *R.s. plumbeus*. Confined to Florida, where has now withdrawn to Lake Okeechobee. Despite careful wardening, and a refuge at Loxahatchee, the stock was down to 10 birds in 1965.

Gundlach's hawk, *Accipiter gundlachi*. Very rare and localized in Cuba, where under shooting pressure from farmers.

Galápagos hawk, *Buteo galapagoensis*. Formerly bred on most islands of this archipelago 600 miles west of Ecuador, but has lately become extinct on 3 and survives as a breeder only on 8, though on some tenuously, with a total population of under 200 birds (in 1962).

Hawaiian hawk, *Buteo solitarius*. Indigenous to the island of Hawaii (only), where steadily reduced in the present century to a population estimated in 1965 to be fewer than 200, perhaps even fewer than 100 birds.

Monkey-eating eagle, *Pithecophaga jef-*

E Crested shelduck

F Monkey-eating eagle

G Mauritius kestrel

feryi. Philippines, where formerly bred on Leyte and Samar but now restricted to Mindañao and (tiny population) Luzon. Under terrible hunting and collecting pressure: fewer than 100 birds may survive. Its future dpends on wardening and the enforcement of hunting and export regulations, and of new laws. **F**

Imperial eagle, *Aquila heliaca*, 2 races. Spanish race, *A.h. adalberti*. Formerly bred in Algeria, Morocco and Portugal, but now probably survives as a breeder only in Spain, where the population is about 100. It is doubtless the most endangered bird in Europe. Fortunately about 7 nests are yearly active in the great Coto Doñana Reserve.

Family FALCONIDAE, caracaras and falcons.

Guadalupe caracara, *Caracara lutosa*. Guadalupe Island off Baja California, Pacific México; extinct by 1900.

Mauritius kestrel, *Falco punctatus*. Reasonably common in this Indian Ocean island early in the preset century, this species may not have numbered more than 10–15 birds in 1963. **G**

Seychelles kestrel, *Falco araea*. Up to 1940 nested on at least 5 islands of this Indian Ocean archipelago; by 1959 restricted to Mahé, where very rare.

Order GALLIFORMES
Family CRACIDAE, curassows, guans and chachalacas.

Horned guan, *Oreophasis derbianus*. Resident in México and southwest Guatemāla, where so far recorded from only 24 localities. Has been reduced in numbers by human pressure. Not more than 13 occupied areas have been lately identified, and a reserve is projected at El Triunfo in Chiapas, where hunting has been illegal lately.

Family MEGAPODIIDAE, megapodes.

Kermadec megapode, *Megapodius* sp. An undescribed megapode inhabited the floor of the crater of Sunday Island, Kermadecs, New Zealand Pacific, disappearing in the eruption of 1876.

La Pérouse's megapode, *Megapodius laperouse*, 2 races. Palau (West Carolines) race, *M.l. senex*, was common in the whole Palau group in *c*. 1880, but has withdrawn, with the advance of human population, from at least 3 islands, and survives on perhaps 4 or more others with a population perhaps under 100. The Marianas race, *M.l. laperouse*, once lived on at least 9 islands from Asuncion in the north, to Guam in the south. It now survives only on 5. From the largest island, Guam, it probably disappeared by 1890.

219

Pritchard's megapode, *Megapodius pritchardi*. Endemic only on volcanic Niuafo'ou off the Tongan group between Samoa and Fiji, where a small population holds its own and has survived 7 eruptions since 1953. **A**

Family TETRAONIDAE, grouse.

Prairie chicken, *Tympanuchus cupido*, 4 races.

Heath hen, *T.c. cupido*, formerly ranged from New England to Virginia. By 1830 confined to Martha's Vineyard island off Massachusetts, where it finally became extinct in 1926 or perhaps 1932.

Greater prairie chicken, *T.c. pinnatus*, formerly widespread over the prairies of southern Canada and central U.S.A., this race has been vanishing and is probably extinct in Saskatchewan and 6 of the United States. Big efforts are being made to establish reserves. Attwater's prairie chicken, *T.c. attwateri*, extinct in Louisiana by 1919, is now confined to 11 counties in central Texas, with a population of fewer than 750 in 1965. Lesser prairie chicken, *T.c. pallidicinctus*, is still found in all 4 states of its old range, eastern New Mexico, southeast Colorado, west Oklahoma and panhandle Texas; has a fluctuating population around 30,000.

Family PHASIANIDAE, quail, partridges, pheasants and fowl.

Himalayan mountain quail, *Ophrysia superciliosa*. Northwest Himalayas (Punjab, Kumaon), extinct 1868. B

Western tragopan, *Tragopan melanocephalus*. Formerly endemic in parts of northwest Pakistan, west Kashmir and Garhwal, this sub-Himalayan pheasant may now have only a tiny relict population in Himachal Pradesh.

Blyth's tragopan, *Tragopan blythi*, 2 races. Southern race, *T.b. blythi*, now lives in a very reduced zone on the Assam-Burma border. Northern race, *T.b. molesworthi*, has been lately found in old range from Bhutan to northern Assam; its status in Tibet is unknown.

Cabot's tragopan, *Tragopan caboti*. Confined to the forests of Fukien and Kwangtung, perhaps also Kiangsi and Hunan, in China; decreasing.

Sclater's monal, *Lophophorus sclateri*. A montane bird of southeast Tibet, north Assam, Burma and west China; has not been seen in the wild since 1938.

Chinese monal, *Lophophorus lhuysi*. Highland China; range may now have contracted to west Szechwan; extremely rare.

Imperial pheasant, *Lophura imperialis*. Endemic on the borders of North and South Vietnam near the Laos frontier;

A Pritchard's megapode

B Himalayan mountain quail

C Swinhoe's pheasant

D Elliot's pheasant

E Mikado pheasant

the present status of this last of the pheasants to be discovered is unknown.

Edwards's pheasant, *Lophura edwardsi* Northernmost South Vietnam; status unknown.

Swinhoe's pheasant, *Lophura swinhoei* Hill forests of Taiwan, where under hunting and lumbering pressure. Aviculture bred birds from England have been liberated as an experiment. **C**

White eared pheasant, *Crossoptilon crossoptilon*, 4 races. Szechwan race, *C.c. crossoptilon*, central Szechwan, eastern and central Sikang to northwest Yunnan Tibetan race, *C.c. drouyni*, southeast Tibet, northern and western Sikang Dolan's race, *C.c. dolani*, southern Tsing hai. Harman's race, *C.c. harmani*, south east Tibet and northern Assam. The populations are very low, but informa tion is scarce.

Brown eared pheasant, *Crossoptilon mantchuricum*. Has a confined, and now withdrawn and small distribution in montane China and northern and west ern Hopeh and northwest and central Shansi. Is extinct in Chihli.

Cheer pheasant, *Catreus wallichi*. Rare and relict in Hazaran Afghanistan, Kash mir, Punjab, Himachal Pradesh and northern Uttar Pradesh in India, and western and central Nepal.

Elliot's pheasant, *Syrmaticus ellioti*. Has a shrinking distribution in Chekiang Fukien and southern Anhwei in south east China; is extinct in Kwangtung. **D**

Hume's pheasant, *Syrmaticus humiae*, 2 races. Typical race *S.h. humiae*, Assam northeast India, Burma west of Irra waddy; and Burma race *S.h. burmanicus* northern Burma east of Irrawaddy, south west Yunnan and northern Thailand The range may persist, but the population in certain areas is declining.

Mikado pheasant, *Syrmaticus mikado* Mountains of Taiwan between 6,000 and 10,000 feet, where rare and declining perhaps only a few hundred survive. **E**

Palawan peacock pheasant, *Polyplectron emphanum*. Once fairly common, now rare on this Philippine island since clearance of the forests began 20 year ago.

Order GRUIFORMES
Family GRUIDAE, cranes.

Japanese crane, *Grus japonensis*. For merly bred in Manchuria and Russian Ussuriland, but now breeds perhaps on the Asian mainland only by Lake Khanka in Ussuriland. The world breeding head quarters is the Kucharota National Re fuge in Hokkaido, Japan where the popu lation, under protection management grew from under 20 birds in 1924 to 172 in 1965. The 134 birds in zoos in 1966 (abou

) per cent captive bred) may have repre-
nted a third of the world population. **F**

hooping crane, *Grus americana*. For-
erly bred in central and western provin-
al Canada and the middle west United
ates south to Iowa, and Louisiana;
igrated to winter on the Gulf coast of
.S. and México, as far south in México
Tamaulipas and central México. Since
40 has bred only in the extensive Wood
uffalo muskegs south of the Great Slave
ake in Mackenzie, Canada and has
intered only on the Aransas Refuge
id sometimes Matagorda and other
ar-by coastal islands of Texas. Enjoys
gal protection with maximum enforce-
ent in Canada and U.S.A. and, as
idenced by annual winter census in
exas and careful studbook of captive
pulation which is now breeding, had a
orld wild population of 30 in 1933, only
14 in 1937, 29 in 1938, 35 in 1939, 31 in
40, 25 in 1941, 28 in 1942, in 30s 1943–51,
20s 1952–57, in 30s 1958–63, 33 in 1959,
in 1960, 38 in 1961, 32 in 1962, 33 in
63, 42 in 1964, 44 in 1965, 43 in 1966, 48
1967 and 50 in 1968, By 1965 there were
in captivity, in 1967 5 young were zoo-
ed, in 1969 18 were captive, 12 at the
sh and Wildlife Service Station at
tuxent. **G**

amily RALLIDAE, rails.

hatham Island banded rail, *Rallus
effenbachi*. **Chatham Island, east of
ew Zealand, extinct by 1840.**

Jake Island rail, *Rallus wakensis*. **Not
und since 1945, extinguished by
apanese garrison in this Pacific
land.**

ahiti red-billed rail, *Rallus ecaudata*.
ather doubtfully survived on the
ahiti Pacific archipelago until c.
25.

hatham Island rail, *Rallus modestus*.
hatham and Mangare Islands east
f New Zealand, where extinct c.
00.

ew Caledonian wood rail, *Tricho-
nnas lafresnayanus*. **New Caledonia;
st found in 1904.**

ord Howe wood rail, *Tricholimnas syl-
estris*. **Lord Howe Island, 400 miles
ist of New South Wales, Australia,
here restricted to highlands and rare.**

apata rail, *Cyanolimnas cerverai*.
nown only from a limited zone of the
apata Swamp in Cuba north of Santo
omás, where confined to a few square
iles of bog threatened by drainage
hemes.

iji bar-winged rail, *Nesoclopeus poeci-
pterus*. **Ovalau and Viti Levu in Fiji,
here extinct 1890.**

an den Broecke's red rail, *Aphanap-*

F Japanese crane

G Whooping crane

H Takahé

teryx bonasia. **Mauritius in Indian
Ocean; extinct c. 1675.**

Flightless blue rail, *Aphanapteryx
leguati*. **Rodriguez in Indian Ocean;
extinct c. 1730.**

Ascension flightless crake, *Crecopsis*
**sp. Ascension Island, South Atlantic;
extinct 1656.**

Laysan rail, *Porzanula palmeri*. **Laysan
Island, where became extinct after
introduction to Midway Island, North
Pacific, where extinct 1944.**

Hawaiian rail, *Pennula sandwichensis*.
Hawaii Island; extinct 1893.

Kusaie rail, *Aphanolimnas monasa*. **Kusaie Island, Pacific; extinct 1827.**

Samoan wood rail, *Pareudiastes pacificus*. **Savaii Island in Samoa, Pacific;
extinct 1873.**

Takahé, *Notornis mantelli*. Formerly
fairly widespread in North and South
Islands, New Zealand. The last (and
only) North Island sighting by Europeans was in 1894. Now reduced to a
small population in the Lake Te Anau
area of South Island where rediscovered
in 1948, having been thought extinct for
years. The main colony in Takahé Valley,
now protected, is stable and has a population of *c*. 200–300 birds scattered in
groups over *c*. 200 square miles. **H**

Family RHYNOCHETIDAE, kagu.

Kagu, *Rhynochetos jubatus*. Confined to
New Caledonia, where in 1860 probably
widespread over the forest of the whole
island. Now has a relict distribution,
supported by legal protection and a
reserve project. It is very rare, and the
only member of an unique suborder.

Family OTIDIDAE, bustards.

Great Indian bustard, *Choriotis nigri-
ceps*. Formerly endemic to most of India
from Punjab to Mysore and northern
Madras, this had its range halved by
about 1924 and since *c*. 1938 has been
reduced to a tiny population in West
Pakistan and east Punjab, with a very
scattered population in Rajasthan, Madhya Pradesh, Gujarat, Maharashtra and
probably Mysore. Now officially protected by all Indian states, the status of
this great bird depends on law enforcement and public education.

Order CHARADRIIFORMES
Family CHARADRIIDAE, plovers and
turnstones.

New Zealand shore plover, *Thinornis
novaeseelandiae*. Up to 1880 was endemic in North and South Islands of New
Zealand and had been recorded from the
Auckland Islands; but since then has
been confined to the Chatham Islands,

221

where by 1937 was apparently confined to Rangatira (540 acres only) with a population of *c.* 140 birds. It was "holding its own" there in 1961 but is one of the rarer and most localized birds in the world, and needs sanctuary protection as well as the present law.

Family SCOLOPACIDAE, snipe, sandpipers and allies.

Cooper's sandpiper, *Calidris cooperi.* **Known from one specimen collected on Long Island, New York, in 1833.**

Tahiti sandpiper, *Prosobonia leucoptera.* **Otaheite and Eimeo; extinct 1777.**

Hudsonian godwit, *Limosa haemastica.* Breeds in Mackenzie and Manitoba and possibly in Keewatin and Franklin, Canada and migrates to southern South America. Was reduced by hunting pressure, mainly in eastern North America on passage migration, to a very small population in the 1920s but since the National Resources Pan-American Treaty of 1941, has recovered and has been considered out of danger since 1958. A

Eskimo curlew, *Numenius borealis.* One of the rarest birds in the world. Formerly bred in northern Canada (only Mackenzie proved, 1823 and the 1860s) and known from passage flocks (some big) in the United States in declining numbers (under hunting pressure) until the 1930s, since recorded only on autumn passage in South Carolina 1956, New Jersey 1959, and Barbados 1963. No spring migrant has been seen anywhere but in Texas since 1926; Texan records are 1945(2), 1950(1), 1952(1), 1959(1), 1960(1), 1961(2), 1962(2), 1963(1), 1964(2) and 1965(1). The last bird in the winter range was seen in Argentina in 1939. The last nesting ground may be in Franklin, or Keewatin, but has not been found.

New Zealand *or* sub-antarctic snipe, *Coenocorypha aucklandica,* 6 races. The 5 surviving races of this snipe are now confined to, and rare in the smaller islands of New Zealand. These are: *C.a. pusilla,* now confined to South-east Island in the Chatham archipelago; *C.a. iredalei,* now confined to South Cape Islands off Stewart Island; *C.a. huegeli,* Snares Island; *C.a. meinertzhagenae,* Antipodes Island; and *C.a. aucklandica,* now confined to Ewing and Adams Islands, Auckland Islands. *C.a. barrierensis,* **Little Barrier Island, extinct 1870.**

Family GLAREOLIDAE, coursers and pratincoles.

Jerdon's courser, *Cursorius bitorquatus.* **Central India, where last collected in Andhra Pradesh in 1900.**

Family LARIDAE, gulls and terns.

Audouin's gull, *Larus audouini.* Confined to the Mediterranean, where for-

A Hudsonian godwit

B Great auk

C Dodo

D Night parrot

E Ground parrot

merly fairly widespread. Now has population estimated at not much mor than 1,000 birds. Its present breedin distribution is on the west of Morocc and Tunisia, on the Chaffarine arch pelago east of Melilla in Spanish Moro co (where *c.* 500 pairs 1966), on islets nea Corsica and Cyprus and in a few sma colonies in the Aegean Sea.

Family ALCIDAE, auks.

Great auk, *Pinguinus impennis.* **Las known living pair killed on Elde Iceland 1844 June 4. B**

Order COLUMBIFORMES.
Family COLUMBIDAE, pigeons.

Mauritius blue pigeon, *Alectroenc nitidissima.* **Mauritius, Indian Ocea extinct 1830.**

Rodriguez blue pigeon, *Alectroena rodericana.* **Rodriguez, Indian Ocea extinct 1693.**

Cloven-feathered dove, *Drepanoptila holosericea.* New Caledonia; relict an reduced.

Giant imperial pigeon, *Ducula goliatl* New Caledonia; relict and reduced.

Mindoro imperial pigeon, *Ducula mi dorensis.* Restricted to Mount Halco on Mindoro in Philippines, where relic

St Helena blue dove, *?Columba* **sp. blue dove seen on St Helena, Sout Atlantic, in 1775, but not since matches with subfossil bones dis covered on the island in 1959, as ye unnamed.**

Bonin wood pigeon, *Columba vers color.* **Bonin Islands (Japan); last see Nakondo Shima, 1889.**

Mauritius pink pigeon, *Columba mayer* Rare and local in the relict forest c southwest Mauritius, Indian Ocean.

Bourbon pink pigeon, *Columba d boisi.* **Réunion, Indian Ocean, extinc 1669.**

Passenger pigeon, *Ectopistes migr torius.* **North America; last died i Cincinnati Zoo 1914 September 1.**

Grenada dove, *Leptotila wellsi.* End mic to Grenada, West Indies, whe has been considered virtually extin though a bird may have been heard i 1929, 2 were shot in 1961, and othe were seen in 1963. Barely survives.

Tana ground dove, *Gallicolumba fe ruginea.* **Tana, New Hebrides, extinc 1774.**

Crested Choiseul pigeon, *Microgour meeki.* **Choiseul, Solomon Islands; ex tinct 1904.**

Family RAPHIDAE, dodo and solitaire

Dodo, *Raphus cucullatus.* **Mauritius Indian Ocean; extinct c. 1681. C**

olitaire, *Raphus solitarius*. Réunion, ndian Ocean; extinct c. 1746.

odriguez solitaire, *Pezophaps soli- ria*. Rodriguez, Indian Ocean; ex- inct c. 1791.

rder PSITTACIFORMES amily PSITTACIDAE, parrots.

lew Caledonian lorikeet, *Vini dia- ema*. New Caledonia; extinct 1860.

Kakapo, *Strigops habroptilus*. Formerly videspread over North and South slands, New Zealand, and possibly also he Chatham Islands. Extinct in the North Island by 1930 (a reintroduced bird urvived till 1934), is now probably estricted to 4 areas of Southland, South sland, with a population probably under 00 birds in all.

light parrot, *Geopsittacus occidentalis*. ormerly endemic in South and Western Australia, is now confined to Western Australia if it still survives. A record rom here in 1960 is unconfirmed; the ast certain sightings are northeast of Mount Farmer between 1912 and 1935. **D**

round parrot, *Pezoporus wallicus*, 3 aces. Tasmanian race, *P.w.leachi*, has rithdrawn somewhat in range, but sur- ives well on the west coast. Eastern ace, *P.w. wallicus*, formerly ranged om Brisbane to beyond Adelaide; is ow probably extinct in Queensland and are and local in New South Wales, outh Australia and Victoria. Western ace, *P.w. flaviventris*, formerly distri- uted along the coastal plain from Perth o Albany, is now known from but two mited areas in Western Australia. **E**

range-fronted kakariki, *Cyanoram- hus malherbi*. South Island, New Zea- and, with a contracted range in high ill scrub from Nelson to Fiordland; are and local.

ahiti kakariki, *Cyanoramphus zea- ndicus*, Tahiti; extinct in c. 1844.

aiatea kakariki, *Cyanoramphus ulie- nus*. Raiatea (South Pacific); never een since first collected in 1774.

Iorned parakeet, *Eunymphicus cornu- is*, 2 races. New Caledonia race, *E.c. ornutus*; very few records in the last 00 years. Uvéa race, *E.c. uvaeensis*, was onfined to Uvéa in Loyalty Islands here very rare; has been lately trans- cated to neighbouring Lifu, where tatus unknown.

range-billed grass parakeet, *Neophema hrysogaster*, 2 races. Tasmanian race, J.c. chrysogaster*, is seldom identified nd probably very rare. Australian race, J.c. mab*, is now probably extinct in New outh Wales and Victoria, and rare in outheast South Australia.

F Turquoise grass parakeet

G Queensland *or* golden-shouldered race of paradise parakeet

H St Lucia parrot

Turquoise grass parakeet, *Neophema pulchella*. In the first third of this cen- tury ranged through southern Queens- land, New South Wales, Victoria and South Australia; has decreased and may now be extinct in the last, but has lately recovered in parts of Queensland. **F**

Beautiful parakeet, *Psephotus pulcher- rimus*. Southeast Queensland and north- central New South Wales; has with- drawn to border area where may have had a population in early 1960s of less than 150 birds.

Paradise parakeet, *Psephotus chrysop- terygius*, 2 races. Arnhem Land *or* hooded race, *P.c. dissimilis*, has been found only, and rarely, in a restricted area of the Northern Territory's Melville Peninsula. Queensland *or* golden-shouldered race, *P.c. chrysopterygius*, has always been very local and rare in a limited area of north Queensland and in the last decade may have numbered less than 250 birds. **G**

Mascarene parrot, *Mascarinus mas- carinus*. Réunion, Indian Ocean; the last known example died in a Munich aviary in 1834.

Broad-billed Mauritian parrot, *Lop- hopsittacus mauritanus*. Mauritius, Indian Ocean; extinct in 1638.

Rodriguez parakeet, *Necropsittacus rodricanus*. Rodriguez, Indian Ocean; extinct c. 1730.

Bourbon parakeet, *Necropsittacus bor- bonicus*. Réunion, Indian Ocean; ex- tinct in 1669.

Rodriguez ring-necked parakeet, *Psittacula exsul*. Rodriguez, Indian Ocean; extinct c. 1875.

Puerto Rican parrot, *Amazona vittata*, 2 races. Puerto Rico race, *A.v. vittata* formerly as widespread as the forests since 1931 has been virtually confined to the 5,600- acre Luguillo National Forest, and had a population of perhaps only 20 in 1970 January. **Culebra race, *A.v. gracilipes*, formerly inhabited Culebra and Vieques islands off Puerto Rico; was extinct by 1912.**

St Vincent parrot, *Amazona guildingi*. Confined to the forests of this 18×11- mile island in the West Indies where has decreased but not with such rapidity as some other island parrots.

St Lucia parrot, *Amazona versicolor*. St Lucia, West Indies. Formerly wide- spread, became restricted to the central forests of the island in the 1950s and is still decreasing. **H**

Imperial parrot, *Amazona imperialis*. Dominica, West Indies. Has now re- treated to the forests of the higher moun- tains where it has been scarce since the

1920s and is now undoubtedly dangerously rare. **A**

Guadeloupe parrot, *Amazona violacea.* **Guadeloupe, West Indies; extinct c. 1722.**

Martinique parrot, *Amazona martinica.* **Martinique, West Indies; extinct c. 1722.**

Guadeloupe conure, *Aratinga labati.* **Guadeloupe, West Indies; extinct c. 1722.**

Carolina parakeet, *Conuropsis carolinensis,* **2 races. Southeast U.S.A.; last died in captivity 1914.**

Thick-billed parrot, *Rhynchopsitta pachyrhyncha,* 2 races. Western race, *R.p. pachyrhyncha,* rare in Sierra Madre Occidental; eastern race, *R.p. terrisi,* nearly if not quite extinct in the Sierra Madre Oriental; in the high Méxican plateau.

Cuban red macaw, *Ara tricolor.* **Cuba; extinct c. 1885. B**

Jamaican red macaw, *Ara gossei.* **Jamaica; extinct c. 1765.**

Jamaican green-and-yellow macaw, *Ara erythrocephala.* **Jamaica; extinct c. 1810.**

Guadeloupe red macaw, *Ara guadeloupensis.* **Gaudeloupe, West Indies; extinct c. 1722.**

Dominican green-and-yellow macaw, *Ara atwoodi.* **Dominica, West Indies; extinct c. 1791.**

Martinique macaw, *Ara martinica.* **Martinique, West Indies; extinct c. 1658.**

Order MUSOPHAGIFORMES
Family MUSOPHAGIDAE, turacos.

Prince Ruspoli's turaco, *Tauraco ruspolii.* Known with certainty from an area of juniper woodland of only c. 10 square miles in highland southwest Ethiopia.

Order CUCULIFORMES
Family CUCULIDAE, cuckoos.

Red-faced malkoha, *Phaenicophaeus pyrrhocephalus.* Peculiar to Ceylon, where range is now reduced to a few patches of heavy jungle in the Central and Uva provinces to c. 5,000 feet.

Delalande's Madagascar coucal, *Coua delalandei.* **Madagascar; extinct 1930.**

Order STRIGIFORMES
Family TYTONIDAE, barn owls.

Soumagne's barn owl, *Tyto soumagnei.* Northeast Madagascar, where not recorded since before 1929 and may be extinct; much of its forest habitat has gone.

A Imperial parrot

B Cuban red macaw

C Seychelles owl

Family STRIGIDAE, typical owls.

Seychelles owl, *Otus insularis.* No confined to Mahé in the Seychelles arch pelago, Indian Ocean. Not found o searches 1931–36 and considered extin but rediscovered in 1959 in very sma numbers at one place in the hills. **C**

Commerson's scops owl, *Otus con mersoni.* **Mauritius, Indian Ocean extinct 1837.**

New Zealand laughing owl, *Sceloglau albifacies,* 2 races. Formerly found o North and South Islands; and Chatha Islands, where extinct.
North Island race, *S.a. rufifacies;* **ex tinct c. 1890. D**
South Island race, *S.a. albifacies,* wa found in Otago, Canterbury and Nelso for most of 19th century; taken for th only time on Stewart Island c. 1880; la fully substantiated record south Cante bury 1914. Since then unconfirmed r cords from Nelson, Southland and Ca terbury (last Nelson c. 1939) sugge the species may just survive.

Rodriguez little owl, *Athene murivor* **Rodriguez, Indian Ocean; extinct 1730.**

Forest spotted owlet, *Athene blewitt* **Central India; extinct c. 1872.**

Order CAPRIMULGIFORMES
Family AEGOTHELIDAE, owlet fro mouths.

New Caledonian owlet frogmout *Aegotheles savesi.* **New Caledonia; e tinct 1880.**

Family CAPRIMULGIDAE, nightjars.

Least pauraque, *Siphonorhis amer canus,* 2 races. Hispaniolan race, *S. brewsteri,* now rare and localized i Hispaniola, and on Gonave confined arid hills.
Jamaican race, *S.a. americanus;* **e tinct 1859.**

Puerto Rican whip-poor-will, *Caprimu gus noctitherus.* Described from foss material in Puerto Rico caves and ident fied with bird collected in 1889. Redi covered (thought extinct since 1911) i 1961 when small but apparently flouris ing population identified near San Jua

Order CORACIIFORMES
Family ALCEDINIDAE, kingfishers.

Ryukyu kingfisher, *Halcyon miyakoe sis.* **Miyako Island in Ryukyu arch pelago, west Pacific, extinct 1887.**

Family BRACHYPTERACIIDAE, grou rollers.

Long-tailed ground roller, *Uratelorn chimaera.* Coastal southwestern Mad gascar, where rare relict population b tween Lake Iotry and Manombo.

Family BUCEROTIDAE, hornbills.

Narcondam hornbill, *Aceros narcondami*. Restricted to Narcondam Island in the Andaman Islands in the Indian Ocean. The population was estimated at *c*. 200 birds in 1927 and needs rechecking.

Order PICIFORMES
Family PICIDAE, woodpeckers.

Fernandina's flicker, *Nesoceleus fernandinae*. Cuba; a rare relict population in Las Villas and Camagüey provinces.

Noguchi's Okinawa woodpecker, *Sapeopipo noguchii*. A very rare resident of virgin forest on Okinawa Island.

Ivory-billed woodpecker, *Campephilus principalis*, 2 races. United States race, *C.p. principalis*, formerly ranged through the heavily wooded bottomlands of the Mississippi river system north to beyond its junction with the Ohio River, and through the wooded bottoms of other great rivers of Mississippi, Louisiana, Alabama, Georgia and South Carolina and the heavily wooded swamps of Florida. By 1930 it was restricted to 1 tract in Louisiana, 1 in South Carolina and perhaps 7 in Florida. In the 1950s the only sightings in the U.S. were unconfirmed records from the Apalachicola swamp in Florida in 1950 and possibly 1952. In 1961–63 there were unconfirmed reports from eastern Texas, and in 1963 an unconfirmed report from Louisiana. A new search campaign is under way for this finest of North American woodpeckers. It may not yet be extinct. The Cuban race, *C.p. bairdi*, formerly ranged all over Cuba, but with forest clearance the population was down to 12 or 13 birds only in the Oriente province by 1956. Sightings have been logged in 1963 and 1968 but no new population information is available. The species, as a whole, is one of the most endangered in the world.

Imperial woodpecker, *Campephilus imperialis*. The world's largest woodpecker; formerly inhabited all the pine-oak forests of the western Sierra Madre, the western backbone of the northern half of México. Since 1960, after much forest clearing and shooting, it has been found in but 5 localities – in Chihuahua, Durango and Nayarit; and is in a serious, relict, danger situation.

Order PASSERIFORMES
Family ACANTHISITTIDAE, New Zealand wrens.

Bush wren, *Xenicus longipes*, 3 races. North Island race, *X.l. stokesi*, was described on 2 specimens taken 1850 on Rimutaka Range in North Island, New Zealand, and never encountered again until rediscovered just below Lake Waikareiti in 1949. There are unconfirmed reports from 4 other North Island places

D North Island race of New Zealand laughing owl

E Bourbon crested starling

F Rothschild's starling

but the race must be relict. South Island race, *X.l. longipes*, has withdrawn since 1880 from probably the whole wooded mainland of South Island and is now scarce and relict in the hills of Fiordland. Stewart Island race, *X.l. variabilis*, once widespread over this southern New Zealand archipelago, seems to have been confined to the South Cape islands since the 1950s, where it survived lately on South Cape Island, Solomon and perhaps Kotiwhenu, and perhaps on Kaimoku whence it was translocated in 1964 from Big South Cape Island where it is now extinct.

Stephen Island wren, *Xenicus lyalli*. Stephen Island, New Zealand, where extinguished by the lighthouse cat in 1894.

Family ATRICHORNITHIDAE, scrub birds.

Noisy scrub bird, *Atrichornis clamosus*. Western Australia, where discovered in 1843 and last collected near Albany in 1889, after which it was thought to be extinct despite unconfirmed reports in 1897 and 1920. It was rediscovered at Two People Bay near Albany in 1961, and by 1966 a population of at least 50 and probably 80 was confirmed; protection has been deployed and the new town site at Two People Bay has been shifted away from the scrub habitat.

Family STURNIDAE, starlings.

Ponapé mountain starling, *Aplonis pelzelni*. Upland Ponapé in Caroline Islands, West Pacific, where very rare.

Kusaie starling, *Aplonis corvina*. Kusaie in Caroline Islands; none recorded since 5 collected 1827 December.

Mysterious starling, *Aplonis mavornata*. Collected on Cook's second voyage probably by J. R. Forster in 1774 on Raiatea in Society Islands, Pacific, though locality and date are not absolutely certain. Never seen again.

Leguat's starling, *Fregilupus rodericanus*. Rodriguez, Indian Ocean; extinct 1832.

Bourbon crested starling, *Fregilupus varius*. Réunion, Indian Ocean; extinct 1862. E

Rothschild's starling, *Leucopsar rothschildi*. Localized and under collection pressure in Bubunan area in northern Bali, East Indies. **F**

Family CALLAEIDAE, wattled crows.

Saddleback, *Creadion carunculatus*, 2 races. North Island (New Zealand) race, *C.c. rufusater*. Formerly widespread on mainland of North Island but probably confined to off-lying islands by 1907.

Here there were probably over 2,000 birds on Hen Island in 1963. Bred on Middle Chicken in 1965 after introduction in 1964. South Island race, *C.c. carunculatus*, was widespread in South and Stewart Islands in early European times. Declined and by 1930s probably confined to Solomon and Big South Cape Islands in Stewart group. In 1960s it was successfully translocated to at least 2 other islands in the group.

Huia, *Heteralocha acutirostris*. North Island, New Zealand, where extinct 1907. A

Kokako, *Callaeas cinerea*, 2 races. North Island (New Zealand) race, *C.c. wilsoni*. Widespread in early European times, this race has now withdrawn to over 15 areas in the remoter parts of the interior of North Island; some of these relict populations appear to be thriving.

South Island race, *C.c. cinerea*. Formerly widespread over South Island and the Stewart Island group, this race was scattered and rare by 1889 and collapsing fast in the 1940s'. Since then it has been reported seldom, from Southland, Nelson, Otago and perhaps Marlborough.

Family CORVIDAE, crows.

Hawaiian crow, *Corvus tropicus*. Confined to the western or Kona coast of Hawaii in Hawaiian Islands, where much reduced in population since forest clearance began in 1890s. An estimate of *c.* 25–50 birds in 1961 has been replaced by a later one of *c.* 250, but the species is clearly very rare. **B**

Family CAMPEPHAGIDAE, cuckoo shrikes.

Mauritius cuckoo shrike, *Coracina typica*. Rare and localized in the relict forest of Mauritius, Indian Ocean.

Réunion cuckoo shrike, *Coracina newtoni*. Réunion, Indian Ocean, where relict and declining in high forested areas; "unlikely that more than 10 pairs . . . survive," according to report in 1965.

Family MIMIDAE, thrashers and mocking birds.

White-breasted thrasher, *Ramphocinclus brachyurus*, 2 races (West Indies). Martinique race, *R.b. brachyurus*. Not uncommon *c.* 1818, was thought extinct after 1886; but a very small population was rediscovered in 1950. St Lucia race, *R.b. sanctaeluciae*. Fairly numerous in 1886, rare and local by 1927, rarer 1932 and tiny population 1961.

Family PYCNONOTIDAE, bulbuls.

Olivaceous bulbul, *Hypsipetes borbonicus*, 2 races.
Réunion (Indian Ocean) race, *H.b. borbonicus*, was on the danger list after the cyclone of 1948 January but had recovered and was common by 1966.

A Huia

B Hawaiian crow

C Tinian monarch

Mauritius (Indian Ocean) race, *H.b olivaceus*. Population has been rare and local since 1912.

Family MUSCICAPIDAE
Subfamily TURDINAE, thrushes.

Seychelles magpie robin, *Copsychus seychellarum*. Endemic to the Seychelles Islands in the Indian Ocean where was known from at least 8 islands and was introduced into another. Now surviving only on Frégate, where a careful count in 1965 found only 12 birds.

Kittlitz's ground thrush, *Zoothera terrestris*. Peel Island in Beechey group of Bonin Islands in west Pacific extinct 1828.

Hawaiian thrush, *Phaeornis obscurus*, races.
Hawaii race, *P.o. obscurus*, was common in 1891 at least around 2,000 feet though rare in 1936–37, and not rare in the Hawaii National Park area in 1968.
Kauai race, *P.o. myadestinus*. Common in the late 19th century, but was found to have retreated to *c.* 3,710 feet on Kaholuamani Mountain in the 1930s where still thrives.
Lanai race, *P.o. lanaiensis*, extinct 1931.
Molokai race, *P.o. rutha*. Until a sighting was recorded in 1967 had not been encountered since 1936 and was thought extinct; is clearly relict and in danger.
Oahu race, *P.o. oahensis*, extinct 1825

Puaiohi, *Phaeornis palmeri*. Endemic to Kauai in Hawaiian Islands, and apparently not seen after first description (1893) until 1940; was believed extinct by 1950 but rediscovered in 1960. It is now known to have a tiny population, of the order of 30 birds, on the Kawaiiki Ridge and adjacent valleys of the Alakai Swamp area.
Grand Cayman thrush, *Turdus ravidus*. Extinct on this island in West Indies 1938.

Raiatea thrush, *Turdus ulietensis*. Raiatea in Society Islands, South Pacific extinct 1774.

Subfamily PANURINAE, bearded tit and parrotbills.

Lower Yangtze Kiang crow tit, *Paradoxornis heudei*. Restricted to the reed beds of less than 70 miles of the Lower Yangtze Kiang River in China between Nanking and Chinkiang. Had this very local distribution in 1914 and may even be extinct.

Subfamily SYLVIINAE, Old world warblers and gnatwrens.

Laysan miller bird, *Acrocephalus familiaris*. Laysan in Hawaiian Islands extinct in 1923.

Nihoa miller bird, *Acrocephalus kingi* Nihoa in Hawaiian Islands, where rang s no more than 156 acres. The 1967 opulation was estimated as 500–600 irds; previous estimates were lower.

eychelles warbler, *Nesillas sechellensis*. eychelles, Indian Ocean, where form- rly found on Marianne, perhaps Cousine nd Cousin Islands. Now found only on ousin where never not more than 30 birds 959, *c*. 45 1965.

odriguez warbler, *Bebrornis roderica- us*. Confined to Rodriguez Island, Indian cean, where perhaps 10–20 survivors in 964 and in danger of early extinction.

ong-legged warbler, *Trichocichla ufa*. **Viti Levu in Fiji, extinct c. 1890.**

ubfamily MALURINAE, Australian arblers.

yrean grass wren, *Amytornis goyderi*. escribed from 2 specimens collected 875 near Lake Eyre in South Australia; ot reported again until 1931, and hought extinct 1958 until local group ediscovered 1961 *c*. 25 miles north of ake Eyre.

ubfamily MUSCICAPINAE, Old World ycatchers and fantails.

hatham Island robin, *Petroica traversi*. Vhen discovered in the Chatham archi- elago, New Zealand, in 1871 this species vas found on Pitt and Mangare Islands. bout 20 years later others were collec- d on Little Mangare which had become, arly in the 20th century, the sole habitat f the species. In 1938 January the popu- ation in this island's single acre of uitable habitat was estimated at 20 to 5 pairs. In 1962 the robins were in ontinued occupation.

ubfamily MONARCHINAE, monarchs.

inian monarch, *Monarcha takatsuka- ae*. Tinian in Marianas in Micronesia, Vest Pacific, where population estimated t 40–50 birds 1945 by one observer, a ttle commoner by another. **C**

eychelles black paradise flycatcher, *erpsiphone corvina*. Seychelles archi- elago, Indian Ocean, where formerly ound on Praslin, Curieuse (1906), Feli- ité (to 1936) and probably Marianne. Iow confined to La Digue where re- orted as decreasing 1940, but tolerably umerous 1960.

ubfamily PACHYCEPHALINAE, whist- rs.

iopio, *Turnagra capensis*, 2 races. North land (New Zealand) race, *T.c. tanagra*. Videspread except perhaps in the north the time of European settlement; egan to decrease 1887; not more than 6 mall populations recognized in middle ird of present century; the survival of ach of these needs confirmation. South

D Hawaii oo

E Oahu oo

F Ponapé great whiteye

Island race, *T.c. capensis*. Since this vanished from Resolution Island in Fiord- land in *c*. 1900 only about 5 small popu- lations have been detected in the middle third of present century; the survival of each needs confirmation. The last record is from West Otago in 1963 May.

Family DICAEIDAE, flowerpeckers.

Four-coloured flowerpecker, *Dicaeum quadricolor*. **Cebú in Philippines, where extinct 1906.**

Family MELIPHAGIDAE, honeyeaters.

Kauai oo, *Moho braccatus*. Common all over the forests of this Hawaiian island in the last decade of the 19th century, this was extremely rare and only twice heard since 1928 (in 1936 and 1940) until rediscovered in 1960 in the high (4,000 foot) Alakai Swamp forest, where 12 were seen or heard; birds have been recorded since.

Molokai oo, *Moho bishopi*. **Molokai, Hawaiian Islands; extinct 1915.**

Hawaii oo, *Moho nobilis*. **Hawaii, Hawaiian Islands; extinct 1934. D**

Oahu oo, *Moho apicalis*. **Oahu, Hawai- ian Islands; extinct 1837. E**

Kioea, *Chaetoptila angustipluma*. **Hawaii, Hawaiian Islands; extinct 1859.**

Stitchbird, *Notiomystis cincta*. North Island, New Zealand, where generally distributed (except in extreme north) in *c*. 1840; by *c*. 1885 extinct on mainland and confined as breeding species to Little Barrier Island (7,000 acres), a bird sanc- tuary since 1896. Here the present small (not yet censused) population appears stable since it increased in the 1940s.

Family ZOSTEROPIDAE, whiteyes.

Lord Howe whiteye, *Zosterops strenua*. **Lord Howe Island, Australia; extinct 1918, or before 1928.**

Truk great whiteye, *Rukia ruki*. Truk Island in Carolines in Micronesia, West Pacific, where discovered in 1895 but not seen by ornithologists in 14 months *c*. 1900 and 2½ years 1957–60. Very rare and local.

Ponapé great whiteye, *Rukia sanfordi*. Ponapé Island in Carolines in Micro- nesia, West Pacific where discovered in 1931, when over 7 birds were collected. In 1947 only 4 birds were seen and 1 was collected. The population is probably dangerously small. **F**

Family DREPANIDIDAE, Hawaiian honeycreepers.
All belong or belonged to the Hawaiian archipelago; where "Hawaii" is cited for members of the family that follow it refers strictly to the island of Hawaii.

Green solitaire *or* **greater amakihi,** *Loxops sagittirostris*. **Hawaii; extinct 1900.**

Hawaiian creeper *or* alauwahio, *Loxops maculata*, 6 races. Hawaii race, *L.m. mana*, reduced in numbers since 19th century but still quite common in places. Maui race, *L.m. newtoni*, not uncommon 1928, less common 1936, much reduced though surviving 1951.
Lanai race, *L.m. montana*; **extinct 1937.** Molokai race, *L.m. flammea*, still quite common 1907, but became so rare that thought extinct 1950s; but 2 birds seen 1961, 3 1962, 1 1963.
Oahu race, *L.m. maculata*, fairly common 1890s, sought in vain 1935, reported 1950 as still to be found (and rare). Kauai race, *L.m. bairdi*, remains common round 4,000 foot contour; several hundred seen Alakai Swamp 1960.

Akepa, *Loxops coccinea*, 4 races.
Hawaii race, *L.c. coccinea*, still a small but stable population in the highlands.
Maui race, *L.c. ochracea*, not seen between 1894 and 1950 and thought extinct before rediscovery 1950 November on Haleakala volcano. **A**
Oahu race, *L.c. rufa*; extinct c. 1900.
Kauai race, *L.c. caeruleirostris*, has a small but apparently fairly stable population mainly in the Alakai Swamp area.

Akialoa, *Hemignathus obscurus*, **3 races. Hawaii race,** *H.o. obscurus*; **extinct 1895 (1940 unconfirmed). Lanai race,** *H.o. lanaiensis*; **extinct 1894 (1911 or later unconfirmed). Oahu race,** *H.o. lichtensteini*; **extinct 1837 (records 1892, 1937, 1940 unconfirmed).**

Kauai akialoa, *Hemignathus procerus*. Kauai, where quite numerous 1891 but already rare 1920; had retreated to the upper plateau 1941 where small population survives around the Alakai Swamp.

Nukupuu, *Hemignathus lucidus*, 3 races. Maui race, *H.l. affinis*, discovered early 1890s and last collected 1896, after which was for long thought extinct until rediscovered in the Kipahulu Valley in 1967.
Oahu race, *H.l. lucidus*; **extinct c. 1860.** Kauai race, *H.l. hanapepe*, discovered in c. 1887, seen to 1899, since when thought extinct until rediscovered in Alakai Swamp in 1960 (2 seen), since when 2 seen 1961, 3 1964, 1 1965.

Akiapolaau *or* Hawaii nukupuu, *Hemignathus wilsoni*. Common on Hawaii 1825–1860s; by 1891 had withdrawn up-hill with forest clearance and was uncommon by 1937; relict around the Hawaiian National Park with a low population. **B**

Maui parrotbill, *Pseudonestor xanthophrys*. Maui, where discovered in the early 1890s, and already relict on the northwest slope of Haleakala Mountain by 1894. In present century has been

A Maui race of akepa

B Akiapolaau *or* Hawaii nukupuu

C Mamo

possibly seen in c. 1928 and certainly seen in 1950 December and in 1967 August on Haleakala.

Ou, *Psittirostra psittacea*. Common on all 6 major islands in early 1890s, is extinct now on Lanai (c. 1932), Molokai (c. 1910) Oahu (c. 1900) and perhaps Maui. Relict on Hawaii in the Upper Olaa Forest Reserve in the Hawaii National Park and on Kauai in the Alakai Swamp where 3 were seen in 1900, 2 in 1963, 3 in 1964 and 2 in 1965.

Laysan "finch," *Psittirostra cantans*, races. Nihoa race, *P.c. ultima*, population estimated 3,000–4,500 1964.
Laysan race, *P.c. cantans*, increasing population reached c. 10,000 in 1958.

Palila, *Psittirostra bailleui*. Hawaii where has withdrawn since discovery; was deserting Kona on west side island in early 1890s; now virtually relict on Mauna Kea and Mauna Loa; the total number reported in 1965 was c. 100 birds.

Hopue *or* **great koa finch,** *Psittirostra palmeri*. **Hawaii; extinct 1896 (unconfirmed reports to 1937).**

Lesser koa finch, *Psittirostra flaviceps*. **Hawaii; extinct 1891.**

Grosbeak finch *or* **kona finch,** *Psittirostra kona*. **Hawaii; extinct 1894.**

Crested honeycreeper, *Palmeria dolei*. Formerly inhabited Molokai (where last seen 1907); now survives only on Maui where at least locally abundant until 1895. Is now relict on the high northern slopes of Haleakala.

Ula-ai-hawane, *Ciridops anna*. **Hawaii; extinct 1892 (report 1937 very doubtful).**

Mamo, *Drepanis pacifica*. **Hawaii; extinct 1898. C**

Perkins's *or* **black mamo,** *Drepanis funerea*. **Molokai; extinct 1907.**

Family PARULIDAE, American wood warblers.

Bachman's warbler, *Vermivora bachmani*. An extraordinarily rare summer visitor to the southeastern U.S.A.; has been proved to nest in Missouri (1897), Arkansas, Alabama, Kentucky and possibly Indiana, and has occupied territories in Virginia, North and South Carolina, Louisiana and Mississippi. In no years of the present century have more than a few birds been recorded anywhere, most often odd singing males.

Kirtland's warbler, *Dendroica kirtlandi*. The breeding range of this bird is confined to the jack pine stands of the Lower Peninsula of Michigan. The first nest was found in 1903 in Oscoda County and no subsequent nest has ever been found more than 60 miles away. The census of

51 found 432 singing males occupying
rritories, that of 1961 502. This warbler,
hich winters in the Bahamas, has a
eeding population of the order of 1,000
ept stable now by the positive conserva-
on of the U.S. Forest Service, the local
udubon Societies and the Michigan
atural Areas Council and Conserva-
on Department. **D**

emper's warbler, *Leucopeza semperi*.
onfined to the West Indian island of St
ucia in the Lesser Antilles, this warbler
as formerly not uncommon in the hill
rests but has been seen lately only in
34, 1947 and 1961, and reportedly heard
1962. It is perhaps the rarest living
ood warbler.

amily PLOCEIDAE, weavers.

o Thomé grosbeak weaver, *Neo-*
iza concolor. **São Thomé Island in**
frica's Gulf of Guinea, extinct 1888.

eychelles fody, *Foudia sechellarum*. The
ly indigenous weaver of the Seychelles
the Indian Ocean. Formerly lived on
aslin, La Digue and Marianne, is now
stricted to Frégate, Cousin and Cousine
tal area *c*. 10,000 acres) with a popula-
n estimated 1959 as 400–500 birds. Is
otected on Frégate, and may be holding
own.

éunion fody, *Foudia bruante*. **Reunion**
land in Indian Ocean, extinct 1776. E

amily FRINGILLIDAE, finches.

onin grosbeak, *Chaunoproctus ferreo-*
stris. **Bonin Islands, Pacific, where**
tinct; collected on Peel Island in
27; may have lingered in Bailley
oup to c. 1890. F

amily ICTERIDAE, New World orioles
d "blackbirds."

ender-billed grackle, *Cassidix palu-*
ris. Collected last in 1910 in marshes at
e headwaters of the Rio Lerma, State
México, México, and apparently not
countered since; may be extinct.

icaraguan grackle, *Cassidix nicara-*
ensis. Restricted to the shores of the
o great lakes of Nicaragua – Managra
d Nicaragua, where evidently a
esently viable population in this limited
nge.

amily EMBERIZIDAE, buntings, Ameri-
n sparrows, Darwin's finches, cardi-
ls, etc.

apata sparrow, *Torreornis inexpectata*,
races. Zapata race, *T.i. inexpectata*, is
nfined to the small Santo Tomàs area
the Zapata Swamp in Villas province
Cuba. Baitiquiri race, *T.i. sigmani*,
as only discovered 1959 in a small area
desert country near Baitiquiri on the
uth coast of Oriente province in Cuba,

D Kirtland's warbler

E Réunion fody

F Bonin grosbeak

G Tasmanian wolf

450 miles east of Zapata, and also doubtless has a small population.

Dusky seaside sparrow, *Ammospiza nig-
rescens*. The breeding range of this
species is restricted to a small area of
salt marshes near Cape Kennedy in
Florida, where the population was estimated as under 500 in 1964, 900–1,200 in
1968 when the majority were on the St
John's River marshes and *c*. 60 breeding
birds on Merritt Island, where the population was less than 200 in 1964. Draining
to improve the human conditions at the
space centre may threaten habitat.

Cape Sable sparrow, *Ammospiza mira-
bilis*. Described in 1919 January, this
may be the last new species of living bird
to have been discovered in the United
States. It no longer breeds at its type
locality, Cape Sable in Florida's Everglades National Park, but nests from the
Ochopee marshes towards the Huston
River and from Gum Slough to the Shark
River with a population estimated as
under 1,000 and probably under 500
birds.

Townsend's bunting, *Spiza townsendi*.
Known only from one specimen taken
1833 May 11 near New Garden in
Pennsylvania.

MAMMALS

Order MARSUPIALIA
Family DASYURIDAE, marsupial "mice,"
dasyures, thylacine and numbats.

Speckled marsupial mouse, *Antechi-
nus apicalis*. **Last collected in Western**
Australia in or before 1910; consid-
ered extinct.

Red-tailed phascogale, *Phascogale cal-
ura*. Formerly recorded from South
Australia, New South Wales and perhaps
Victoria, this animal was not observed
for nearly a century since 1867 and
believed extinct. Lately specimens have
been occasionally collected by house
cats and seen in the Narrogin-Kojonup-
Pingrup area of inland Western Australia.

Thylacine or "Tasmanian wolf," *Thyla-
cinus cynocephalus*. Formerly inhabited
Australia, where primitive aboriginals
and their dingos may have been the
agents of its extinction. In Tasmania it
was common 100 years ago but is now
confined to the dense western bush where
it has been recorded perhaps only twice
in the 1960s; it is protected by law and
the South-West District Game Reserve of
1.6 million acres. **G**

Family PERAMELIDAE, bandicoots.

Eastern barred bandicoot, *Perameles
fasciata*. **Recorded only from New**
South Wales, where discovered in
1840 at the junction of the Darling
and Namoi rivers. Recorded on the

Liverpool Plains in 1841, and along the Murray River in 1857, where fairly common; but last collected at the junction of the Murray and Darling rivers in 1867. **A**

Western or little barred bandicoot, *Perameles bougainvillei*, 3 races. *P.b. bougainvillei* is now apparently confined to Bernier and Dorre Islands in Shark Bay, Western Australia, where fluctuating population is presently abundant. There are no recent records of *P.b. notina* of southern South Australia.
P.b. myosura **of mainland Western Australia has not been collected since 1906 and is presumed extinct.**

Rabbit bandicoot *or* bilby, *Macrotis lagotis*, 6 races. Now probably extinct in Victoria (last recorded 1866), New South Wales (last record 1912) and Western Australia (last record *c*. 1950 or before); rare but surviving in northern South Australia, southwestern Queensland and Northern Territory where it has been recorded from 36 localities in the last two decades. All races are rare, and at least one is doubtless extinct:
M.l. grandis, **which has not been recorded from its type locality in southern South Australia (Nalpa, Lake Alexandrina), or from anywhere else, since early in the present century.**

Pig-footed bandicoot, *Chaeropus ecaudatus*, 2 races. Both races are probably extinct. Recorded from Western and South Australia, from Northern Territory and from New South Wales, the last New South Wales specimen was taken in 1880, and no confirmed sighting has been recorded since, though the possibility that a population may survive in Central Australia has been discussed. The Western Australian race, *C.e. occidentalis*, is based on two specimens, one of them taken in 1843; another "dried skin" was reported in 1927.

Family PHALANGERIDAE, phalangers.

Leadbeater's possum, *Gymnobelideus leadbeateri*. Known only from Victoria, where recorded from about 8 places – from 5 of these in the 1960s, where a relict population appears to have lately somewhat recovered in an area about 100 miles square since the devastating bush fires of 1939, after which it was for some time believed extinct. **B**

Scaly-tailed possum, *Wyulda squamicaudata*. Known only from the Kimberley Division of Western Australia; a relict species recorded from only 3 other places, none over 300 miles apart, since its first description from Violet Valley. **C**

Western ring-tail *or* ring-tailed possum, *Pseudocheirus occidentalis*. Never recorded outside the South-west Division of Western Australia, this animal is now

230

A Eastern barred bandicoot

B Leadbeater's possum

C Scaly-tailed possum

D Brown hare wallaby

relict and probably in real surviv danger.

Family MACROPODIDAE, wallabies, ka garoos and rat kangaroos.

Brown hare wallaby, *Lagorchestes lep rides*. Formerly New South Wales ai South Australia, now presumed e tinct. Though still fairly common New South Wales in 1857, no specim has been taken there (nor anim seen) since 1890. D

Western hare wallaby, *Lagorchestes h sutus*. Formerly distributed over Weste Australia and islands of Shark Bay, ai into South Australia, this species ma now be extinct on the continent, ai survives in small and fluctuating nui bers on Bernier and Dorre Islands.

Banded hare wallaby, *Lagostrophus fa ciatus*. Formerly distributed rath widely over southwestern Australia, th species has not been certainly report on the continent since 1906, but surviv in substantial though fluctuating pop lations on Bernier and Dorre Islands.

Ring-tailed rock wallaby, *Petrogale xa thopus*, 2 races. The southwest Queer land race may be in no danger. T typical race, *P.x. xanthopus*, formerly South Australia and the extreme west New South Wales has not been observ in the latter state since 1924, but st occurs in one relict population of reaso able numbers in South Australia's Fli ders Range.

Bridled nail-tailed wallaby, *Onychoga fraenata*. Formerly distributed from ce tral Queensland through inland N South Wales perhaps into adjacent are of South Australia, this species has n been recorded in continental New Sou Wales since 1924 and is of quite unkno\ status elsewhere. However, a colony b been lately established on Bulba Isla near Newcastle, New South Wales.

Crescent nail-tailed wallaby, *Onychog lea lunata*. Formerly found in southe Western Australia and South Australi this animal may survive on and arou\ the Nullarbor Plain; the last specim (the last recorded) was killed between t Tarlton and Jervois Range in 1956.

White-throated wallaby, *Macropus pa ma*. Probably extinct in Australia: t species has been recorded only in t Illawarra District north of the Shoa haven River, where none has been r ported in the present century, and fro the Dorrego District (also in New Sou Wales) about 300 miles northwest, whe it was last collected in 1932. None h been encountered since in Australia. colony was reported in 1967 as havii recently been identified on Kawau Islar (5,120 a.) in Hauraki Gulf about 30 mil north of Auckland, North Island, Ne

aland, descended from animals ap-
arently introduced from Australia in
1870.

oolache wallaby, *Macropus greyi*.
**uth Australia; last recorded 1938
ad believed extinct. E**

rush-tailed rat kangaroo, *Bettongia
nicillata*, 2 races. Formerly distributed
astern and western races have been
scribed) from the Cape York Peninsula
Victoria, and in Central and Western
ustralia, this animal probably now
rvives only in 3 widely separated
lonies in north Queensland, the West-
n Centre, and southwest Western
ustralia.

e Sueur's rat kangaroo, *Bettongia lesu-
r*. Formerly ranging over almost the
hole of Australia, this is virtually
tinct on the continent, though relict
pulations may possibly survive in
rthwestern and Central Australia. It
still fairly common, however, on
rnier and Dorre Islands in Shark Bay,
estern Australia.

aimard's rat kangaroo, *Bettongia gai-
ardi*, 2 races. Tasmanian race, *B.g.
niculus*, is still widespread but be-
ming split into smallish, localized
pulations.

**ustralian race, *B.g. gaimardi*, was
rmerly confined to the Fox area of
astern Australia and the western
ains of New South Wales; it may
ave extended to southern Queens-
nd. It became extinct early in this
ntury.**

ng-nosed rat kangaroo, *Potorous tri-
ctylus*. Formerly ranging from South
ustralia through Victoria and New
uth Wales to South Queensland, is
w extinct in South Australia and rare
the rest of its range, having probably
more than 3 or 4 relict colonies in
ctoria, 2 in New South Wales and a
w in Queensland.. **F**

ilbert's rat kangaroo, *Potorous gil-
rti*. **Discovered at King George's
und in Western Australia (2 speci-
ens) by John Gilbert in 1840 and
ever seen alive since; considered
tinct.**

road-faced rat kangaroo, *Potorous
atyops*. **Known from 3 Western Aus-
alian specimens collected in 1840
Valyema swamps near Northam,
ng George's Sound) and 1908 (Mar-
aret River) and considered extinct. G**

der INSECTIVORA
mily NESOPHONTIDAE.

astern Cuban nesophontes, *Neso-
ontes longirostris*.

estern Cuban nesophontes, *Neso-
ontes micrus*. **Extinguished respec-
vely in eastern Cuba; and Cuba and
e Isle of Pines, before 1800.**

E Toolache wallaby

F Long-nosed rat kangaroo

G Broad-faced rat kangaroo

H Hispaniolan solenodon

St Michel nesophontes, *Nesophontes
paramicrus*.

Atalaye nesophontes, *Nesophontes
hypomicrus*. **Bone material found in
1930 in barn owl pellets in a rock
shelter on Monte Culo de Maco in
Dominican Republic, Hispaniola, was
so fresh that it had doubtless been
swallowed lately. The species were
both described from skeletal remains
in Haiti caves near St Michel. Glover
M. Allen assigns the Dominican
material to the late 19th century, and
Gerrit S. Miller Jr believes from it
that the peculiarly West Indian Neso-
phontids (known from Cuban, Hispaniolan and Puerto Rican Flandrian
bones) may still exist.**

Hispaniolan nesophontes, *Nesophontes zamicrus*. **Extinguished in
Haiti and the Dominican Republic
before 1800.**

Puerto Rican nesophontes, *Nesophontes edithae*. **Extinguished in
Puerto Rico before 1800.**

Family SOLENODONTIDAE, solenodons.

Cuban solenodon, *Atopogale cubana*, 2
races.
**Typical *or* Bayamo race, *A.c. cubana*,
occupied the Sierra Maestra and
Pinar del Rio Province, has not been
reported since about 1890 and is presumed extinct.**

Race *A.c. poeyana*, survives in very small
numbers; formerly of the hills of eastern
Cuba it now occurs only in the mountains
of Sagua-Baracoa in northeast Oriente
province.

Hispaniolan solenodon, *Solenodon paradoxus*. Formerly confined to Hispaniola
this animal was thought extinct until
rediscovered in the stony forest of the
north eastern Dominican Republic in
1907; it is rare and survives only in the
lightly human-populated areas in northwest, southwest, north-central and
eastern parts of the Dominican Republic.
In the late 1960s 40 were captured for
zoos, and this most interesting insectivore is under serious human pressure,
notwithstanding legal protection from
1967 March. **H**

Family SORICIDAE, shrews.

Christmas Island shrew, *Crocidura
trichura*. **Indigenous to the Christmas
Island in the Indian Ocean, off Java,
where collected in 1886 and 1897, but
considered to be probably extinct in
1908 after the settlement of the island.**

Family TALPIDAE, moles and desmans.

Pyrenean desman, *Galemys pyrenaicus*.
Relict and rare in the fast trout rivers
of the Pyrenean region of southwest
France, and in Spain and Portugal.

231

Order CHIROPTERA
Family PHYLLOSTOMATIDAE, flower bats, etc.

Hispaniolan fig-eating bat, *Phyllops haitiensis.* **Described from a skull from Caña Honda, Dominican Republic, and material found in late owl pellets on Monte Culo de Maco, Dominican Republic (as** *Nesophontes,* **p. 231), in caves near St Michel and in late owl pellets in a cave at Diquini, Haiti. May have survived to c. 1917.**

Red fig-eating bat, *Stenoderma rufum.* Described in 1818 from a specimen of unknown locality otherwise known to 1943 only from prehistoric bones in the Cueva Catédral near Morovis, Puerto Rico. Believed extinct until 1 taken 1943 St Thomas, 3 taken 1957 St John; both islands in Virgin Islands.

Haitian flower bat, *Phyllonycteris obtusa.* **Known only from prehistoric bones near Atalaye, near Port-de-Paix; and from owl pellets at Diquini; all in Haiti. The last are highly probably late, and doubtless post-1600.**

Jamaican flower bat, *Phyllonycteris aphylla.* **Based on a single specimen taken in Jamaica some time before 1898 and on Jamaican fossil fragments. Considered extinct.**

Family VESPERTILIONIDAE, typical bats.

Indiana bat, *Myotis sodalis.* Has a cave-living population in the mid-west and eastern U.S.A. under grave new pressures from vandals and other cave-explorers.

Spotted bat, *Euderma maculatum.* Known only from 22 records in the western United States – one of North America's rarest mammals.

Order PRIMATES
Family LEMURIDAE, lemurs.

Grey gentle lemur, *Hapalemur griseus.* Formerly widely distributed over all Madagascar save the north, this animal is now relict in high bamboo 'thickets in a few parts of the surviving eastern and western forests.

Mongoose lemur, *Lemur mongoz,* 2 races. The typical *L.m. mongoz* formerly lived on Anjouan and Moheli in the Comoro Islands, where its present status is unknown, and in the Sihanaka country on the Madagascar mainland where its range has shrunk to two localities in the northwest which are fortunately nature reserves, the Plateau de l'Ankarafantsika and Tsingy de Namoroka. The crowned race, *L.m. coronatus,* formerly inhabited a large area of wooded savanna in north Madagascar but is now relict. Part of its range is in the protected Parc National de la Montagne d'Ambre. **A**

Weasel lemur, *Lepilemur mustelinus,* at least 4 races. All but the typical race are

A Mongoose lemur

B Fork-marked mouse lemur

C Indris

in some possible survival danger. T red-tailed race, or sportive lemur, *L. ruficaudatus,* is now much reduced range in the forested west of Ma gascar and appears to be confined the Narinda Bay-Onilahy River str and to the Ankarafantsika Reserve a its neighbourhood. Nosy-bé race, *L. dorsalis,* is confined to Nosy-bé Isla where it is still common in Lokobé fore though threatened by clearance. T white-footed race, *L.m. leucopus,* former occupied the dry regions of the extrem southeast, where it was particular common near Lake Anongy and Amb vombé. It appears now to be reli between the Manambovo and Mandra rivers.

Ruffed lemur, *Lemur variegatus.* Fo merly widespread in all eastern Mad gascar, is now much reduced by ove hunting and of relict status. It has population in the Nosy-Mangabé Reser and another in the Lokobé Reserve o Nosy-bé.

Hairy-eared mouse lemur, *Allocebus tr chotis,* was known only from the typ specimen collected somewhere betwee Tamantave and Murunduva, Madaga car, and two other skins. None havin been collected or reported for 90 yea the species was firmly believed to extinct when André Peyrieras red covered the living animal on the ea coast near Mananara in 1966.

Fat-tailed lemur, *Chirogaleus mediu* 2 races. Has contracted in range fro a formerly wide area extending to sout east and west Madagascar to reli populations in the Ankarafantsika R serve, in dry forest near Mont d'Amb and west of Fort Dauphin, and oth dry forests in the west. In danger fro forest clearance.

Coquerel's mouse lemur, *Microceb coquereli.* Formerly widely distribute in western Madagascar, this speci may now have but 1 relict populatio between the rivers Onilahy and Ma goky in southwestern Madagascar.

Fork-marked mouse lemur, *Phaner fu cifer.* Once widespread in western a northern Madagascar, has declined wit forest clearance and may have but relict populations, near Tulear in t southwest, round Ambasindava Bay an on Mont d'Ambre. **B**

Family INDRIIDAE, indrises and sifaka

Verreaux's sifaka, *Propithecus verreaux* 5 races. Typical race, *P.v. verreaux* formerly inhabited virtually all sout west Madagascar from the Tsiribihin River on the west to Fort Dauphin the southeast; now ranges west on as far as St Augustin's Bay and is decl ning, though the range embraces 2 (o 3) nature reserves. Coquerel's race, *P. coquereli,* formerly inhabited more

orthwest Madagascar, now occupies
nly the area round Mahajamba Bay
nd at least part of the Nature Reserve
f the Plateau de l'Ankarafantsika. Van
er Decken's race, *P.v. deckeni*, lives still
a relatively large area between the
Manambolo and Mahavavy rivers, at
etsina south of Lake Kinkonky, but is
ery scarce and local. Part of the Tsingy
e Namoroka Nature Reserve is within
s range. Crowned race, *P.v. coronatus.*
northwest Madagascar, where now
educed to an area west of the Mahavavy
iver. Part of the Tsingy de Namoroka
within its range. **D**

orsyth Major's race, *P.v. majori.* All
ces of this sifaka are in danger, but
nis most of all. Formerly its range
xtended from south-central to south-
est Madagascar; but it is now confined
the Sakaraha forest near Lamborma-
andro in the southwest.

ndris, *Indri indri.* Confined to the
rests of the eastern Malagasy moun-
ains from Antongil Bay to the Masora
iver, this fine animal has declined with
rest clearance and hunting pressure
nd has become relict in the same gross
ange; is protected by 2 nature reserves.

amily DAUBENTONIIDAE, aye-ayes.

ye-aye, *Daubentonia madagascariensis.*
ormerly lived in the northwest and
ost of the eastern forests of Madagas-
ar; now restricted to the northeast
rests between Antalaha and Manan-
ary; it is guessed that the world populaon of this monotypic and extraordinary
mily is no more than 50. In 1967 4
ales and 5 females were translocated
the island of Nosy Mangabé off the
ortheast coast, and have apparently
ettled well in this designated nature
serve. **E**

iant aye-aye, *Daubentonia robusta.*
Vest and south Madagascar, known
rom subfossil bones, teeth in
rchaeologically dug ornaments, and
skin seen near Andranomavo in the
oalala district in c. 1930.

amily CEBIDAE, New World monkeys.

ald uakari, *Cacajao calvus.* Formerly
anged in Brazil in forests from north
f the Rio Solimoes from near Tefé al-
ost as far west as the mouth of the Rio
a, northeast to the Rio Japura, and to
e Rio Toapana. Now relict between the
io Amazon and the Rio Japura in wes-
ern Brazil, where under severe hunting
nd live-collecting pressure.

ed uakari, *Cacajao rubicundus.* For-
erly replaced *C. calvus* from north
f the Rio Solimoes and west of the Rio
a in west Brazil, into Peruvian Ama-
nia, is now relict between the Amazon
nd the Rio Putumay in west Brazil
nd east Peru. Under severe hunting
nd live-collecting pressure.

D Crowned race of Verreaux's sifaka

E Aye-aye

Black-headed uakari, *Cacajao melanocephalus.* Formerly widespread in the
Rio Branco and Rio Negro systems of
northern Brazil into Amazonas Venezuela as far as the Casiquiare; now
confined to a narrow strip along the Rio
Negro from below the Rio Branco junction up to Marabitanas, where under
severe hunting and live-collecting pressure.

White-nosed saki, *Chiropotes albinasus.*
A very rare species confined to the Upper
Rio Tapajoz system in Brazil.

Woolly spider monkey, *Brachyteles ara-
chnoides.* Now confined to a very restricted area of southeast Brazil, to coastal
mountains and the Tupi forest from
southern Bahia to São Paulo, and to
Minas Gerais; formerly reached north
to Rio Grande do Norte. Possibly the
rarest living New World monkey, and
under strong pressure from forest clearance.

Goeldi's tamarin, *Callimico goeldii.* A
rare and curious monkey known from
Acre and the Rio Xapury in western
Brazil; may extend into Amazonian Peru
and Bolivia. Under live-collecting pressure.

Family CALLITHRICIDAE, marmosets
and tamarins.

Golden lion marmoset, *Leontideus rosa-
lia.* Restricted to the coastal montane
rain forest of the States of Rio de Janeiro
and Gunabara in southeast Brazil. Is
practically extinct in Gunabara and rare
everywhere. Decline marches with forest
clearance and live-collecting.

Golden-headed tamarin, *Leontideus chry-
somelas.* Known from under 10 specimens (1 alive in London Zoo 1869), from
coastal Bahia State, eastern Brazil,
where now may be relict south of Rio
de Contas, east of Sierra de Periperi and
north of Rio Pardo (between 14° and 16°
S.), if not extinct.

Golden-rumped tamarin, *Leontideus
chrysopygus.* Known scientifically from
3 specimens collected near Ipanema in
1822, at Vitoria in Botucatu in 1902,
and at Bautu in 1905, all in the State of
São Paulo, Brazil; a few other skins were
collected by 1820 and up to 1938. May be
extinct.

Family CERCOPITHECIDAE, Old World
monkeys.

Douc langur, *Pygathrix nemaeus.* Rare
and unstudied in Indo-China (Laos and
Vietnam); has been recorded once (1892)
from Hainan.

Snub-nosed monkey, *Rhinopithecus roxel-
lanae*, 3 races. This remarkable and
hardy monkey ranges, or ranged,
through the high mountain forests of
China in Szechwan (Yaochi district),
southern Kansu, Yunnan and Kwei-

chow, and over the neighbouring borders of eastern Tibet and, according to a recent report, Assam. Despite this wide range, it is among the rarest primates living.

Pig-tailed langur, *Simias concolor.* Known only from South Pagi, Sipora and Siberut in the Mentawi archipelago off West Sumatra, where heavily hunted.

Green colobus, *Colobus verus.* Rare and very localized in the High Forest zone of West Africa from Sierra Leone and Guinea in the west to Togo in the east.

Family PONGIDAE, apes.

Dwarf gibbon, *Hylobates klossi.* Confined to islands of North and South Pagi, Sipora and Siberut in Mentawi archipelago off West Sumatra, where heavily hunted.

Orang utan, *Pongo pygmaeus.* In Pleistocene times extended to northwest India, China, Java and Celebes; now confined to a restricted and declining range in Sumatra (estimated population *c.* 1,000), Borneo (*c.* 4,000) and captivity (*c.* 500). Nominally protected, but under great hunting pressure mainly for zoo, pet and laboratory trade which involves smuggling. The future of the species depends on law enforcement, primarily by the Governments of Indonesia, Sarawak and Sabah. **A**

Pygmy chimpanzee, *Pan paniscus.* Restricted to a relatively small area of humid rain forest on the south bank of the Congo River in Congo (Kinshasa) south to the Kasai and Sunkuru rivers. Threatened by forest clearance. **B**

Gorilla, *Gorilla gorilla*, 2 races. Mountain race, *G.g. beringei*, occupies *c.* 8,000 square miles of a *c.* 35,000 square mile triangle based on the Equator with its southern apex near Fizi, separated from the lowland race by a 650-mile gap. It lies in Congo (Kinshasa), Rwanda and Uganda. The key area round the Virunga volcanoes is protected by the Albert National Park in Congo and the gorilla sanctuary of Mounts Muhavura, Gahinga and Sabinio in Uganda. The population, estimated between 5,000 and 15,000 individuals, is under the threat of habitat destruction by farming developments. **C**

Order EDENTATA
Family MYRMECOPHAGIDAE, anteaters.

Giant anteater, *Myrmecophaga tridactyla*, 3 races. Has a wide distribution from British Honduras and Guatemala south through Central and South America to Peru and northern Argentina, in which it is declining partly under the pressure of trophy-hunters and settlers.

Family DASYPODIDAE, armadillos.

Giant armadillo, *Priodontes giganteus.* Has a wide distribution from Colombia and Venezuela southeast of the Andes

A Orang utan

B Pygmy chimpanzee

C Mountain race of gorilla

to Amazonian Peru and northern Argentina in which it is declining, rare, and under hunting pressure.

Lesser pichiciego, *Chlamyphorus truncatus.* Central and western Argentina where "singularly scarce."

Greater pichiciego, *Burmeisteria retusa*, 2 races, both rare and under hunting pressure. *B.r. clorindae* of western Formosa province in Argentina may extend to near Salta and the Chaco and probably into the south Paraguayan Chaco. *B.r. retusa* lives in central and south Bolivia and the extreme north of Jujuy and Salta provinces in Argentina.

Order LAGOMORPHA
Family OCHOTONIDAE, pikas.

Sardinian pika, *Prolagus sardus.* **Known from numerous Pleistocene and Flandrian localities in Corsica and Sardinia, including Tavolara off Sardinia where F. Cetti (1774) mentions the presence "of giant rats whose burrows are so abundant that one might think the surface of the soil had been recently turned over (remuée) by pigs." No evidence of survival after this record.**

Family LEPORIDAE, rabbits and hares.

Ryukyu rabbit, *Pentalagus furnessi.* Confined to the islands Amami Oshima and Toku-no-Shima south of Kyûshû, with present population estimated at 500–900 after hunting pressure. Is nearly extinct on Toku-no-Shima, despite official protection since 1921. **D**

Volcano rabbit, *Romerolagus diazi* México, where occupies perhaps the most limited range of any indigenous animal, is confined to the middle slopes of Popocatépetl and Ixtacihuatl and adjoining ridges bordering the Valley of México on east and south and declining under the pressure of cultivation and hunting despite nominal legal protection.

Assam rabbit, *Caprolagus hispidus.* **Formerly ranging in India from Uttar Pradesh to Assam, at the base of the Himalayan foothills, and south to Dacca in East Pakistan, this animal was last collected in 1956 and perhaps seen in 1958 and is now probably extinct.**

Short-eared rabbit, *Nesolagus netscheri.* Confined to the Barisan Range in southwestern Sumatra, where known from 15 specimens, and known to be endangered by forest clearance.

Order RODENTIA
Family SCIURIDAE, squirrels.

Kaibab squirrel, *Sciurus kaibabensis.* Confined to an area *c.* 70×30 miles of the Kaibab Plateau of the north rim of the Grand Canyon, Arizona, which has a fluctuating population around 1,000 individuals. Is fully protected in the National Park and may not be endangered. **E**

Black-tailed prairie dog, *Cynomys ludovicianus*. Rapidly declining in the short grass southern prairie from south Saskatchewan and North Dakota to southeast Arizona, south-central Texas, and northern Chihuahua in México. Extermination largely by cattlemen. It is preserved in at least three nature reserves.

Méxican prairie dog, *Cynomys mexianus*. Confined to southeast Coahuila, adjacent Nuevo Leon, San Luis Potosí, and probably Zacatecas between 5,500 and *c.* 7,000 feet, a relict population.

Utah prairie dog, *Cynomys parvidens*. Utah only, where occurred in 9 counties in 1935–36, and in only 5 in 1962 (in south-central Utah). The 1968 towns contained possibly 6,000 animals on 8,000 a. Has been poisoned and infected with sylvatic plague, but the Bureau of Sport Fisheries and Wildlife is now encouraging a moratorium on control measures of this rarest of the prairie dogs.

Family HETEROMYIDAE, pocket mice and kangaroo rats.

Big-eared kangaroo rat, *Dipodomys elephantinus*. Has a relict distribution in the hills of San Benito and Monterey counties in central California.

Texan kangaroo rat, *Dipodomys elator*. Has a relict distribution in southeast U.S.A., lately known from but 1 county in Oklahoma and 5 in Texas.

Family CRICETIDAE, New World mice, hamsters, lemmings, voles and gerbils.

Jamaican rice rat, *Oryzomys antillarum*. **Last collected in Jamaica c. 1877, since when believed extinct.**

St Vincent rice rat, *Oryzomys victus*. Known from a single specimen collected on St Vincent, West Indies, in or before 1897; believed extinct.

Martinique rice rat, *Oryzomys desmaresti*. Extinct; probably wiped out by the eruption of Mont Pelée on Martinique, West Indies, in 1902.

Barbuda rice rat, *Oryzomys audreyae*. Believed extinct on Barbuda, West Indies, in 1902.

St Lucia rice rat, *Oryzomys luciae*. Last collected St Lucia, West Indies, some time before 1881; considered extinct.

Chatham rice rat, *Oryzomys galapagoensis*. Chatham Island, Galápagos Islands, collected by Charles Darwin in 1835 and not apparently seen since.

Indefatigable rice rat, *Oryzomys indefessus*. Indefatigable and South Seymour Islands, Galápagos Islands, probably extinct since c. 1945.

James rice rat, *Oryzomys swarthi*. James Island, Galápagos Islands, collected in 1906; apparently never seen since.

Darwin's rice rat, *Oryzomys darwini*. Indefatigable Island, Galápagos Islands, probably extinct since c. 1945.

D Ryukyu rabbit

E Kaibab squirrel

F Jamaican short-tailed hutia

Salt marsh harvest mouse, *Reithrodontomys raviventris*, 2 races. Declining in the salt marshes of San Francisco Bay and Marin County, California, which are rapidly becoming limited by "reclamation."

Beach meadow vole, *Microtus breweri*. Confined to Muskegat Island, Massachusetts, off the extreme west end of Nantucket Island. Fluctuates in numbers, as is typical of voles; but has shown a general decline which has been attributed to erosion, hurricanes, building construction, predation and other factors.

Gull island vole, *Microtus nesophilus*. A form from Gull Island, off the eastern extremity of Long Island, New York, which seems to have become extinct around the time of its scientific description in 1898.

Family MURIDAE, typical mice and rats.

Maclear's rat, *Rattus macleari*. Indigenous to Christmas Island in the Indian Ocean, off Java, where collected in 1886 and 1887 and swarming in 1897, but probably already extinct by 1908, after the settlement of the island.

Bulldog rat, *Rattus nativitatis*. Indigenous to Christmas Island, above; a burrowing rat of the interior hilly jungle, discovered in 1887, which had also vanished by 1908. Both species may have been extirpated by disease introduced by the man-brought roof rat *R. rattus*.

Family CAPROMYIDAE, hutias and coypu.

Bushy-tailed hutia, *Capromys melanurus*, 2 races. Has a circumscribed range in Cuba in the Sierra Maestra forests, in the low country north of Santiago de Cuba, in Oriente and west Pinar del Rio provinces, and possibly in the Isle of Pines. This is a relict distribution after hunting pressure and forest clearance.

Dwarf hutia, *Capromys nana*. Described from fossil bones from caves, this species was found alive in the Cienaga de Zapata, the Zapata Swamp in Cuba, in 1937. This area is now a nature reserve and the population, under legal protection, may survive. A living population has not been recorded elsewhere.

Jamaican short-tailed hutia, *Geocapromys browni*, 2 races. Little Swan Island race, *G.b. thoracatus*, is confined to this island in the Gulf of Honduras.

Jamaican race, *G.b. browni*, confined to Jamaica where formerly doubtless common, now survives only in rocky and inaccessible areas, the principal (and possibly only) relict population being found in the John Crow Mountains. **F**

Bahaman hutia, *Geocapromys ingrahami*, 3 races. **Abaco Island race, *G.i. abaconis*. Extinct.**

Crooked Island race, *G.i. irrectus.* **Extinct.**

Typical race, *G.i. ingrahami,* is now confined to the Plana Cays between Mariguana and Acklins Island in south Bahamas, where evidently fairly common.

Cuvier's hutia, *Plagiodonta aedium.* No specimen was obtained between Cuvier's in 1836 and the next in 1947, and the species was thought extinct; it is extremely rare and confined to Hispaniola.

Dominican hutia, *Plagiodonta hylaeum.* Now probably confined to the Samana Bay forests in northeast Dominican Republic, Hispaniola. Rare. **A**

Order CETACEA

Family PHYSETERIDAE, sperm whales.

Sperm whale, *Physeter catodon.* All temperate and tropical oceans; much reduced by whaling which decimated this species, particularly in the Atlantic between the end of the 18th and the middle of the 19th century; the peak of New England-based whaling was in 1846. Still under whaling pressure in the Azores and other areas. **B**

Family ESCHRICHTIDAE, grey whale.

Grey whale, *Eschrichtius gibbosus,* 2 races.

Pacific race, *E.g. glaucus,* was practically exterminated by over-fishing by the early 20th century; but is now totally protected and has increased to a population estimated at over 8,000; is agreeably common off the coast of California.

Atlantic race, *E.g. gibbosus,* **seems extinct, having evidently been last taken off New England in the early 18th century, and last washed up dead 1864 in Babbacombe Bay, Devon, England.**

Family BALAENOPTERIDAE, rorquals.

Sei whale, *Balaenoptera borealis.* The smallest of the rorquals now commercially fished and under new pressures. The pelagic whalers in southern waters took *c.* 5,000 in 1963–64 and *c.* 20,000 in 1964–65; it is estimated that the take of 17,583 in 1965–66 reduced the Antarctic stocks by more than a third; 12,368 were taken in 1966–67.

Fin whale, *Balaenoptera physalus.* All oceans, with a population of the order of 110,000 in 1955–56, down to 32,400 in 1963–64, as a consequence of over-fishing. **C**

Blue whale, *Balaenoptera musculus,* 2 races. All oceans; the biggest animal that has ever lived.

The typical race, *B.m. musculus,* had a world population of the order of 30,000–40,000 in the middle 1950s, mainly in the Southern Hemisphere, reduced by over-fishing to *c.* 1,000 in the middle 1960s. **C**

Pygmy race, *B.m. brevicauda.* Inhabits the southern Indian Ocean with an estimated population reduced from *c.* 4,000 to *c.* 2,000–3,000 by 1963.

A Dominican hutia

B Sperm whale

C Fin whale and blue whale

D North Atlantic right whale and humpback whale

The species is now the world's most endangered whale and needs complete international protection.

Humpback whale, *Megaptera novae angliae.* A cosmopolitan whale which appears to be increasing in the North Atlantic where it is fairly numerous on the west side. In the North Pacific, where it is rapidly declining, 2,339 were killed in 1963 and it is now rare with a population probably under 5,000. In the Southern Hemisphere there were estimated to be *c.* 22,000 in Antarctic waters alone in the 1930s; now there are probably under 3,000 in all waters south of the Equator where, since 1963, the International Whaling Commission has agreed to a complete cessation of their hunting: in the North Atlantic, where the IWC introduced prohibition in 1900 this measure has provedly paid off already. **D**

Family BALAENIDAE, right whales.

Greenland right whale, *Balaena mysticetus.* Confined to the Arctic Ocean, this whale was a main target of the old wooden whaling-ship industry of half a century ago, and more, which practically exterminated it in over 100 years of over-fishing. The relict population is now fully protected by all Arctic nations and all hunting is forbidden except locally by aborigines. Its main surviving population, of the order of 1,000 and reportedly now increasing, is in the Bering Chukchi-Beaufort Sea area, and tiny populations have been lately in evidence in the northeast Pacific, near Spitsbergen and in the Beaufort Sea. The situation in Greenland waters and in the Okhotsk Sea, where it formerly flourished, is uncertain.

North Atlantic right whale, *Eubalaena glacialis.* Confined to the North Atlantic where it formerly ranged north to the Arctic Ocean at the border of the range of the Greenland right whale. Has been hunted since at latest the 12th century originally in the Bay of Biscay but later on both North Atlantic coasts north to Iceland and the Norwegian Arctic. Was over-fished to near-extinction on the European side by the early 18th, on the American side by the early 19th century. Internationally protected since 1937, rare sightings have disclosed a relict population, possibly of a few hundred, which may be slowly increasing. **D**

North Pacific right whale, *Eubalaena sieboldi.* Formerly ranged the North Pacific on the west to Formosa (Taiwan) in winter, the Japanese archipelago and Kamchatka, on the east to Baja California in winter, the US (including Alaska) and British Columbia. Was fished until the 1930s when protected internationally and over-fished since the 1840s. Survives as a relict population of unknown size, but there is no evidence from the (fairly regular) sightings that any recovery has got under way.

Southern right whale, *Eubalaena austra-lis*. Formerly ranged the southern oceans mainly between 30° and 60° S. Lat. Over-fishing began in the first decade of the 19th century and became marked in Chile, the Argentine Republic and West Africa, and positive in New Zealand and Australia, and appears to have brought the population to near-relict status over a century ago. Protected internationally since 1935, this species show no important signs yet of positive recovery but has been sighted lately off Chile, South Georgia, Tristan da Cunha, Australia and New Zealand.

Order CARNIVORA

Family CANIDAE, dogs.

Red wolf, *Canis niger*, 3 races.

Western race, *C.n. rufus*. Formerly inhabited central Texas and Oklahoma, extreme southeast Kansas, southwest Missouri and northwest Arkansas. Tiny population surviving in parts of east-central Texas, Oklahoma and Arkansas may be of this, or of next race.

Central race, *C.n. gregoryi*. Formerly inhabited central and western Indiana, southern Illinois, western Kentucky, western Tennessee, southeastern Missouri, most of Arkansas, Mississippi and Louisiana, southeastern Oklahoma and eastern Texas. Now reduced to tiny relict populations in Texas, Louisiana and possibly also Arkansas. Species may number not more than *c.* 150 living individuals, after heavy trapping and hunting pressure.

Eastern race, *C.n. niger*. Formerly inhabited southeastern Tennessee, Alabama, most of Georgia and Florida; last probably survived in the Okeefenokee Swamp of Georgia until *c.* 1918.

Falkland fox, *Dusicyon australis*. Falkland Islands, where last one said to have been killed at Shallow Bay on West Falkland in 1876.

Maned wolf, *Chrysocyon brachyurus*. Rare, endangered and reduced from a wide former range to the interior of Brazil from Piaui to Rio Grande do Sul and Matto Grosso, extending into eastern Bolivia (possibly), Paraguay and north-eastern Argentina. Extinct before the end of the 19th century in Uruguay and Argentina south of the Rio de la Plata. Has an estimated population of *c.* 1,500–2,200 individuals in a gross survival area of 650,000 square kilometres. **E**

Family URSIDAE, bears.

Spectacled bear, *Tremarctos ornatus*. Ranges or ranged, from Colombia (possibly Panama), through the forested highlands of northern South America to southern Peru and northwestern Bolivia, possibly (formerly) northern Chile. Now rare as a consequence of forest destruction, and in serious need of investigation. **G**

Brown and grizzly bears, *Ursus arctos*, c. 17 races? As here listed this species

E Maned wolf

G Spectacled bear

H Mexican race of grizzly bear

incorporates the brown bears of Eurasia and the big brown bears and grizzlies of North America (and northern México) for which the earliest name available is *Ursus horribilis*. At least 93 Linnaean names have been given, at one time or another, to specimens or populations of indigenous North American and Mexican grizzlies, no less than 84 of them by Clinton Hart Merriam between 1896 and 1929. The formidable task of arranging the American forms into valid races has not been lately tackled. Grizzlies are now extinct in the areas from which at least 22 of these forms were named. To bring the grizzlies into a comparison with the Eurasian brown bears (taken as having 7 races living, and 1 extinct) the American forms have been here lumped into 9 groups (6 living and 3 extinct) representing geographical populations of this highly variable bear which appear separable, and most of which have vernacular names in current use. They are not offered as firm subspecies so much as collections of the forms as they might be arranged for a critical study, listed under their senior Linnaean names. The number of Linnaean names, as listed by Hall and Kelson in 1959, that have been given to the members of each group is shown in brackets. These marked * are considered to be in survival danger.

Big brown bear, *U.a. alascensis* (14). Alaska (excluding southern panhandle) and some off-lying islands (not Kodiak).

Kodiak bear, *U.a. middendorfi* (2). Kodiak Island.

Western grizzly, *U.a. dalli* (23). Southern Alaska, western British Columbia and northern Washington. Extinct in southwest British Columbia 1883 and Washington lately.

Barren-ground grizzly, *U.a. richardsoni** (6). Northern Yukon and northern Mackenzie, formerly northern Alaska and Keewatin. Of declining status with an estimated population under 1,000.

Yukon grizzly, *U.a. kluane* (7). Yukon territory.

Grizzly, *U.a. horribilis* (26). Formerly from eastern British Columbia to Manitoba tier of Canadian Provinces south to Utah-Kansas tier of United States. Now withdrawn into Rocky Mountain highlands and foothills from B.C. to Alberta south to Colorado, and now extinct in the Prairie. Became extinct in eastern Montana 1893; in eastern Wyoming 1887; in Utah 1911; and in eastern Colorado lately.

California grizzly, *U.a. californicus* (7). Formerly most of California. Extinct; the last 1933, in the north.

New Mexico grizzly, *U.a. horriaeus* (6). Formerly Arizona, New Mexico and western Texas. Extinct, the last in Texas in the 1910s and in Arizona and New Mexico lately (1950s).

Méxican grizzly, *U.a. nelsoni* (2). H

Formerly México in northern Baja California, northeastern Sonora, most of Chihuahua and Coahuila, and northern Durango. Extinct, the last in northern Sonora in 1855, the last of all in northern Chihuahua in 1962 (subject to a planned resurvey).

Besides these American groups, one of the 8 Old World races is in danger:
Syrian brown bear, *U.a. syriacus.** Formerly ranged throughout the mountains of the east end of the Mediterranean south into Israel; now probably extinct in much of its former range and survives in relict populations on Mount Hermon (Lebanon/Syria) on the Alawit Mountains in Syria, in northern Iraq, in Transcaucasia in Armenia and in Caucasian Georgia near Sukhumi in the Abkhazkaya S.S.R. – and another is extinct:
Atlas brown bear, *U.a. crowtheri*. Formerly inhabited western North Africa; last recorded in mountains of north Morocco near Tetuan in 1841.

Polar bear, *Ursus maritimus*. Declining in its native Arctic and the subject of much international study and concern; has been under human pressures and may now have a world population no more than *c.* 10,000 – over half in Canada, slightly increasing in Siberia under U.S.S.R. protection, and under protection or harvest control by the other Arctic countries – Norway, Denmark, U.S.A. and Canada. **A**

Family PROCYONIDAE, raccoons and pandas.

Giant panda, *Ailuropoda melanoleuca*. Lives in the Chuing-lai and Ta-liang Mountains of western Szechwan in China, and perhaps also in southwestern Shensi and in part of Tibet. Is strictly protected by China, and there is no evidence of a population decline; though fossil evidence from eastern Szechwan and northern Burma shows its range is a relict of what it enjoyed in Pleistocene times. **B**

Family MUSTELIDAE, weasels, badgers, skunks and otters.

Black-footed ferret, *Mustela nigripes*. Probably the rarest North American indigenous mammal; a prairie animal now extinct in Texas, Kansas and Oklahoma and with a highly fragmented range in the Dakotas, Montana, Nebraska and Colorado; has been doubtless brought into decline by the destruction of its prairie dog prey. **D**

Sea mink, *Mustela macrodon*. Coast of Maine, U.S.A., where became extinct in c. 1860, or possibly not until c. 1894.

La Plata otter, *Lutra platensis*. Ranges from southern Brazil into the Matto Grosso, Paraguay, Uruguay and to northern Argentina where it lived in the Rio de la Plata system but has now almost disappeared; under severe hunting pressure.

A Polar bear

B Giant panda

C Giant otter

Giant otter, *Pteronura brasiliensis*. Has or had, a wide range in the rivers of South America from Venezuela to northeastern Argentina and is everywhere becoming rare through hunting pressure; its fur, equal with that of a jaguar, fetches the highest price ($1,800 lately) of any South American animal. Fur statistics from Peru show a decline of the crop by ten times in the period 1946–6? doubtless directly due to overhinting. C

Cameroun clawless otter, *Paraony? microdon*. May be confined to the river systems of Bamenda and Bamoun in Cameroun, and is in grave danger from overhunting for the developing pelt trade.

Sea otter, *Enhydra lutris*, 2 races. Southern race, *E.l. nereis*, formerly occupied the kelp beds of the west coast of North America from Washington to Baja California. By 1876 the pelt trade had exterminated it in Washington and Oregon and it was thought to have been extinguished in California by 1911; but in 1938 it was rediscovered off Bixb? Creek off the Monterey Coast of California; since then under protection and good enforcement it has extended it? range along the California coast from Santa Barbara to Santa Cruz counties and had a population estimated in 1965 at *c.* 850–900.

Family VIVERRIDAE, civets and mon? gooses.

Large-spotted civet, *Viverra megaspil?* 2 races.
Travancore race, *V.m. civettina*, once very common in the wooded plains and adjoining hill slopes of coastal Malaba? and Travancore, is now very rare indeed in the coastal district and Western Ghat? of south India, and may even be extinct?

Foussa, *or* Malagasy civet, *Fossa foss?* Formerly found in all the eastern forest zone of Madagascar, this animal is now confined to the surviving dense forest stands. Reduced by habitat destruction it is also under hunting pressure and in definite decline.

Falanouc, *Eupleres goudoti*. Madagasca? forests, where has a relict distribution after a decline attributed to hunting and habitat destruction.

Fossa (*or* Fosa), *Cryptoprocta ferox*. Distributed all over Madagascar (except high plateaux) but scarce and relict in distribution after hunting pressure.

Family FELIDAE, cats.

Pardel lynx, *Felis pardina*, cf. 2 races? The surviving form, found only in the Iberian Peninsula is by most authorities classed as a race of the northern lynx *F. lynx*; but in Pleistocene times its range extended to central Europe where it coexisted and overlapped with the larger species. It may still possibly survive in the Carpathians and Caucasus.

panish race, *F.p. pardina*, may now
urvive only in the delta of the Guadal-
uivir in southern Spain where an esti-
nated 150 to 200 in the Coto Doñana
Reserve may be the largest remaining
opulation.

ardinian race, described in 1908 as
ynx sardiniae, **is referred to this**
pecies as *F.p. sardiniae* **and is pro-**
ably extinct.

ion, *Panthera leo*, 11 races. Asiatic race,
Panthera leo persica: in Pleistocene times
he lion ranged beyond Africa through
ost of continental Europe and Asia,
ncluding England and Wales. Though
till in Europe during the classic times
f ancient Greece and early Rome, it
as, outside Africa, confined to Asia by
ate historical time; and the last inhabi-
ed countries appear to have been, or be,
srael (to 13th century), Pakistan (to
842), India outside Kathiawar (to 1884),
ersia where single lions were last seen
y the Kharki River in the southwest
1941 and 1942 (*possibly* the race may
ere survive) and Kathiawar in India
here the only recognizable surviving
opulation is based on the *c.* 309,000 a.
ir Forest. Here censuses have estimated
89 lions in 1936, 240 in 1950, 290 in 1955,
50 in 1960, 250 in 1961 and 1962, 285 in
963, and only 162 in 1968. The populaon is under some protection and ecolo-
ical analysis, and three lions were
anslocated to the Chandraprabha
anctuary in Uttar Pradesh in 1957
here they have bred and flourished.
he main danger is the forest degrada-
on of Gir which is used by 7,000 human
habitants and 57,000 domestic stock,
f which the lions kill 10–20 a day,
ainly water buffalo. **E**

arbary race, *P.l. leo*, **Africa north of**
e Sahara, extinct 1922.
ape race, *P.l. melanochaitus*, **south-**
nmost Africa, extinct 1865.

iger, *Panthera tigris*, 7 races. Bengal
ce, *P.t. tigris*, is the only race without
present sheet in the Red Data Book;
may soon earn one as its status in
dia is deteriorating.

aspian race, *P.t. virgata*, once ranged
om Persia and Chinese Turkestan to
e Altai and the Caspian, Aral Sea
d Lake Balkhash areas of Russia. By
48 this race was extinct around Lake
alkhash and along the Syr Dar'ya in
azakhskaya S.S.R.; indeed while it is
ill recorded in the U.S.S.R. from eastern
zerbaidzhan to the Tadzhikskaya S.S.R.
is has been so close to the Persian and
fghan borders that the tigers could
ve been immigrant foragers. There is a
ny relict resident population, which
as been estimated at 15–20 animals, in
aspian north Persia, and another of
known size but probably larger in
rthern Afghanistan.
mur race, *P.t. altaica*. The largest race,
e long-haired "Siberian tiger," once

D Black-footed ferret

E Asiatic race of lion

F Amur *or* "Siberian" race of tiger

G Barbary race of leopard

ranged north to the Upper Lena basin
in Siberia, east to the Amur-Ussuri
river systems, south to Korea and the
Hwang Ho in China and west to eastern
Mongolia and Lake Baikal. Now the
population is relict and fractionated,
with headquarters only in Amurland
(Primorskaya Oblast), mountains of
North Korea (*c.* 40–50 animals on last
estimate and mountains of north Manchuria. It is under hunting pressure for
the pharmaceutical and zoo trade. **F**
Chinese race, *P.t. amoyensis*, has a
wide range in China north and west to
the edge of the high plateau, west to
Shensi and Kweichow, formerly but no
longer to Szechwan and Kansu, but within it is very rare and fractionated into
relict populations under considerable
hunting pressure. Sumatran race, *P.t.*
sumatrae formerly flourished in northern and montane southwest Sumatra
but since the Second World War has
been hunted to relict status in most areas.
Javan race, *P.t. sondaica*, numerous
in many parts of Java a century ago,
is now confined to about 5 small populations, mostly in the east part of the
island; it has lately become extinct in
the Udjung Kulon Peninsula Reserve
at the west end of the island.
Bali race, *P.t. balica*, is fully distinct
racially from the Javan form, though is
rumoured to have been derived from
introduced Javan stock. Formerly widespread over most of the island except
the east end it is now so rare that it has
not been collected since 1937 or reported
since 1952. Pending exploration of the
dense and inaccessible northern forests
this race is logged as an endangered
survivor; but it may prove to be extinct.

Leopard, *Panthera pardus*, *c.* 30 races.
Barbary race, *P.p. panthera*. Was formerly abundant in Morocco, Algeria
and Tunisia but has now been reduced
by hunting pressure to just 1 part of
Morocco in the central Atlas and the
high forests of the Oulms region, where
it is doubtful whether 100 survive. **G**
Sinai race *P.b. jarvisi*. Sinai in Egypt
and perhaps northern Saudi Arabia;
is presently extremely rare, and under
investigation; may prove to be extinct.
Arabian race, *P.p. nimr*, of the southern
part of the Arabian Peninsula extending
to Yemen and Oman is now everywhere
scarce and under hunting pressure, some
of it organized.
Anatolian race, *P.p. tulliana*, was formerly widespread through western Asia
Minor to Russian Transcausia; now
has relict populations lately identified
in a handful of places in Turkey, survives in Israel, and may survive in small
numbers in Syria, Jordan, and possibly
Lebanon; it is extinct in Russia. Under
severe hunting, trapping and poison
pressure; but attempts are being made to
organize reserve protection in Turkey.

Amur race, *P.p. orientalis*, formerly widespread in Korea, Manchuria and the Primorskaya Oblast (Amurland) of Russia is now practically extinct in Manchuria and reduced to relict populations in North Korea and in Primor'ye, mostly south of Lake Khanka.

Snow leopard, *Panthera uncia*. May formerly have extended to highland Persia; now rare and relict in the central Asian highlands of U.S.S.R., China, Himalayan India, West Pakistan and Afghanistan. Protected in India (except Kashmir) and U.S.S.R.; may have a population of only 400 ± 200 individuals in the Himalayas.

Cheetah, *Acinonyx jubatus*, 9 races.
Asiatic race, *A.j. venaticus*, once widely distributed from Israel and Arabia to Turkmenistan, Afghanistan, Baluchistan and northern India; is now reduced to relict populations in Turkmenistan, Kazakhstan, Afghanistan, southwest Persia (estimated under 100) and possibly Baluchistan, northern Saudi Arabia and Oman. It became extinct in India in the 1950s, is probably extinct in Jordan, and has been extinct in Israel for over a century; after long hunting pressure and the human destruction of habitat and prey. A

Order PINNIPEDIA
Family OTARIIDAE, fur seals and sea lions.

Philippi's fur seal, *Arctocephalus philippii*, 2 races. Juan Fernandez race, *A.p. philippii*, formerly bred off Chile on the Juan Fernandez archipelago west of Valparaiso and perhaps on the San Felix/San Ambrosio archipelago west of Taltal. Since the 1890s it was unrecorded for so long that it was presumed to have become extinct through over-slaughter (3 million skins were taken on Masafuera in the Juan Fernandez group in only 7 sealing years). But in 1968 30 seals were discovered on Masatierra and a larger population was reported from Masafuera; already the "recolony" is legally protected by the Chilean Government. Guadalupe race, *A.p. townsendi*, formerly bred on the principal islands along the coast of California, and on the Islas San Benito and Isla de Guadalupe off México's Baja California. Nearly extinct by 1900 and later believed to be entirely so, after fur slaughter, the subspecies has recovered. A breeding population returned to Guadalupe (the most distant island from the continent) in 1954, and 600 fur seals were estimated on the beaches there in 1965.

Walrus, *Odobenus rosmarus*, 2 races. Atlantic race, *O.r. rosmarus*, formerly bred on the beaches of the Arctic islands west to Canadian Franklin and east to the Laptev Sea, south to the Belcher Islands in Hudson's Bay, Sable Island off Nova Scotia, Bear Island and Arctic Finland. From these southern limits

A Cheetah

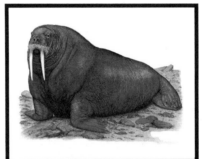

B Atlantic race of walrus

C Caribbean monk seal

D Hawaiian monk seal

(except the Belcher Islands) it has now withdrawn, and its population has become fragmented and declining, mainly under aboriginal hunting pressure. The average annual kill in the European Arctic sector of the range has been c 2,666 lately. Protective legislation is being deployed by the Arctic countries responsible but the permitted aboriginal take in many areas still exceeds the replacement capacity of the breeding walruses. **B**

Kurile harbour seal, *Phoca kurilensis* A close relation of the common (harbour seal, *P. vitulina*, confined to the Kurile Islands (U.S.S.R.) and northern Hokkaido (Japan) where now breeds mainly on Shiashkotan, Iturup, Urup and Simushir with a population estimated as c 2,000–2,500 in 1956. Has been hunted in the past but may now enjoy planned protection under ecological advice.

Ringed seal, *Phoca hispida*, 8 races Saimaa race, *P.h. saimensis*, has been confined to the freshwater lake Saimaa system in southeast Finland between the Baltic and White seas since early post glacial times, and has become isolated by geological and physiographical change of the terrain. Has 2 or 3 separate populations in Saimaa and at least 4 inter connecting lakes, with a total number estimated in 1960 as c. 200–250, under some threat from pollution and shooting by fishermen.

Ross seal, *Ommatophoca rossi*. The only seal entirely confined to the Antarctic seas, with a total population estimated in 1958 as 20,000 to 50,000 of which 10,000 were estimated in 1953 as living in the Falkland Islands Dependencies (*not* Falkland Islands). No breeding beaches have been discovered and the young are doubtless born on the pack-ice. Is protected under the conservation amendment of 1964 to the international Antarctic Treaty.

Mediterranean monk seal, *Monachus monachus*. Formerly distributed throughout the Black Sea, Mediterranean, along the northwest African coast south to Cape Blanc, and round Madeira and the Canaries, this seal is now confined to between 20 and 30 breeding beaches, only 2 of which (in Rio de Oro and Morocco) have largish populations. The declining world population probably does not exceed 500 animals; protected in 6 countries it is threatened by (often illegal) hunters.

Caribbean monk seal, *Monachus tropicalis*. Formerly bred in the Caribbean Sea and Gulf of México on the islands, and on the shores from Texas to Honduras. No breeding colony has been recorded since 200 seals were exterminated off México Yucatán in 1911. Was last seen in Jamaican waters in 1952 and off Yucatán in 1962 and may still survive, but is in serious danger. **C**

Hawaiian monk seal, *Monachus schaunslandi*. Still breeds in what may be its original range – on 6 atolls in the Leeward chain of the Hawaiian archipelago from Kure to French Frigate Shoals. Its world population was estimated in 1958 at 1,350 and may have slightly increased since. **D**

Order SIRENIA
Family DUGONGIDAE, dugong and sea cow.

Dugong, *Dugong dugon*. Confined to the shores of the Indian and West Pacific Oceans; browses on marine vegetation in shallow water. Is nearly everywhere declining under human hunting pressure, and now has small populations in Madagascar, Mozambique and Tanzania, a slightly more flourishing population in Kenya, small populations in Somalia and the Red Sea and Gulf of Aden. In India is still recorded from the Gulf of Kutch and the Andaman Isles, and has a relict population in the Gulf of Manna and Palh Strait between India and Ceylon where overhunting has been marked. In Burma and Malaysia there are now few, and in Borneo and the Philippines it now appears to be extinct. It is still recorded from Taiwan and the Ryukyu Islands and (rumours need confirmation) from Japan and Korea. Further south, in Palau Islands, a proposed national park could improve the population; and there are colonies also in the Carolines, the Solomons (furthest east) and the Marshalls. The dugong is also found round New Caledonia and the south coast of New Guinea. Its most stable population is along the east, north and west coasts of Australia where under government protection and a restriction of hunting permits to aboriginals a recovery of population could develop. **E**

Steller's sea cow, *Hydrodamalis stelleri*. **Bering Strait region, where bred at Bering Island and believed extinct by 1768; though an unconfirmed report alleges a sighting of a group of 6 near Cape Navarin in 1962 July. F**

Family TRICHECHIDAE, manatees.

West Indian manatee, *Trichechus manatus*. 2 races. Caribbean race, *T.m. manatus*, formerly ranged from the Bahamas and Greater Antilles to the mangrove rivers of the Caribbean mainland countries, including the Orinoco, and east to the rivers of the Guianas. The present distribution is mostly relict and fragmented. In Cuba hunting pressure has reduced the population to 3 estuaries only. In southern México, including Yucatán, a fair population survives, as it also does in British Honduras where its prospects are not bad. In Guatemala, especially at Lake Izabal, a decline has been fast, as it has been also in the lagoons of Costa Rica; a few may survive

E Dugong

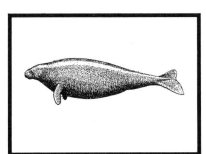

F Steller's sea cow

G Przewalski's horse

H Onager *or* Persian race of Asiatic wild ass

in Panama. The Orinoco is still a stronghold, but in Guyana hunting has made this an endangered species. In Surinam a small population survives, as possibly does one in Cayenne. Florida race, *T.m. latirostris*, formerly ranged up the rivers of the southeastern U.S. from North Carolina to the Rio Grande (Texas/México). It is now found only in Florida up the Suwanee River and in the south, where a small population is well protected.

Amazonian manatee, *Trichechus inunguis*. Formerly native to virtually the whole Amazonian river system, now seriously reduced and declining in the Lower Amazon, and even in some uninhabited upper reaches in Peru.

West African manatee, *Trichechus senegalensis*. Coastal lagoons and lower reaches of West African rivers from Senegal to Angola, everywhere slowly diminishing and tending to split into isolated relict populations.

Order PERISSODACTYLA
Family EQUIDAE, horses.

Przewalski's horse, *Equus przewalskii*. Horses of this type were much in evidence in the European fossil record until Late Pleistocene times, and the species is an ancestor of the domestic horse. In late historical times there is no evidence of wild survival of this steppe horse outside a Mongolian centre, from which its range extended into the Altai and into northern Sinkiang, China. As recent time went on, the populations became fragmented and relict under human pressure, and in the last decades the main sightings have been in the Takhin Shar-nuru highlands in southwestern Mongolia between 1942 and 1967. The captive stock in zoos and animal parks, mainly in Europe, had reached 153 by 1968 when it doubtless outnumbered the wild population, which is now strictly protected and under close observation by the University of Ulan Bator. **G**

Tarpan, *Equus gmelini*. Doubtless the direct ancestor of at least the European and West Asian domestic horses, this horse survived latest in Russia, where the last survivor died in the Ukraine in 1851.

Asiatic wild ass, *Equus hemionus*, 5 races. Mongolian race, *E.h. hemionus* (the kulan), was once widely distributed from Amurland through Siberia, Manchuria, Mongolia and Chinese Turkestan to the steppes of European Russia at least as far as Odessa. It is now restricted to Mongolia in the south and southwest extending over the frontier into China where a population of some thousands may be ceasing to decline under Mongolian and Chinese protection. Persian race, *E.h. onager* (the onager), formerly ranged over the south Russian steppes, northwest Afghanistan and north Persia. It is now extinct in Afghanistan and much reduced in Russia where, confined to the 290-square mile Badkhyz Reserve, established specially for it in 1941, it has stabilized at *c.* 700 population after some vicissitudes. In Persia small isolated populations may survive near Gum and Meshed and number a few hundred. **H** p. 241. Indian race, *E.h. khur* (the khur), formerly ranged widely over the dry plains of northwest India and West Pakistan, but is now reduced to under 1,000 animals, mostly in the Little Rann of Kutch, a few in southern Sind. Tibetan race, *E.h. kiang* (the kiang), formerly ranged over the Tibetan Plateau north to the Kuku Nor and south to Ladakh, Nepal and Sikkim, and probably keeps the same range, perhaps with a reduced and scattered, but not presently with an endangered population. **A Syrian race, *E.h. hemippus*, was last seen in 1927 in the Jabal Sinjar, north of the Euphrates, and is doubtless extinct; it formerly ranged through Syria, Palestine, Arabia and Iraq.**

African wild ass, *Equus asinus*, 2 (wild) races since 1600. Nubian race, *E.a. africanus*, formerly was distributed over Sudan east of the Nile to the Red Sea, and into Eritrea; only a small population may survive (and this needs confirmation) in the Sudan-Eritrea border region. Populations reported in 1960 near Tibesti-Enni in Chad, and in 1965 not far from Giarabub in Libya, may, like others west of the Nile, be groups of gone-wild feral asses; this species is the domestic donkey's ancestor. **B** Somali race, *E.a. somalicus*, formerly extended from Eritrea south of Massawa through much of Ethiopia to Somalia. The main population in Ethiopia was reported in 1965 as 200–350 animals in the Sardo region. Other herds may have survived at Lake Hertale in Ethiopia, Buri in Eritrea and in Wadi Nogal in north Somalia. The race needs conservation reserves and ecological investigation. **C**

Mountain zebra, *Equus zebra*, 2 races. Cape race, *E.z. zebra*, the first zebra known to Europeans was, at its discovery, confined to the montane area of Cape Province, and had some measure of protection as early as 1656. But after farming and human development pressures it was down to *c.* 47 animals in 1937. Largely due to the development of the Mountain Zebra National Park the population of the race had been brought up to 75 strictly protected individuals by 1965. **D.** Hartmann's race, *E.z. hartmannae*, ranged from southern Angola through southwest Africa to the Orange River, on the western edge of the Namid Desert. The population has declined from a large one to *c.* 7,000 in 1967, partly due to a

A Kiang *or* Tibetan race of Asiatic wild ass

B Nubian race of African wild ass

C Somali race of African wild ass

D Cape race of mountain zebra

programme of game-proof fencing which has restricted access to grazing and water. The race is protected from hunting but needs ecological management.

Quagga, *Equus quagga*. Formerly Cape Colony; the last certain one died in the Amsterdam Zoo in 1882 August 12.

Family TAPIRIDAE, tapirs.

Mountain tapir, *Tapirus pinchaque*. Rare and substantially declining in the temperate forests and grasslands of Andean Colombia, Ecuador, northern Peru and possibly western Venezuela.

Central American tapir, *Tapirus bairdi*. Formerly ranged from southern México to Colombia and Ecuador west of the Andes; is now grossly fragmented in range and lives only in the few remaining undisturbed substantial forest stands; it is becoming very rare indeed in México.

Family RHINOCEROTIDAE, rhinoceroses.

Great Indian rhinoceros, *Rhinoceros unicornis*. Formerly ranged over most of the northern Indian subcontinent, including Nepal, from Peshawar in West Pakistan and Kashmir east to the Burma border and south through the Ganges Plain. Retreated with human land development and under some hunting pressure to a relict-type distribution over 50 years ago and has now declined to a population of *c.* 740 in the 1960s, of which about 160 were in the Chitawan Sanctuary in the Rapti Valley of Nepal, and the rest in India, where no less than 400 were estimated in the 166-square mile Kaziranga Sanctuary in Assam, the rest in Assam (most in 7 sanctuaries) and West Bengal (2 sanctuaries). Strict protection devised by the Governments of India and Nepal has stabilized the population.

Javan rhinoceros, *Rhinoceros sondaicus*. In Pleistocene times extended in Asia to India and Ceylon, and but 100 years ago was still in northeast India and southwest China; in the early decades of the present century it survived in Thailand, Laos and Vietnam. It lasted in Sumatra until the early 1940s, but since then has been confined to Java where it now survives only in the Udjong Kulon Reserve in the extreme west. In its 11 square miles there were not more than 40 Javan rhinos in 1967. Here under management aided by the WWF, the Fauna Preservation Society and IUCN another classic animal is making its last stand.

Sumatran rhinoceros, *Dicerorhinus sumatrensis*, 2 races. Was once distributed from East Pakistan through Assam, Burma, much of Thailand, Cambodia, Laos, Vietnam, and Malaya to Sumatra and Borneo. Small relict populations of the mainland race, *D.s. lasiotis*, still survive in Burma (*c.* 20–30), Thailand (*c.* 6), Malaya (*c.* 30) and Cambodia (*c.* 10), and perhaps in Assam, East Pakistan, Laos nd Vietnam. The Sumatran race, *D.s.* *umatrensis*, survives in Borneo (*c.* 10–30 n Sabah) and Sumatra (possibly 60) vhere an headquarters is in the swamp egions of Riau (*c.* 25), and it is also resent in the Löser (north; *c.* 20), and outh Sumatran (*c.* 15) nature reserves. he future of the species depends as much on ecological research as on international sanctuary management and conservation law enforcement. **E**

quare-lipped *or* white rhinoceros, *Ceratotherium simum*, 2 races. **F**
Southern race, *C.s. simum*, was formerly videspread in southern Africa, being ound in southern Angola, southwest Africa, Bechuanaland, Rhodesia, southvest Zambia, Transvaal, Zululand and art of Mozambique. Its southernmost imit appears to have been the Orange River. By the end of the last century it vas widely extinct, and a third the way hrough the present century had been viped out everywhere except in Zululand in Natal) in the Umfolozi and Hluhluwe Reserves. Here the Parks, Fish and Game Preservation Board of Natal has deployed such excellent rhino management hat by 1965 the Umfolozi population was 06 – beyond the optimum capacity of the Reserve, the Hluhluwe population was '5 and that of the rest of Zululand *c.* 130; nd 330 had already been translocated afely to other national parks in South Africa, Rhodesia, and even Kenya, and 3 had been sold to mainstream zoos ikely to produce a captive-bred stock!
Northern race, *C.s. cottoni*, was in the 9th century widely distributed in northast tropical Africa west to Chad and orth to the Nile in the Sudan: it now as populations in the Sudan (Bhar-elhazal and Equatoria, where estimates ary from a few hundred to 2,000); in arts of the west Nile Province of Uganda *c.* 350 1955, under 80 1962); in northeast Congo (Garamba National Park *c.* 1,000 963, of which invading rebels from the Sudan may have destroyed at least 900 s under 100 were reported surviving in 966); and in northern Ubangui in the Central Africa Republic (Nolende and Birao, present but under 10 reported 965). By translocation, a small breeding roup has been established since 1961 in Uganda's Murchison Falls National Park; and it is on safely managed national arks that the future of this seriously eclining race depends.

Black rhinoceros, *Diceros bicornis*. Formrly inhabited virtually the whole of Africa outside the rain-forest belt from Cameroun, Chad, southwest Ethiopia nd Somalia south to Angola and the Cape Province of South Africa. IUCN's Survival Service Commission census undertaken in 1960 lists the surviving vild populations thus:
Cameroun 400, Congo (Kinshasa) a few in Kagera and Upemba national parks),

E Sumatran rhinoceros

F Square-lipped *or* white rhinoceros

G Black rhinoceros

H Pygmy hippopotamus

Chad 500, Zambia 400, Central African Republic 300, Rhodesia 1,500, Sudan 200–300, Mozambique 500, Ethiopia a few, Angola 150–200, Somalia almost extinct, South-West Africa 280, Kenya 2,500, Botswana 20, Uganda 500, Malawi 12?, Tanzania 3,000–4,000, Republic of South Africa 408.

The total (11,000–13,500) indicates that the black rhino has the highest population of the living species; but these figures represent a strong decline as a consequence of bush-clearing and hunting, even in Kenya. There is still much illegal hunting of rhinos for the trade in their horn, to which folklore attributes aphrodisiac properties. International plans of the national park authorities of Africa look forward to a wide restocking, with the use of translocation where possible. **G**

Order ARTIODACTYLA
Family SUIDAE, Old World pigs.

Pygmy hog, *Sus salvanius*. Formerly restricted to the Terai swamp-grass lands of Nepal, Sikkim, Bhutan and northwest Assam, this animal has not been recorded since 1959. Until the Nepal Terai has been further explored it cannot, however, be held extinct.

Family HIPPOPOTAMIDAE, hippopotamuses.

Pygmy hippopotamus, *Choeropsis liberiensis*. Has a discontinuous distribution in West Africa which appears relict. In Nigeria it is confined to the Rivers and Owerri Provinces; in the Ivory Coast it has not been recorded further east than the River Bandama; in Liberia it is generally distributed in the river systems; in Sierra Leone it is local but fairly widely distributed in the east; in Guinea it lives in the extreme southeast; and in Portuguese Guinea a small population was recorded in 1958 near the River Corubal. In the present century declines have been recorded at least in Liberia and Nigeria. The wild surviving population needs extensive survey. The species breeds well in captivity, especially at the Basle Zoo in Switzerland. **H**

Family CAMELIDAE, llamas and camels.

Vicuña, *Vicugna vicugna*. Has a now relict distribution in the puna, or 12,000–16,000 foot Andean plateau of southern Peru, eastern Bolivia, northeastern Argentina and northern Chile. Has declined under hunting pressure in last 3 decades and is still killed for meat and wool despite legal protection in all 4 countries.

Bactrian camel, *Camelus bactrianus*, 2 races. The typical race, *C.b. bactrianus*, is the domestic form. Wild race, *C.b. ferus*, was already a relict in historical times, confined to the Gobi Desert. It is now fractionated into two populations, one in northwest China in the Tarim region between Lob Nor and Bagrach Kol which is very rare and little known, and the other in southwest Mongolia. The Mongolian population is based on the high plains of the Ederengin Nuru Mountains in the southwest, west of longitude 100° E. and was reported in 1963 as stable and around 400–500 animals. A small herd of semi-domesticated wild stock is kept in the Gobi-Altai Province of Mongolia. **A**

Family CERVIDAE, deer.

Persian fallow deer, *Dama mesopotamica*. Fossil evidence shows that this deer ranged to Cyprus in Neolithic and Bronze Age times, to Iraq in the Bronze Age, to Israel in the Middle Pleistocene, to Lebanon in the Upper Pleistocene and to Turkey (Troy) in the Bronze Age. In historical times it still extended from Syria and Palestine through Iraq to south and southwest Persia. The last report from Iraq, in 1955, suggests that a tiny population may then have survived between Maidan and Halabja near the Persian border. Otherwise this deer is known wild only from Persia, where it was reported in 1964 as surviving in only two small patches of riverside thicket on the Karkheh River west of Haft Tapeh and on the Dez River east of it, in Khuzestan. In 1968 a survey indicated a population of under 30 on the Dez and at least 5 on the Karkheh. The captive population, which is a breeding population, consists of a small herd in the Dasht-e-Naz Park in Mazandaran, Persia and 11 animals (in 1969 June) at the Kronberg Zoo in Germany, and may equal the wild population; much depends on the fortunes of the zoo population and good management in Khuzestan. **B**

Swamp deer *or* barasingh, *Cervus duvauceli*, 2 races. Northern race, *C.d. duvauceli*, formerly widespread in the Indian subcontinent north of the Ganges, is now confined to relict populations in Nepal where 500–1,300 were estimated 1965 in southwest and (a few) in Chittawan Valley; in Uttar Pradesh where 1,400–1,800 were estimated 1965 along the Nepal border and Sarda River with a few survivors further west along the base of the Himalayas; and in West Bengal (a few in Jaldapara Sanctuary) and Assam (main population in Kaziranga Sanctuary and perhaps outliers on the Bhutan border), where 500–600 estimated in 1965. Southern race, *C.d. branderi*, formerly doubtless more widely spread in central India, is now confined to Madhya Pradesh, mainly in and around Kanha Park which had a population of *c.* 3,000 in 1938, 500 in 1958, 98 in 1968 and 70 in 1969. The world population

A Wild race of Bactrian camel

B Persian fallow deer

C Schomburgk's deer

of 3,000–4,000 has been brought to its low state mainly by heavy poaching and hunting in Madhya Pradesh, and generally also by habitat destruction for cultivation.

Schomburgk's deer, *Cervus schomburgki*. **Confined to Thailand, where now regarded as having become extinct. The last one appears to have been shot in 1932 September in the forests near Sayok along the Qwe Noi River. C**

Brow-antlered deer, *Cervus eldi*, 3 races. Manipur race, *C.e. eldi*, formerly ranged over this state of India, is now confined to the Keibul Lamjao Sanctuary (so designated 1953) at the south end of Logtak Lake where the population, reported at about 100 in 1961, has been legally protected since 1934 and is under pressure of farming habitat change, rival grazing and human disturbance and, perhaps, poaching. It is hoped that the Manipur Government will encourage an ecological survey and deploy a management policy. Thailand race, *C.e. siamensis*, "formerly abundant in the plains and forests from southern Thailand and Cambodia through Laos and Vietnam to Hainan, is now reduced and split into relict populations in all areas, excepting parts of Cambodia." (N. M. Simon.)

Sika, *Cervus nippon*, 7 races.
Taiwan race, *C.n. taiouanus*, had a good population in the high central mountains of Taiwan (Formosa) until the end of the Japanese occupation when protection was lifted and hunting pressure and habitat destruction brought the wild population to near extinction. The semi-captive population must now outnumber the wild population and constitute the chief survival insurance; it consists of over 300 animals in Western zoos (particularly England), *c.* 50 at the Taipei Zoo in Taiwan, and a managed herd of 100–200 on Lu-tao, an island near Taitung in Taiwan. **D**
North China race, *C.n. mandarinus*, was once probably widespread in northeastern China, but during the present century has become reduced to tiny relict populations, possibly all "farmed," in Chengteh and eastern Shansi, about which very little is known.
South China race, *C.n. kopschi*, formerly ranged widely from the Lower Yangtze system into Chekiang, Kiangsi and northern Kwangtung but is now virtually extinct, though a few were reported in 1965 as surviving in the Yangtze Valley. Shansi race, *C.n. grassianus*, formerly ranged throughout the whole of the western mountains of Shansi, including the mountains of the Chihli border. Was last reported in 1937 as positively surviving in the high west Shansi forest (whence last specimen 1920), and may have been hunted to extinction, though

few Chinese zoos have living specimens. ryukyu race, *C.n. keramae*, has subspeciated since its introduction from apan into the Ryukyu archipelago before 1757; and exists on Yakabi-, Kuba- nd Keruma-Shima. The population has eclined from *c.* 160 in 1955 to *c.* 30, but ow enjoys legal protection and some eserve management.

hite-lipped *or* Thorold's deer, *Cervus lbirostris*. A Tibetan species that ranges to China in Szechwan and Kansu, and now much persecuted and very rare.

ed deer, *Cervus elaphus*, 19 races. wedish race, *C.e. elaphus*, formerly idely distributed in Sweden, was reorted as reduced to a world population some 150 animals in 1961 confined to 3 olated localities in Skåne. actrian race, *C.e. bactrianus*, the "Bacian wapiti," has a now limited populaon in the riverine forest strips of Amuarya, Turkmenistan, Uzbekistan, Tadkistan and northern Afghanistan. The .S.S.R. population, mostly (*c.* 100) in e Tigrovaya Balka Reserve in Tadjikisn, is estimated as *c.* 300–400 and the tal population *c.* 400–500.

arbary race, *C.e. barbarus*, the "Barbary ag," the only North African race, now rvives only in a narrow strip of forest the Algero-Tunisian border and may umber no more than 200 or 300. Corsican ce, *C.e. corsicanus*, Corsica and ardinia; is now confined to one private tate in the Casabianda-Pinia area of orsica, where only 5 individuals were ported in 1964; and possibly survives in ardinia only in the southeast in perhaps ly 2 areas. ashmir race, *C.e. hanglu*, "barasingha hangul," now has a precariously reicted range on the north and east of e Vale of Kashmir, and a tiny populaon (perhaps only 6) in Himachal Prash; it was reported in 1968 that it ould be surprising if more than 150 were ft. **E**

'Neill's race, *C.e. macneilli*, is much ersecuted and decreasing in Tibet, westn Szechwan and Sinkiang, and is now otected by the Chinese Government. utan race, *C.e. wallichi*, the "shou," rmerly had a wide range over the ntral Asiatic highlands, but is now nfined (if it survives) to the Chumbi alley of Bhutan/Tibet, and is known to ve occurred in neighbouring valleys of hutan; the King of Bhutan (in 1965–67) convinced that it is extinct. arkand race, *C.e. yarkandensis*, was rmerly found in Chinese Turkestan on e lower courses of the Kashgar, Yarknd and Khotan rivers and on the main arim. After heavy hunting pressure, it now confined to the Lob Nor area of e Tarim basin.

apiti *or* American elk, *Cervus canaden- s*, 6 races. Tule race, *C.c. nannodes*,

D Taiwan race of sika

E Hangul *or* Kashmir race of red deer

F Père David's deer

"the Tule elk," formerly ranged over most of central California but now is reduced to 3 relict populations in the Owens Valley, Colusa County and Kern County, numbering in all 450 individuals in 1970 February, all under protection and control.

Merriam's race, *C.c. merriami*, the "Merriam elk," formerly of Arizona, southern New Mexico, north Chihuahua in México, northwest Texas and southwest Oklahoma has been extinct since 1906.

Père David's deer, *Elaphurus davidianus*. China, where probably ceased to exist wild at the time of the Shan Dynasty (1766–1122 B.C.) when the Chihli Plains were brought under cultivation. Survived in parks until its scientific discovery by Abbé Armand David in 1865 in the Imperial Hunting Park near Peking. Became extinct in China in 1921 in the aftermath of the Boxer Rebellion in which the Imperial herd (the last surviving) were virtually destroyed; but before the end of the 19th century live stock had been shipped to Europe from which the Duke of Bedford established a herd of 16 in Woburn Park in Bedfordshire, England. The Woburn herd increased to 64 by 1922 and the Dukes of Bedford began to distribute stock to other zoo parks; by 1963 the European population, still with its biggest herd at Woburn, exceeded 400. In 1964 living stock was returned to China from the London Zoo and is breeding in the Peking Zoo. This species has been saved by captive culture. **F**

Marsh deer, *Blastocerus dichotomus*. Ranged north in Brazil to western Bahia, Goyaz and Matto Grosso, west to east Bolivia, Paraguay, and the Argentinian Chaco, south to Entre Rios in Argentina. Now reduced, in Argentina only to Formosa, where rare under hunting pressure.

Pampas deer, *Ozotoceros bezoarticus*, 3 races. Still more or less fills its former range on the open campos of Brazil, Paraguay, Uruguay and Argentina, but in such reduced numbers in some areas that it is considered seriously endangered, especially in Pampas Argentina, where it survives only on a few private estates in Buenos Aires province.

Chilean pudu, *Pudu pudu*. Bolivia and Chile, on the western Andean slopes, and in forested valleys of Patagonian Andes in Argentina; is now critically rare in some areas.

Reindeer and caribou, *Rangifer tarandus*, *c.* 24 races. North American and Eurasian Arctic and Subarctic. Some races have small populations. Novaya Zemlya race, *R.t. pearsoni*, had

245

a population of about 20,000 on the two islands of Novaya Zemlya in the Russian Arctic at the end of the 19th century, but only just over 1,000 in 1930. By 1950 it survived only on the eastern north island with a population of only a few dozen. Hunting is now prohibited by the U.S.S.R. Government.

Family ANTILOCAPRIDAE, pronghorn.

Pronghorn, *Antilocapra americana*, 5 races.
Lower California race, *A.a. peninsularis*, formerly ranged in México's Baja California from below San Felipe on the east and San Quintin on the west south to near Magdalena Bay; may now be restricted to the Vizcaino Desert near Scammons Lagoon and the Magdalena Desert and but a few hundred strong.
Sonora race, *A.a. sonoriensis*, formerly ranged from Sonora in México south to the Sonora River and north into southwest Arizona, now has a very fractionated and decreasing range in northwest Sonora and but 2 herds, perhaps, over the Arizona border amounting to not more than 100 animals which are protected, and managed in the Cabeza Prieta Game Reserve and the Organ Pipe Cactus National Monument.

Family BOVIDAE, antelopes, cattle, goats and sheep.

Mountain nyala, *Tragelaphus buxtoni*. Southeast Ethiopia; over 9,000 feet in the mountains of Arussi and some of those of Bale and Sidamo, where the total world population, not very seriously diminished since the species' discovery in 1908, is of the order of 2,000.

Giant eland, *Taurotragus derbianus*, 4 races.
Western race, *T.d. derbianus*, formerly ranged through Senegal, Gambia, Portuguese Guinea, Mali and north Ivory Coast, is now in grave danger under hunting pressure in Mali, practically extinct in Gambia, probably only a wanderer to Portuguese Guinea and probably extinct in the Ivory Coast. The surviving population in Senegal may be of the order of 180, largely in the Niokolo Koba National Park; other herds have been lately identified in the Haut-Bafing region and Bakoy on the Mali/Senegal/Guinea border. A

Asiatic buffalo, *Bubalus bubalis*. Domesticated originally in south Asia this is now a very rare wild animal. It formerly occupied most of the Brahmaputra and Ganges Plains of India and East Pakistan but now survives mainly in Assam. Of the world population estimated in 1966 as a little under 2,000, *c*. 1,425 were in Assam, particularly in the Sanctuaries of Kaziranga (700), Manas (400) and Pabha (100), and at Laokhowa (50), Sankos-Manas (75) and East Lakhimpur

A Giant eland

B Asiatic buffalo

C Tamaraw

D Anoa

(100). In the rest of India the Godava River headquarters held 400–500; ar Nepal held *c*. 100 on the Kosi River. B

Tamaraw, *Anoa mindorensis*. Indigeno to the Philippines, on Luzon and Mi doro, but found on Mindoro only historical times where, once widely d tributed, it has been reduced from abu dance to critical rarity in the prese century, primarily as a consequence overhunting, since 1936 illegal. It is no according to Tom Harrisson, restrict almost entirely to Mount Iglit, Mou Calavite and the hinterland of t Sabloyon Penal Settlement, where fe of convict escapes has accorded far mo effective protection than is obtainab under the law. Iglit and Calavite a official reserves, but more tamaraws ha been killed there than anywhere else.

Anoa, *Anoa depressicornis*, 3 races. D Lowland race, *A.d. depressicornis*, for erly had a wide distribution in northe Celebes; is now found in a severe threatened relict distribution in son swampy forests, after uncontrolled hun ing. Mountain race, *A.d. fergusoni*, is small form restricted to the mountains west Celebes where it still survives reduced numbers under hunting pressu in the Bonthain Peak, Toradja Highlan and central mountain areas. Quarles race, *A.d. quarlesi*, is a dwarf form whi formerly inhabited the whole southwe peninsula of Celebes, but has now r treated to central Toradja and uplar Binoewang under hunting and probab also forest-clearance pressure.

Aurochs, *Bos primigenius*. The dire ancestor of European domestic catt survived latest in Poland, where th last survivor died in 1627, in the gan preserve of Jaktorowka in Masovia

Kouprey, *Bos sauveli*. Known from Ca bodia, from an area of 12,000 squa kilometres on the right and another, 2 kilometres apart, of 6,000 square kil metres on the left bank of the Meko River; may also survive in northeaste Cambodia and western Vietnam. In 19 the population of central Cambodia w estimated at *c*. 800 (500–600 r., 200 l.) a in 1940 *c*. 1,000, in 1952 *c*. 500, in 1964 *c*. 2 and 1966 probably a slight increase. Hur ing pressures have produced a cris which legal protection by the Cambodi Government and the establishment of chain of sanctuaries may, it is hoped, in time to cure.

Yak, *Bos grunniens*, 2 races. Wild rac *B.g. mutus*, distinguished from the do estic form, once appears to have rang widely over the great Asiatic Plate from Chinese Turkestan through Tib and over the Karakorum and Himala to Kashmir and Sikkim. It is now survival danger, restricted to northe and northeastern Tibet above 4,5

etres; it occasionally wanders into
ikkim and more frequently into India
y the Chang Chen Mo Valley; the
ibetan headquarters is the Chang Tang.

uropean bison, *Bison bonasus*, 2 races.
robably a Flandrian (postglacial) in-
der of Europe, sharing a common
ncestry most recently with the Ameri-
in bison, *B. bison*; evidently reached
ngland (presumably before the Channel
reak *c.* 7000 B.P.) where lasted till Late
ronze (or Iron) Age; reached Denmark
9500 B.P.: at its heyday ranged through
estern and southern Europe and into
e Caucasus and northward in Siberia
s far as the Lena River system. **E**
ithuanian *or lowland race*, *B.b. bona-
s*, was, by hunting pressure and forest
earance, reduced in the early present
ntury to the wild herd in the Bialo-
ieza Forest; this had 737 animals in 1914
ıt not one survived the First World
`ar; fortunately some Bialowieza ani-
als had been sent to Pszczyna, in
lesian Poland since 1923, where the
ipulation reached over 70 in 1921; but
ıly a cow and 2 bulls survived the
litical troubles of that year. With
me 200 park stock from Sweden and
ermany these were translocated to
ialowieza in 1929 and are the ancestors
the present feral stock there. In the
20s an International Society for the
rotection of the European Bison was
rmed, with a stud-book and intelli-
nce files on every living animal. By
38 Jan Zabinski's studbook listed 97
lmissibly pure-bred European bison in
Polish parks and European zoos. The
ipulation had far fewer losses in the
cond World War than in the First
orld War and the zoo and park man-
ement persisted. By 1947 it was 99, by
55 over 200 for the first time since 1918,
rgely due to buildup at Bialowieza, by
63 *c.* 550. It is now of the order of 800.
ıis is a singular triumph for the Euro-
an conservation and zoo fraternity.

aucasian race, *B.b. caucasicus*, be-
me extinct in about 1925, though
ucasicus genes are present in some
the present semi-captive stock in
ussia.

merican bison, *Bison bison*, 2 races.
ains race, *B.b. bison*, the "plains
son," was the main sufferer of the
palling overhunting which brought the
son population down from a climax
pulation estimated at 60 million to
w hundred by 1889. The rehabitation of
e plains bison is one of the first great
iployments of positive North American
nservation and has been so successful
at the plains bison no longer needs a
eet in the Red Data Book.

ood race, *B.b. athabascae*, the "wood
son," formerly extended perhaps into
ntral Alaska, certainly from east
ıkon and south Mackenzie through

E European bison

F Blaauwbok

G Arabian oryx

H Scimitar-horned oryx

northeast British Columbia and most of
Alberta to Rocky Mountain U.S.A. south
to Utah and Colorado. By 1891 the wood
bison had been reduced to *c.* 300 animals
on the borders of Mackenzie and Alberta
south of Great Slave Lake and west of
Slave River. By 1893 there were *c.* 500 in
this area; but by 1907 the population was
reported at its lowest. On the appointment of rangers in 1911 the population
recovered and had reached 1,500–2,000 in
1922 when the range was designated
Wood Buffalo Park by the Canadian
Government. But in 1925–28 6,673 plains
bison were released in the Park, and it
was soon thought that the race was
being destroyed by hybridization. Fortunately a discrete herd, isolated from the
rest by 75 miles of almost impassable
country, was discovered in 1957 and soon
found to consist of *c.* 200 animals on the
Upper Nyarling River. In the 1960s new
satellites of this colony of pure wood
bison were translocated to, and established in the Fort Providence area of
Mackenzie and Elk Island Park in Alberta. Meanwhile the Wood Buffalo
Park population, hybrids included, had
risen to over 10,000 animals. Careful
management must surely ensure the survival of *B.b. athabascae* and *B.b. bison* as
good races, as it has certainly already
ensured that of *B. bison* as a species.

**Blaauwbok, *Hippotragus leucophaeus*.
Formerly known from the neighbour-
hood of Swellendam, Cape of Good
Hope; exterminated in 1799 or 1800. F**

Arabian oryx, *Oryx leucoryx*. Formerly
ranged over the whole Arabian Peninsula
as far west as Sinai, north as the Syrian
desert and east as Iraq. Under wide
hunting pressure withdrew from northern range – last Jordan *c.* 1930, Nefud in
northern Saudi Arabia early 1950s – and
is now virtually confined to the Oman
sector of the Rub' al Khali and the Duru
and Wahiba country to the east, with a
population reported in 1969 as under 200.
Operation Oryx (1962 onwards) of IUCN
and Fauna Preservation Society with
much local and international support
contrived a planned wild-capture campaign to establish a breeding zoo-bank,
which by 1969 consisted of (mostly breeding) herds of 16 in Arizona, 7 in California,
23 in Slamy in northwest Qatar (Persian
Gulf of Arabia), 1 in Kuwait and others
in Riyadh and Taiz zoos (Saudi-Arabia) –
a total of over 47. The object of the
operation is to build up a stock which
can be liberated when a planned national
park and sanctuary system is deployed
successfully in Arabia. G

Scimitar-horned oryx, *Oryx tao*. A Saharan species formerly widespread over the
deserts and dry districts of North Africa
from the Nile to Senegal, not north of the
Grand Atlas. Under hunting pressure

(report dates in brackets), is extinct in Morocco (1957), probably only a seasonal visitor to Algeria (1967), extinct in Tunisia *c.* 1906, not recently reported from Libya, extinct in Egypt *c.* 1850, scarce in Sudan (1954), and apparently extinct in Rio de Oro after 1963. Populations (*c.* 10,000 in all) survive in northern Chad (*c.* 4,000), in Air and Ténéré in Niger and in the Adrar des Iforas in Mali. So far the species is officially protected only in Sudan. **H**

Addax, *Addax nasomaculatus*. Formerly ranged from Senegambia over virtually the whole Sahara to Egypt and Sudan. Now broken into relict populations in Sahara Español (Rio de Oro; may be extinct), Mauritania, Mali, Algeria (rare), Libya (disappearing fast), Sudan (1 small herd in Darfur only) and Chad (3 main herds); and has become extinct in Tunisia (by 1962 report) and Egypt (by 1932 report). Hunting pressure is the direct cause of the decline and a law-enforcement system and reserve mosaic is urgently necessary; neither is yet deployed.

Bontebok, *Damaliscus dorcas*, with blesbok 2 races.
Blesbok, *D.d. albifrons*, is extinct in the wild but has so large a population on South African farms that it does not rate a Red Data Book sheet.
Bontebok, *D.d. dorcas*, at the colonization time (late 17th century) was confined to a narrow strip between Swellendam and Caledon in southwest Cape Province. Hunting and land development reduced the once-abundant population rapidly, and from 1864 private conservation-minded farmers enclosed herds on private estates; legal protection followed. In 1931 the National Bontebok Park was set up not far from Bredasdorp to enclose 22 bontebok. By 1953 the stock had increased to *c.* 120; but owing to disease a new park was set up at Swellendam in 1960. The estimated total population was 17 in 1931, 33 in 1935, 57 in 1936, 69 in 1938, 525 in 1961, *c.* 600 in 1962 and *c.* 750 in 1965. There are now 6 separate managed herds and the fate of the race seems secure.
Hunter's hartebeest, *Damaliscus hunteri*. Ranged and ranges from the Tana River in Kenya to the Dera area west of the Juba River in Somalia, with an estimated population reported in 1964 as a maximum of 1,500 of which 200 were in Somalia. Since the extension of an irrigation land-development scheme to the east side of the Tana has been dropped the species has been considered to be no longer endangered.

Hartebeest, *Alcelaphus buselaphus*, 15 races.

Swayne's race, *A.b. swaynei*. When discovered in 1891–92 the population confined to Somalia between Hargeisa and the neighbouring area over the Ethiopian border was of the order of 4,000 in about a dozen great herds. By 1905 the population was down to *c.* 880, after a rinderpest outbreak. Overhunting has since reduced the population which was evidently confined to *c.* 200 animals in 1966 on the Alledeghi Plains in Ethiopia; in 1967 the population was reported as down to 40 or less on the Alledeghi Plains, 26 west of Lake Awassa and not more than 130 at Lake Chamo, where a reserve is proposed.
Tora race, *A,b, tora*, is now rare, with *c.* 200–300 in Sudan, along the eastern border, and unknown but small population in neighbouring parts of Ethiopia and Eritrea.
Bubal race, *A.b. buselaphus*, the "bubal antelope" of North Africa from Morocco to Egypt, became extinct in the present century, the last known specimen dying in the Jardin des Plantes, Paris, in 1923.
Cape *or* red race, *A.b. caama*, formerly of the Cape area of southernmost Africa, became extinct in about 1938.

Black wildebeest *or* white-tailed gnu, *Connochaetes gnou*. Formerly widespread in South Africa in the Karoo of Cape Province and the high veld of the Orange Free State and southern Transvaal. Came under intensive hunting pressure and was probably extinguished in Transvaal by 1885; but in Orange Free State was protected by private Boer farmers. In the present century all survivors have been conserved on private land, and in 1936 a system of game reserves was deployed, of which at least 5 now harbour these gnus. The population, carefully logged, climbed from 1,048 in 1947 to 2,117 in 1965. This conservation by private citizens and government agencies of the Republic of South Africa has paid off.

Beira, *Dorcatragus megalotis*. Lives in small parties in north and northwest Somalia as far south as the Nogal Valley, where a population of 1,000 was estimated in 1905, and in east-central Ethiopia. Uncommon, but a decline has not been proved and an ecological survey is desirable.

Slender-horned gazelle, *Gazella leptoceros*. A Saharan species extending south to northwest Chad, extinct in Egypt and very rare and fractionated elsewhere in North Africa, where formerly widespread, after hunting pressure; is in a precarious state in Libya and now known from but few localities in Tunisia and

Algeria (it did not extend to Morocco and is of uncertain status in Sudan).

Pelzeln's gazelle, *Gazella pelzelni*. Maritime region of northern Somalia, where declining in last 2 decades, particularly in former Italian Somaliland, due to uncontrolled hunting.

Red goral, *Nemorhaedus cranbrook*. Confined to a limited area, and probably rare in the Mishmi Hills of Assam and the Adung Valley of extreme northern Burma.

Japanese serow, *Capricornis crispus*, races. Japanese race, *C.c. crispus*, formerly existed throughout most suitable high forest of Honshu, Shikoku and Kyushu, and is now extinct in the Chugoku district of Honshu and rare in Kyushu where very few survive, and restricted to the mountains. The population, declining, was reported at *c.* 2,000–3,000 in 1968; the animal is completely protected as a Special Nature Monument and reserves have been formed. Formosan race, *C.c. swinhoei*, was formerly abundant in the northern range of the higher mountains of Taiwan and grazed down to 2,000 ft. Since the end of the Japanese occupation hunting control has been abandoned and under hunting pressure the distribution has become patchy though the animal is still not uncommon in some areas.

Arabian tahr, *Hemitragus jayakari*. Oman (Arabia); formerly at least on montane ranges, now relict; possibly the only population, doubtless in need of protection, survives on the Jebel Hafit.

Nilgiri tahr, *Hemitragus hylocrius*. Lives in south India at 4,000–6,000 ft from the Nilgiri Hills to the Anamallais and southward along the Western Ghats is much reduced in numbers and now rare; the Nilgiri Hills population reported in 1963 as 420 in 4 sanctuaries may have been over half the total.

Walia ibex, *Capra walie*. Is confined to the 8,000–11,000-foot level on the northwest escarpment of the Semien Mountains in Begemder Province. Here under long and sometimes rough hunting pressure, the range has contracted and the population has declined, and cultivation pressure on the grazing grounds is now also a threat. The solution to the stabilization and increase of the population, now only a few hundred, lies in the designation and management of the Semien as a national park, which is already approved in principle by the Imperial Government.

LLEN, Glover M. (1942). Extinct and vanishing mammals of the western hemisphere with the marine species of all the oceans. New York, American Committee for International Wild Life Protection.

RCHEY, Gilbert (1941 May). The moa a study of the Dinornithiformes. *Bull. Auckland Inst. Mus.* no. 1: 135 pp.

ENNETT, H. H. (1939). Soil conservation. London, McGraw-Hill, 994 pp.

ENSON, C. W. (1967). The birds of Aldabra and their status. *Atoll Res. Bull.* 118/119: 63–111.

RODKORB, Pierce (1963 June, 1964 June, 1967 June). Catalogue of fossil birds. *Bull. Florida State Mus.* 7 (4): 179–293; 8 (3): 195–335; 11 (3): 99–220.

ARLQUIST, Sherman (1965). Island life: a natural history of the islands of the world. New York, Natural History Press, 451 pp.

ARRINGTON, Richard (1957). Mermaids and mastodons a book of natural and unnatural history. London, Chatto & Windus, xvi+ 251 pp.

ARRINGTON, Richard (1967). Great national parks. London, Weidenfeld & Nicolson.

ARSON, Rachel (1962). Silent Spring. Boston, Houghton Mifflin, xvi+368 pp.

LARK, J. Grahame D. (1961). World prehistory an outline. Cambridge, University Press, xvi+282 pp.

OLE, Sonia (1963). Races of men. London, British Museum (Natural History), 131 pp.

OMMITTEE ON RARE AND ENDANGERED WILDLIFE SPECIES (1966 July on). Rare and endangered fish and wildlife of the United States. *Bureau Sport Fisheries Wildlife Resource Publ.* no. 34; periodically revised. A U.S. Govt. publication in a quarto binder with sheets in mimeod style.

RAGG, J. B. *ed.* (1967). Advances in ecological research. London & New York, Academic Press, vol. 4: xii+312 pp.

ROWE, Philip Kingsland (1967). The empty ark. New York, Charles Scribner's Sons, xviii+301 pp.

ARLING, Frank Fraser (1969 Nov.–Dec.). The Reith lectures – wilderness and plenty. *Listener* 82 (2120): 653–56; (2121): 693–96; (2122): 722, 724–26; (2123): 783–84, 786; (2124): 818–21; (2125): 847–48, 851–52.

ARLINGTON, C. D. (1969). The evolution of man and society. London, George Allen & Unwin, 753 pp.

ASMANN, Raymond P. (1959). Environmental conservation. New York, Wiley; and London, Chapman & Hall.

AY, Michael H. (1969). Fossil man. London, etc., Hamlyn, 159 pp.

UFF, Roger (1956). The moa-hunter period of Maori culture. Wellington, *Canterbury Mus. Bull.* no. 1: xx+400 pp. (2nd ed.).

LLERMAN, J. R. and MORRISON-SCOTT, T. C. S. (1951 Nov.). Checklist of palaearctic and Indian mammals 1758 to 1946. London, British Museum (Natural History), iv+810 pp.

MILIANI, Cesare (1955). Pleistocene temperatures. *J. Geol.* 63: 538–78.

FALLA, R. A., SIBSON, R. B., and TURBOTT, E. G. (1966). A field guide to the birds of New Zealand and outlying islands. London, Collins, 245 pp.

FISHER, James (1967 Oct.). Fossil birds and their adaptive radiation *and* Aves. *In* HARLAND, W. B. *et al.* (eds.). The fossil record. London, Geological Society, pp. 133–54 and 733–62.

FISHER, James, SIMON, Noel and VINCENT, Jack (1969 May). The red book wildlife in danger. London, Collins, 368 pp.

FLEMING, C. A. (1962 Apr.). History of the New Zealand land bird fauna. *Notornis 9* (8): 270–74.

FLEMING, C. A. (1962 Dec.). The extinction of moas and other animals during the Holocene period. *Notornis 10* (3): 113–17.

FLINT, Richard Foster (1957). Glacial and pleistocene geology. New York, John Wiley, 553 pp.

GAYMER, R. (1967). Observations on the birds of Aldabra in 1964 and 1965. *Atoll Res. Bull,* 118/119: 113–25.

GLACKEN, Clarence J. (1967). Traces on the Rhodian shore nature and culture in Western thought from ancient times to the end of the eighteenth century. Berkeley & Los Angeles, University of California Press, xxx+763 pp.

GODWIN, Harry (1956). The history of the British flora. Cambridge, University Press, 384 pp.

GRAHAM, Edward H. (1944). Natural principles of land use. London, etc., Oxford, University Press, 274 pp.

GREENWAY, James C. Jr. (1958). Extinct and vanishing birds of the world. New York, American Committee for International Wild Life Protection, x+518 pp.

HACHISUKA, Masauji (1953). The dodo and kindred birds. London, Witherby, 250 pp.

HALL, E. Raymond and KELSON, Keith R. (1959 Mar.). The mammals of North America. New York, Ronald Press, 2 vols., pp. xxx+ 1–546+79 and x+547–1083+79.

HARPER, Francis (1945). Extinct and vanishing mammals of the Old World. New York, American Committee for International Wild Life Protection.

HARROY, Jean-Paul (1967). Liste des Nations unies des Parcs nationaux et Reserves analogues. Bruxelles, *IUCN* (Morges) *Publ.* (n.s.) no. 11; 550 pp.

HARTING, James Edmund (1880). British animals extinct within historic times with some account of British wild white cattle. London, Trübner, x+258 pp.

HOSKINS, W. G. (1955). The making of the English landscape. London, Hodder & Stoughton, 240 pp.

JACKS, G. V. and WHYTE, R. O. (1939). The rape of the earth. London.

KURTEN, Björn (1968 Apr.). Pleistocene mammals of Europe. London, Weidenfeld & Nicolson, viii+317 pp.

LAMBRECHT, Kálmán (1953). Handbuch der

Palaeornithologie. Berlin, Borntraeger, xx+ 1024 pp.

LÜTTSCHWAGER, J. (1961). Die Drontevögel. Wittenberg Lutherstadt, Ziemsens *Neue Brehm Bücherei*, 60 pp.

MARTIN, P. S. and WRIGHT, H. E. Jr. eds. (1967). Pleistocene extinctions the search for a cause. New Haven & London, Yale University Press, x+453 pp.

MELLANBY, Kenneth (1967). Pesticides and pollution. London, Collins *New Naturalist*, 221 pp.

MORCOMBE, Michael (1969). Australia's national parks. Melbourne, Lansdowne Press, 232 pp.

MOREAU, R. E. (1966). The bird faunas of Africa and its islands. New York & London, Academic Press, 424 pp.

MORRIS, Desmond (1965 Aug.). The mammals a guide to the living species. London, Hodder & Stoughton, etc., 448 pp.

MORRIS, Desmond (1967). The naked ape. London, Jonathan Cape.

MOUNTFORT, Guy (1969). The vanishing jungle the story of the World Wildlife Fund expeditions to Pakistan. London, Collins, 286 pp.

NICHOLSON, [E.] Max, (1970 Jan.). The environmental revolution a guide for the new masters of the world. London, Hodder & Stoughton, 366 pp.

OLIVER, W. R. B. (1949). The moas of New Zealand and Australia. *N.Z. Dominion Mus. Bull.* no. 15; 206 pp.

OSBORN, Fairfield (1948). Our plundered planet. London, Faber & Faber, 192 pp.

PETERS, James Lee *et al.* (1931 on). Check list of birds of the world. Cambridge (Mass.), Harvard University. 15 vols., some still to be published.

PETERSON, Roger Tory and FISHER, James (1955 Oct.). Wild America. Boston, Houghton Mifflin, xiv+434 pp.

PILBEAM, David (1970 Feb.). *Gigantopithecus* and the origins of Hominidae. *Nature 225* (5232): 516–19.

RAVEN, Charles E. (1942). John Ray naturalist his life and works. Cambridge, University Press, xx+502 pp.

RITCHIE, James (1920). The influence of man on animal life in Scotland a study in faunal evolution. Cambridge, University Press, xvi +550 pp.

ROTHSCHILD, Lionel Walter, Lord (1907). Extinct birds. London, Hutchinson, xxix+ 244 pp.

DE SCHAUENSEE, R. Meyer (1966). The species of birds of South America and their distribution. Narberth, Pa., Livington Publ. Co. for Acad. Nat. Sci. Philad., 578 pp.

SHEPARD, Paul (1967). Man in the landscape a historic view of the esthetics of nature. New York, Knopf, xx+290+viii pp.

SIMON, Noel (1966 on). Red data book volume 1 – Mammalia. Morges, IUCN, looseleaf progressive slip file.

SIMPSON, George Gaylord (1945 Oct.). The principles of classification and a classification

Selected Bibliography continued

of mammals. *Bull. amer. Mus. nat. Hist. 85:* xvi+350 pp.

STAMP, Sir Dudley (1969). Nature conservation in Britain. London, Collins *New Naturalist*, xiv+273 pp.

STOCK, Chester (1956). Rancho la Brea, a record of Pleistocene life in California. *Los Angeles Co. Mus. Sci. Ser.* no. 20: 83 pp.

UNITED NATIONS GENERAL ASSEMBLY (1968 Dec.). The problems of human environment. Session 23, meetings 1732 and 1733 (A/Pv. 1732 & 1733).

VINCENT, Jack (1966 on). Red data book volume 2. Aves. Morges, IUCN, looseleaf progressive slip file.

VOLLMAR, Fritz and MCGREGOR, Alan *eds.*
(1968). The ark under way second report of the World Wildlife Fund. 1965–1967. Morges, World Wildlife Fund, 323 pp.

VOLLMAR, Fritz and MCGREGOR, Alan *eds.* (1969). World Wildlife Fund Yearbook 1968. Morges, World Wildlife Fund, 319 pp.

WEST, R. G. (1968). Pleistocene geology and biology with especial reference to the British Isles. London, Longmans, Green & Co., xiv+377 pp.

WETMORE, Alexander (1956 Jan.). A check-list of the fossil and prehistoric birds of North America and the West Indies. *Smithson. Misc. Coll. 131* (5): 105 pp.

WHITE, Gilbert (1788 Dec.). The natural history and antiquities of Selborne, in the county of Southampton. London, B. White & Son v+468+13 pp.

WRIGHT, H. E. Jr. and FREY, David G. *ed.* (1965). The quaternary of the United States A review for the VII Congress of the International Association for Quaternary Research. Princeton, University Press, x+922 pp.

ZEUNER, Frederick E. (1958). Dating the past an introduction to geochronology. London Methuen, 516 pp., 4th ed.

ZEUNER, Frederick E. (1959). The Pleistocene period its climate, chronology and faunal successions. London, Hutchinson, 447 pp.

ZEUNER, Frederick E. (1963 Feb.). A history of domesticated animals. London, Hutchinson 560 pp.

Acknowledgments

The publishers are grateful to the following people, who have generously contributed time and talent to the production of this book:

Philippa Scott, Eric Hosking and Donald Paterson for special photographs;

the Photographic Library of the World Wildlife Fund under the guidance of Dr Fritz Vollmar;

Miss Jane Fenton, personal assistant to Peter Scott;

James Orr, C.V.O., for coordinating communications with H.R.H. The Prince Philip, Duke of Edinburgh.

They would also like to thank Kodak Ltd.

The photographs of cheetahs on the jacket is by Norman Myers of Bruce Coleman Ltd.

The endpapers show the Badlands, U.S.A., reproduced from a National Parks Service Photograph by W. S. Keller.

COLOUR PLATES

The World Wildlife Fund supplied the colour transparencies for the following plates:

by F. Vollmar: frontispiece reverse, pages 19, 95, 98

by Thor Larsen: 96–7 top

by François-Edmond Blanc: 96–7 bottom

by E. P. Gee: 135, 136–7, 138, 158–9

and the drawings for the following plates:

by Helmut Diller: 85 both, 107 both, 148, 170, 187, 197, 198–9

by Paul Barruel: 86, 125, 147, 169

by Jörg Kühn: 108, 126, 188, 200.

The photograph for the frontispiece was supplied by National Aeronautics and Space Administration, U.S.A.;

for page 157 top by Donald Paterson; centre by the National Parks Service, U.S.A.; and bottom and for page 160 by Philippa Scott.

MONOCHROME AND DANGER LIST PICTURES

H.R.H. The Prince Philip, Duke of Edinburgh,

took the photographs on pages 25, 28 and throughout his chapter, Observing with Camera.

Eric Hosking photographed Prince Philip on pages 45, 73.

The World Wildlife Fund supplied the original drawings for the following illustrations:

by Josette Gourley 1963–8: 27, 81, 152, 168, 174, 177, 185, 218A, C, D, 219E, F, 221G, 231F, 232A, 234C, 237G, 238A, B, 239E, F, G, 240A, 209G, H, 242B, C, D, 243E, H, 244A, B, 245D

by Paul Barruel 1968–70: 172, 190

by Jörg Kühn 1963–4: 176, 226A

by Helmut Diller 1968–70: 153, 213, 240B, 242A, 243F, G, 245E, 246A.

The Photographic Library of the World Wildlife Fund supplied the originals of the following illustrations: pages 146 by H. Heimpel, 177 by P. Morrison and the New Zealand Department of International Affairs, 181 by the New York Zoological Society, 186 by Dr J. Eibl-Eibesfeldt, 202 by F. C. Sibley, 212 by N. Myers.

The pictures on the following pages are reproduced by courtesy of the IUCN and were drawn for *The Red Book*, London, 1969:

by Cécile Curtis: 165, 237H, 238C, 240C, 246B

by Shigekazu Kobayashi: 218B, 220C, D, E, 221F

by D. M. Henry: 218D, 221H, 224C

by R. M. Fennessy: 219G

by P. Slater: 223F, G

by N. W. Cusa: 220A, 225D, F, 226B, C, 227F

by B. C. Driscoll: 230C, 232A, 233D, E, 235D, E, 236A

by M. Wilson: 232B, 234B, 241E

by D. W. Ovenden: 239D, 240D

John Freeman photographed the pictures reproduced on the following pages: 166, 220B, 222B, C, 223E, 224B, 225E, 227D, E, 228A, C, 229E, F, G, 230A, B, 231E, G, H, 234A, 235 241F, 244C, 245F, 246D

page 26 by courtesy of Tanzania National Park

pages 84, 87, 123 by courtesy of the trustees the British Museum

pages 88, 89 by courtesy of the trustees of the National Portrait Gallery

pages 90, 203 by courtesy of the National Audubon Society

pages 92, 93 by courtesy of the Concord Public Library

pages 100, 103 U.S. Department of the Interior National Park photographs by M. Woodbridge and Ralph H. Anderson

page 123, 142, 143 Barnabys Picture Library

page 128 Aerofilms Ltd

page 129 E. Hosking and J. Fisher

page 133 by courtesy of the National Trust Operation Neptune, photograph by Charles Woolf, M.P.S.

page 140 from the Mansell Collection

page 141 from the French Government Tourist Office

pages 144, 145 from the Swiss National Tourist Office and Swiss Federal Railways

page 145 P. A. Røstad, Oslo

page 179 by courtesy of the High Commission for New Zealand

page 237E and F drawn by Ian Garrard

The drawings for H.R.H. The Duke of Edinburgh's and Stewart L. Udall's text are by Denis Manton.

The extract by W. H. Hudson in chapter 2 of James Fisher's text is reproduced by courtesy of the RSPB and Society of Authors.

Executive editor: Stanley E. Flink

Associate editor: Jean Atcheson

Picture research assistant:
Johanna Morris

The Index is by Roger F. Pemberton

Forest of Ae (Dumfriesshire), 134
Forest of Dean (Gloucestershire), 131, 134; arboretum in, 139
Forest Parks (FPs, *formerly* National Forest Parks), 131, 134, 139
Forestry and forests, 34, 35, 43, 80; "climax forests", 113, 123, 189; economic, and public amenities, 134; pre-historic and historic, 122–30 *passim*; reafforestation, 123
Forestry Commission (FC), 131, 133, 134–9; guides, 134
Formosa (Taiwan), 87
Fossa, 238
Fossil fuels, 10
Foudia, 83, 175, 176, 229, *229*
Fourier, François, 99
Foxes, 28, 83, 121, 193, 237
France, 146
Franklin, Benjamin, 204
Fregata aquila, 61, 217
Frégate island (Seychelles), 146
Fregilupus, 82, 175, 176, 225, *225*
French Revolution (1789), 99
Frigate bird, 61, 217
Frogs, 25
Fulmar, *60*, 61, 123

Gabon, 172
Gadwall, 122, 123
Galápagos Islands NP, 27, 29, 42, 47, 48, 51, 54, 57, 72, 193, 194, 195; wild life in *194*
Galemys pyrenaicus, 231
Gallicolumba ferruginea, 82, 222
Gallinago anthonyi, 184
Gallinule, Hodgen's, 180
Gallirallus minor, 180
Gambel, William, 206
Gambia, 167
Gandhi, Mrs Indira, *quoted*, 216
Gannet, 122, 123, 149
Gazelles, 248
Geocapromys, 185, 189, 235, *235*, 236
Geococcyx conklingi, 201
Geopsittacus occidentalis, 222, 223
George, Lake (near Canberra), 28
Geronticus eremita, 143
Ghana, 168
Giant panda, **frontispiece reverse**, 13, *79*
Gibbon, dwarf, 234
Giraffe, 78, 155
Glacier NP (British Columbia), 208
Glacier NP (Montana, USA), 207
Glen More FP, 134
Glossotherium, 193
Glyptodonts, 191, 193, 196
Goats, 143, 156
Gobi Desert, 196
Godman, John Davidson, 206
Godwits, 91, 123, 222, *222*
Gomphotheriids (*see also* Mastodon), 193
Goosander, 123
Goose: Canada, 122, 123; cereopsis, 178, 218, *218*; graceful, 202; grey-lag, 91, 122, 123; Hawaiian (néné), *133*, 156, **157**, 183, 218; tarepos, 180
Gopher, Sinclair's pocket, 196
Goral, 150, 248
Gorillas, 171, 172, 234, *234*
Gosse, P. H., 206
Goyt Valley (Peak District NP), 133
Grackles, 191, 229
Grahamland Peninsula, 26
Grand Canyon NP (Arizona), 207
Grant, President Ulysses S., 103, 104
Great Rift Valley (East Africa), 48, 66
Great Smoky Mountains NP (North Carolina and Tennessee), 207
Grebes, 91, 122, 123, 191, 217
Greece, 29, 84, 106, 113, 149
Green belts, 130
Grinnell, George Bird, 111

"Grizzly Giant" (big tree), 206
Grosbeak, Bonin, 83, 229, *229*
Ground roller, long-tailed, 174, 224
Grouse, 66, 120
Grus, 143, 189, 208, 220, 221, *221*
Guadalquivir delta (Spain), 18
Guadalupe Island, 191
Guan, horned, 191, 219
Guatemala, 191
Guiana, French, 194
Guillemots, 61, 123
Guinea, Portuguese, 167, 168
Guinea-pigs, Prince Philip's, 25
Gulls, *30*, 59, *59*, 123, 206 222
Guyana (*formerly* British Guiana), 194
Gwydr State Forest (Wales), 134
Gymnobelideus leadbeateri, *177*, 230, *230*
Gymnogyps, 202, *205*, 219

Habitat programmes, 214
Harlan, Richard, 206
Haeckel, E. H., 115
Haiti, 92, 190
Halcyon miyakoensis, 82, 224
Haliaeetus species, 180
Hammerkops, 66
Hammond, J. L. and Barbara, 124, 127; *quoted*, 127
Hamster, hairy-footed, 121
Hapalemur griseus, 174, 175, 232
Hardknott FP, (England), 139
Harriers, 91, 122, 123, 180
Hartebeest, 168, 171, 248
Harvard University (USA), 83, 93, 94, 105
Harvest-mouse, 88
Hauser, Samuel, 102, 103, 105
Hawaii, 81, 156, 176, 182, 183
Hawaii Volcanoes NP, 183, 207
Hawfinch, 122, 123
Hawks, *56*, 56, 189, 194, 202, 219
Hayden, F. V., 101
healdende (conservationists), 116, 134
Hebrides, the, 80; Outer, 29, 58
Hedges, Judge Cornelius, 102, 103, 105
Helena (Montana), 102, 103
Hemignathus, 83, 228, *228*
Hemitragus, 143, 248
Heptaxodon, giant rodent, 185
Heritage Coast area, 139
Herons, 48, *48*, 66, 70, *70*, 82, 173, 176, 217
Heteralocha acutirostris, 82, 180, *180*, 226, *226*
Heteropsomys insulans, 185
Hexolobodon phenax, 185
Hilbre Island, 29
Hillman, John Wesley, 207
Himantopus novaezealandiae, 180
Hipparion, 155
Hippopotamus, 118, *155*, 155, 162, 164, 243, *243*
Hippotragus leucophaeus, 83, 247, *247*
Hispaniola, 192
Hoffman, Dr Lukas, 215
Hog, pygmy, 106, **107**, 243
Hokioi (eagle), 180
Holmesina septentrionalis, 202
Homopsomys antillensis, 185
Homotherium latidens, 121
Honduras, 192; British, 191
Honeycreepers, Hawaiian, 183, 227–8
Honeyeater, 178
Hoplophorus (glyptodont), 193
Hopue, 83, 228
Horn, Cape, 26, 195
Hornbill, Narcondam, 225
Horse, 191, 193, 203; Alaska, 202; domestic, 156; eastern, 201; extinct, 202; Lambe's, 201; plains, 201; primitive, 155; Przewalski's, 94, **95**, 150, 241, *241*
Hoskins, W. G., 124
Hovacrex roberti, 174

Hudson, W. H., 106–9; *quoted*, 106–9
Huia (Callaeid), 82, 180, *180*, 226, *226*
Hungary, 106, 146
hunting: as preservative of wilderness, 110–1; pre-historic, 117–30 *passim*
Hutias, 185, 186, 189, 235, *235*, 236, *236*
Huxley, Sir Julian, 168; *quoted*, 114
Hydrodamalis stelleri, 83, 202, 241, *241*
Hyena, spotted, 121, 143
Hylobates klossi, 234
Hylopetes borbonicus, 175, 226
Hypsipetes borbonicus, 175, 226

IBP (International Biological Program), 78, 213
ICBP (International Council for Bird Preservation), 13, 14, 215
ICI (Imperial Chemical Industries), 132
IPPF (International Planned Parent-hood Federation), 11
IUCN (International Union for Conservation of Nature and Natural Resources, *see also* Survival Service Commission), 11, 13, 14, 18, 30, 43, 77, 81, 114, 211, 213–6 *passim*; Operations Intelligence Unit (and six Commissions of), 215; survival list of, 82 (*see also* Red Data Book)
Ibex, 119, *144*, 168, 248
Ibises, *62*, 63, *63*, 143, 201, 218, *218*
"Ic healde", 116
Iceland, 15, 27, 28, 47, 80, 145
Idaho (USA), 101
Iguanas, 51, *52–3*, 54, *55*, 194
India, 29, 84, 134, 153–4, 156, 201; South, 106
Indian Ocean islands, 173–6
Indians: North American, 104, 105, 203; South American, 36
Indonesia, 153
Indri indri, 174, *232*, 233
Indris, 174, *232*, 233
Industrial Revolution in Britain (c. 1760–1840), 127, *128*
Industry: interest in nature, 132; neglect of nature, 209
Inner Farne islands (Northumbria) nature reserve (c. A.D. 676), 128
International Waterfowl Research Project, 215
Iran (Persia), 29, 154–5, 156
Iraq, 154, 155, 156
Ireland, 149
Isolobodon, Haitian rodent, 185
Israel, 156, 161
Italy, 146
Ivory Coast, 167, 168
Izaak Walton League (USA), 210

Jaguar, fierce, 201
Jamaica, 189, 190
Japan, 106, 151–2
Jay, tufted, 191
Jefferson, President Thomas, 204–5
Jerboa, marsupial, 178
Jericho, 155
Jordan, 161; HM the King of, 162
Josselyn, John, 204

Kagu, 182, **188**, 189, 221
Kaibab squirrel, 207
Kakapo (flightless parrot), 180, *181*, 181, 223
Kakarikis (parakeets), 82, 181, 182, 223
Kangaroos, 177, 178; rat, *see* Rat kangaroo
Kangaroo rat, 235
Kathiawar (India), 134
Katmai national monument (Alaska), 208
Keats, John, 90, 91, 93, 99
Kenya, 28, 48, 64, 171
Kestrels, 124, **125**, 175, 176, 219, *219*
Kingfishers, 66, 82, 224
Kioea, 83, 227
Kites, 91, 122, 186, 189, 219

Kittiwake, 61
Kiwis, 179, *179*
Koala, 177
Kokako (Callaeid), 181, 226
Kouprey, 246
Krüger NP (South Africa), 173

Lack, Dr, 91
Lagorchestes, 83, 178, 230, *230*
Lagorja, Lake (Tanzania), 113
Lagostrophus fasciatus, 230
Lake District, English, 101
Lake District NP (England), 129, 131, 139
lakes, 18–21
land: demands for, 18; uses of, 21; wild, 43
Langford, Nathaniel Pitt, 102, 103
Langurs, 233, 234
Larus audouini, 222
Laurentians (Canada), 27
Leaf-warbler, 88
Lebanon, 161
Lemmings, 120, 121
Lemurs, 174, 175, 232, *232*
Leontideus, 233
Leopards, 119, 143, 150, 154, 161, *162*, 163, 239, *239*, 240
Lepilemur mustelinus, 232
Leptobos, 155
Leptotila wellsi, 186, 222
Lesotho (*formerly* Basutoland), 173
Leucopeza semperi, 186, 229
Leucopsar rothschildi, 225, *225*
Lewis, Meriwether, 206
Liberia, 167–8
Libya, 162
Limosa haemastica, 222, *222*
Linnaeus, Carolus, *80*, 84
Lions, 121, 134, **136–7**, 143, *152*, 154, *164*, 165–6, 239, *239*; marsupial, 177–8
Llamas, 193, 202, 203
Lobster, rock, 173
Loch Ard, 139
Lofoten Islands (Norway), *145*
London, City of, 128
Longfellow, Henry Wadsworth, 105
Lophophorus, 220
Lophopsittacus mauritanus, 82, 175, 223
Lophura, 152, 220, *220*
Lorikeet, 82, 182, 223
Loxops, 83, 228, *228*
Luano Reserve (Angola), 81
Lutra platensis, 238
Luxembourg, 146
Lynx, 18, **19**, 121, 144, 238, 239

Macaws, 82, 185, 186, 224
MacGillivray, William, 92
Macropus, 83, 178, 230, 231, *231*
Macrotis lagotis, 230
Madagascar (Malagasy), 106, 173–5
Magpie, 122
Magpie robin, Seychelles, 146, **147**, 176
Mahé island (Seychelles), 124
Malagasy Republic, *see* Madagascar
Malawi, 172
Malaysia, 152
Maleo, 153
Mali, 168
Malkoha, red-faced, 224
Mallard, 218
mammals extinct since 1600 (and map), 83, *83*
Mammoths, 121, *142*, 143, 150, 191, 201, 202, 203
Mammut, 191, 193, 202
Mamo, 83, 228, *228*
Man: as master of nature, 77, 78–81, 123; as naturalist, 84; his balanced predation, 81
Manatees, 186, 193, 208, 241
Maui (Hawaiian island), 156
MAR, Project, 215